Realities of Foreign Service Life, Volume 2

Realities of Foreign Service Life, Volume 2

Edited by Melissa Brayer Hess, Patricia Linderman and Marlene Nice

An AAFSW Book (Associates of the American Foreign Service Worldwide)

iUniverse, Inc.
New York Lincoln Shanghai

Realities of Foreign Service Life, Volume 2

iUniverse books may be ordered through booksellers or by contacting:

iUniverse
2021 Pine Lake Road, Suite 100
Lincoln, NE 68512
www.iuniverse.com
1-800-Authors (1-800-288-4677)

Because of the dynamic nature of the Internet, any Web addresses or links contained in this book may have changed since publication and may no longer be valid.

The views expressed in this work are solely those of the author and do not necessarily reflect the views of the publisher, and the publisher hereby disclaims any responsibility for them.

ISBN: 978-0-595-45314-6 (pbk)
ISBN: 978-0-595-89627-1 (ebk)

Printed in the United States of America

Contents

Part II   Practicalities of Foreign Service Life

Part III   Family and Relationships

Foreword

When the first volume of "Realities" was published in 2002, it was immediately perceived as a very useful volume, both for new Foreign Service employees and for people who were considering a Foreign Service career.

Since its publication, the Foreign Service has changed radically in order to respond to new circumstances and to new demands being placed upon it. The editors of the first volume soon realized that there were topics and issues which either had evolved considerably since 2002 or which didn't exist at that time. Thus, they concluded that a new volume, "Realities II," would be the best way to reflect the current "Realities of Foreign Service Life."

In this second volume, the editors use a somewhat different point of view. The first volume contained numerous experiences narrated in the first person. For this new collection, the authors (though they usually write from personal experience) have also sought opinions and comments from others, thus providing a multi-person perspective for many topics.

One might ask, "How has the Foreign Service changed?" "Realities II" did not set out to include material on all the changes which have taken place. However, many of them are reflected in these pages. The most dramatic change is the great increase of unaccompanied posts and all the stresses that creates. The Diplomatic Readiness Initiative brought in large numbers of new employees and their spouses, including many more male spouses. The result was an even greater call for family member employment opportunities just as new security restrictions made family members ineligible for many of the consular positions they had previously held. At many posts, things which we used to do with pleasure—getting to know host-country nationals or even holding a big Fourth of July celebration—have taken on a different tone since United States policy has angered so many people. And evacuations have become almost routine.

The Foreign Service is also in the midst of a great turnover in personnel. Many people will be retiring because of age limitations. New people will be taken in more quickly because the modified Foreign Service Examination facilitates hiring. The Department of State is now turning to members of the Civil Service as well to fill overseas positions—something which they had never expected and which is totally new to them. And even the number of foreign-born spouses seems to be on the rise.

Much has been written about the important role of accurate and realistic expectations in helping a person adapt to circumstances. With so many new arrivals, a book like "Realities II" is all the more important because it openly and honestly deals with many of the current and relatively new situations which members of today's Foreign Service community—whether employees or family members—might encounter.

Mette Beecroft
AAFSW President Emerita

Ten Reasons to Read This Book

by Terri Williams, AAFSW President Emerita

Why should you read this book? Well, using the words that anyone in the Foreign Service seems to hear when they ask any question: "it depends." Perhaps …

> You are thinking that a career in the Foreign Service might (or might not) be the right thing for you …
>
> Your spouse or partner is wondering what his or her life would be like if you join the Foreign Service …
>
> You've already joined the Foreign Service but are curious about what lies ahead of you …
>
> You worry how moving around the world might affect your (present or future) children …
>
> You're wondering what it is really like to live in a place you have to look up on a map to learn to spell …
>
> You are curious about the details of everyday life in the Foreign Service:
> housing, cars, schools, spouse employment and much more …
>
> You suspect that people who think diplomacy is all about dinners and cocktail parties may be missing a few details …
>
> You are the parent of a new or prospective member of the Foreign Service, and you want to know what this life is all about …
>
> You have a close friend who is considering joining the Foreign Service …

You want to find out more about life in the Foreign Service, but aren't even quite sure what kinds of questions to ask ...

Well, READ ON....

Introduction

The Foreign Service is much more than a job, or even a career—at overseas postings, it is a 24-hour lifestyle that presents great challenges and opportunities to both employees and accompanying family members.

What is everyday life like at an overseas post? How are Foreign Service children educated? How do employees and family members adjust to moving to a new country every few years? What employment opportunities are available for accompanying partners? What's it like to be a single officer abroad? What happens if you are struck with a serious illness overseas?

These are the kinds of questions that this book attempts to answer. To do so, thirty-one volunteer writers—including Foreign Service officers and specialists, spouses and one talented teen—carefully researched their topics, interviewed others, and added their own perspectives, sometimes very personal ones, to their essays.

This book is not intended to replace the first volume, *Realities of Foreign Service Life*, but to provide additional information on a range of new topics. Although some aspects of Foreign Service life have changed since its publication in 2002—such as the large increase in unaccompanied assignments, reflected in an essay in the present volume—we believe that the first book remains highly relevant. Some of its topics were not repeated in this volume, and we believe they remain "required reading" for new and prospective Foreign Service community members. The essays on accompanying husbands, gay partners, long-distance relationships, divorce in the Foreign Service and depression after a move are among those which should not be missed.

As in the first book, the essays here do not set out to describe the daily work routines and assignments of a Foreign Service officer or specialist. This is admirably accomplished by the book *Inside a U.S. Embassy*, published by the American Foreign Service Association (AFSA).

Amid the praise for the first volume were voices that wondered why we often focused on the negative aspects of Foreign Service life. Clearly, life overseas offers unique and exciting opportunities: traveling far off the beaten path, learning languages, gaining deep insights into other cultures, making friends around the world, and making a difference by working at an embassy or as a volunteer abroad. We have tried to offer more of a sense of this adventure and excitement in the present volume. However, the areas in which new and prospective Foreign Service community members truly need information and guidance—including limited spouse employment opportunities, the threat of evacuation, health issues, the challenges of adjustment, and separated tours—remain on the "minus" side of the ledger.

The Foreign Service is not for everyone. This book is intended to provide an honest and realistic picture of this unusual lifestyle, to help readers make better-informed decisions about whether to embark on this journey—and get the most out of the experience once they have done so.

One very positive aspect of Foreign Service life is the strong sense of community it often fosters. The Associates of the American Foreign Service Worldwide (AAFSW), **www.aafsw.org**, the publisher and nonprofit beneficiary of this book, is among the most active supporters of this sense of community. We would like to thank its President, Judy Felt, for her enthusiastic backing of this project and her ongoing efforts on behalf of Foreign Service partners and family members.

We would also like to profusely thank AAFSW Presidents Emerita Mette Beecroft, who wrote our Foreword, and Terri Williams, who kept our spirits high over the two years it took to complete this book, and then uncomplainingly proofread the entire document (any remaining errors are ours!). Other volunteers whose names do not appear in the book but who provided invaluable editing and other help behind the scenes include Brian Neely, Bert Curtis, Nan Leininger, and many others who responded to our authors' calls for information.

And finally, we would like to thank all of the authors who responded to Marlene's original call to write for this book, professionally researched and prepared their essays, and waited patiently to finally hold this volume in their hands.

Melissa Brayer Hess, Patricia Linderman and Marlene Nice

PART I
Overseas Perspectives

Neighborhood Diplomats: Befriending Host Country Nationals

by John Hosinski

He was probably the first person I saw when we moved into our apartment. There he was, outside his house next door in the middle of the February cold, banging away under the hood of a car. Sawing body parts off and welding all sorts of stuff back on—making all sorts of noise … all day. I wondered if he'd ever stop. He once woke up my 5-month-old up during his (and at the time my) nap. I wanted to throttle him. We didn't say a word to one another for weeks.

But as the spring air warmed, we started with the casual head nods and then full-fledged hellos. Before long, the standard formal introductions to each other's families ensued. His son's wife was pregnant with their first child. He had family in Canada. We'd both lost family members to cancer. Over a year and a half later, I talk to him nearly daily. He always finds time to show my admiring toddler around his garage and insists on giving me a glass of his potent homemade wine. He helps me with the language, which often makes for a shared laugh. I don't even notice the banging and pounding anymore, considering that he's now fixed our car. And as our tour comes to an end, I know I'll miss him and his family.

The process of getting to know someone from your host country is very often a mutually beneficial relationship. We move beyond the easy stereotypes to learn new things about one another as well as more about ourselves and our own cultures. Local friends often provide knowledge of how things work in a country better than any guidebook or country report and can make even the most isolated place feel a bit warmer. By making friends overseas, you grow more comfortable in a foreign setting and in your own skin. And like it or not, interactions with local people give you a great opportunity to explain things from a uniquely American perspective, making you a sort of informal "neighborhood diplomat" conducting public diplomacy person to person.

Settling in

Making friends is not easy and takes time. And just what is considered friendship? Any positive personal contact initiated regularly between people over the course of a tour. So while a relationship that carries on into e-mail, letters, and even phone calls or visits long after a tour is over is rightly considered friendship, so can be any regular communication with someone in which some simple personal information is exchanged.

But before mingling with the locals, you have to get comfortable. Moving in is hard work. The demands of moving and adjusting to the climate, food, and schedule of a new place often take precedence over a social life. In addition, it takes quite a bit of time just to get to know other members of the embassy community.

At most posts, there are networking resources for expats abroad, such as international clubs, parent-teacher associations, baby/toddler playgroups, or professional associations. Embassy colleagues and family members and other expats are a valuable resource and help create a sense of community that is helpful during a transition to a new, unfamiliar place. Our American friends are a large part of our lives overseas—where would we be without our 4th of July, our barbeques, our Community Liaison Office-sponsored events? Meanwhile, our non-American expat friends share our situation and globetrotting lifestyle and help us to view our host country from a different, non-American, perspective. According to Dr. Anne P. Copeland, an expert on cross-cultural communication and Executive Director of the Interchange Institute in Brookline, Massachusetts, spending time with other Americans or expats is very natural and happens across cultures and around the world, since "people get a valuable kind of support from others who share their experience."

But no matter where you are posted, you will come into contact with local nationals. At post, you'll likely get to know a number of locally-hired staff. You might develop good contacts with grocers, shopkeepers, or other service providers. You'll probably have local neighbors. You may meet people at religious services or at volunteer activities, or just on the street. Yet making *friends* is another story requiring a little bit more work than just exchanging pleasantries or being a good customer. In fact, it can be altogether different and even exhausting. The local sense of personal space and personal information may be much different than yours. They may do things (like show up for dinner at 10 pm) that baffle you. You may be asked for help getting a visa. You may have to listen to a detailed five-minute response to the standard "how are you?" greeting. You may be asked to talk about politics or foreign policy, or asked if you are a spy (I have).

How we get together

Although tours last several years, the time will fly. In fact, the short-term nature of overseas tours can sometimes stand in the way of getting to know someone—you, perhaps subconsciously, may never want to fully extend yourself if you know you will have to pull up stakes and leave soon.

Potential friends know this as well, and also may be unwilling to invest much personal time in a relationship with someone they realize will be leaving soon. One Foreign Service spouse suspected that local members of a volunteer project she worked on were wary of getting to know her too well, considering she was leaving in less than two years. My wife and I found this to be the case at our current post, when we moved in and noticed that our neighbors were a bit timid, even cold toward us for the first few months. My wife's locally-hired colleagues at work told her that, first, this was just how some people were here; and second, our apartment had previously been used almost exclusively as temporary housing, so the neighbors were used to Americans showing up, not saying much, and then leaving just as quickly. Once they learned we would be staying for a few years, our neighbors warmed up to us quickly, to the point that we now feel like part of the neighborhood, with them inviting us to their houses for meals and coffee, us hosting them for full-blown American-style Sunday brunches—and that quintessential sign of neighborliness: borrowing each other's stuff.

Though your neighbors or work colleagues at post may be the first local citizens you meet, there are many other opportunities to meet host country nationals. The ways people meet friends normally fall into three categories: proximity, shared interest, and serendipity.

Proximity

If you aren't on a compound, you'll likely develop some sort of regular relationship, if not friendship, with your local neighbors. Foreign Service officers work with and get to know many of the local staff at post and other work-related contacts that may also lead to friendship. The same is true for spouses whose professional networks bring them into contact with locals.

One interviewee even noted that she and her family have become friends with their landlord—perhaps made easier by the reliability of payments and repairs—but also a reflection, again, of good neighborliness. Landlords appreciate tenants who take care of their property, and tenants appreciate a responsive landlord. Having a friendship that allows you to get to know your landlord and discuss things openly is, as anyone who has even been on either side of the rentor/rentee line can attest, a major blessing.

Shared interests

Shared interests usually lead to more substantive talk about ourselves, our backgrounds and cultures. For example, parents have many opportunities to meet locals with children the same age. The PTA, sports and music events, and baby/toddler groups are examples of settings in which parents and their kids get to know one another. Be aware, however: child-rearing techniques differ across cultures. In Croatia, our child's sleep schedule tends to be very different from that of our neighbors and friends, who regularly call or come over during naptime or at bedtime.

Sports or recreation clubs provide an opportunity to meet people. Many note that they've made friends through jogging, tennis, or other athletic activities with local enthusiasts. One foreign-born spouse said she meets her local friends on the golf course—an activity that has forged relationships and opened some business networking opportunities.

Foreign Service officers also meet locals through cultural events (art exhibits, musical performances, etc.), religious services, art classes and language classes. A number of spouses serving in isolated posts with high hardship and/or danger levels noted that volunteering was a good way to get out and meet people when opportunities for interaction with others are limited or constrained.

Serendipity

From time to time, something crops up and you discover something that you hadn't been looking for. How many of us can point to pictures in our albums, souvenirs displayed in our homes, or unique opportunities that arose because we were unexpectedly in the right place at the right time?

This happens with friendships as well. You bump into someone on the street; you overhear someone say something interesting; you go to an event you'd planned to miss and meet someone. The examples are numerous. One spouse noted how a toothache requiring extensive dental care led to a friendship with her dentist and regular participation in her dentist's English-language conversation group. A musically-inclined spouse was at an embassy party when he overheard two local embassy employees lamenting their band's lack of a proper drummer. He volunteered, leading to the formation of more than one band, a number of gigs around the area, and friendships not only with his band mates, but a number of their friends as well. Another Foreign Service officer noted how making time in her hectic schedule to attend a representational event—a traveling exhibit of American artists—led to a friendship with someone she met there.

Getting to know them

We all rely on a certain number of stereotypes to help us grasp the new countries and cultures we are living in. Well-worn, all-inclusive or mostly-inclusive stereotypes help us break down the characteristics of each country and better understand the things we experience day-to-day basis. But the inherent danger of stereotypes is that they can serve as a crutch, preventing us from appreciating the individuals we meet.

Dr. Harlan Wadley, a State Department psychiatrist based in Vienna, notes that local friends serve as "informal trainers" to help us process new cultural information, particularly during the early stages of a tour. Dr. Wadley notes that because of our limited time at each post, most of us don't have the time to fully adapt ourselves to another culture, but simply to learn as much as possible about our host country. The best way to begin this process is not only to meet local citizens, but to observe the salient characteristics of a new culture, he says.

Common examples of salient characteristics are basic social rules such as formal and informal greetings, eye contact, personal space, and non-verbal communications. The most common, and most salient of all cultural characteristics, though, is language. Learning even the basics of a foreign language does wonders for your capacity to live and operate confidently in another country. Although the basics of a language will help you come into more contact with host country nationals, you may find yourself only able to develop friendships with those who share a common linguistic fluency with you, be it in English or another language. One spouse noted that her good, but limited, Russian skills were a significant constraint to her moving to higher levels of friendship in a Central Asian country, while her ability to converse fluently at a French-speaking post resulted in much easier social situations.

How do friends get together in your host country? In Croatia, where café culture is king, inviting someone out for a cup of coffee is the basic first step in a developing friendship. Once that level of ice is broken, most friends will visit one another's homes for dinner or in the summer, for a barbeque. The drummer mentioned previously noted that he and his Croatian band mates have been to each other's homes numerous times. He's even met their grandmothers, which is the Croatian equivalent of getting on someone's Christmas card list.

Of course, meeting foreign friends can also lead to cases of cross-cultural miscommunication. An embassy employee in Uruguay noticed that all the Americans showed up promptly for a 6 p.m. dinner invitation, while the Uruguayans arrived at their normal evening meal hour, 9 p.m. A similar situation occurred when my wife and I nearly offended our neighbors in Zagreb when we got up to head home shortly after New Year's Eve fireworks and champagne. We hadn't realized that a traditional New Year's meal was being prepared, and our hosts were very confused by our casual attempt to leave. Such a thing had never happened to them before, and a speechless stare-down ensued, with them not knowing what to say, and us not knowing why everyone was staring at us. We worked out an acceptable compromise: my wife left to get some rest before our child's dawn wake-up time, while I represented the family over food and drinks until 4 a.m.

Roadblock: Visas

It's inevitable that Foreign Service officers and their families are asked for help in getting a visa, often leading to touchy and uncomfortable situations. One spouse noted that nearly all of her contacts with locals led in some way or another to either the topic of visas or to some other request for a favor (such as obtaining some product not available in the country.) One former Foreign Service officer ended a budding romantic relationship almost as quickly as it started when the "V" word crawled across a candlelit tablecloth like an unwanted cockroach.

Dr. Wadley notes that the visa issue highlights the fact that diplomats are often on an unequal footing with average host-country citizens. A diplomatic position brings with it official status, immunities, high-level contacts, (sometimes) nice housing, and often a higher standard of living compared to most local people. These differences, whether they are highly obvious or mostly in the perceptions of host-county citizens, often form the basis for requests for favors.

According to Dr. Copeland, the most common American reaction to the visa question reflects a mixture of our American individualist ethic ("don't ask anyone for favors"), our universalism (an absolute sense of right and wrong, and the idea that the same rules should apply to all), and our sense of low power distance, leading us to dislike special privileges and prefer egalitarian relationships. Yet in other areas of the world, word of mouth and personal or familial connections are the way that nearly everything gets done.

Neighborhood diplomats

In mid-2004, while our presidential election season was in full swing, I was somewhat stunned when a Croatian acquaintance from down the street asked me to explain the Electoral College. Talk about a curveball. I was expecting questions about tackle football, maybe Michael Jackson at the worst, but the Electoral College? I handled it pretty well, but still had to think really hard about it.

American cultural imports travel the globe. Our movies, TV shows, music, and products—and their numerous local spin-offs—are popular. But these often fail to give a complete view, and sometimes present a misleading picture, of American culture. Thanks to the United States' predominant position in world affairs, our political actions also receive worldwide attention.

Adding to this mix is the impact of official propaganda, less-than-free presses, and persistent conspiracy theories that create, in some countries, an environment of confusion or incorrect information about the United States. There are also nearly always real issues of disagreement between the U.S. and our host countries that get plenty of local airtime.

Friendships between Americans and foreigners can help close the distance between our perceptions and yield positive results for our official bilateral relationships, just as student and cultural exchange programs do. By befriending a host-country national, you're engaging in a highly personal, microcosmic kind of public relations: neighborhood diplomacy.

Saying goodbye

Frequent moves are another aspect of Foreign Service life that can be both a blessing and a curse. Besides the phenomenon noted above—the lack of enthusiasm for constructing friendships when both you and the locals know you will be leaving in a few years—many complain that they never stay in one place long enough to get to know people. Based on interviews, it also seems far less common for Foreign Service officers and their family members to keep in touch with local friends than with other Americans or expats they met on tour.

However, e-mail and improved travel options have made it easier to stay in touch. I know of numerous Foreign Service employees and family members who maintain far-flung networks across the globe and even return to visit old friends or host them for a visit to the U.S.

Saying goodbye is an important process. Dr. Wadley notes that attaching meaning to a tour is a good way to transition from one country to another. When we bid on a country, many of us probably never think about the new friends we will get to know there. Taking time to note the friendships you have made in a place, and making a point to say goodbye to your friends, may be the best way both to reflect on the good times you've had, and to gain a sense of closure at the end of a tour.

A Foreign Service spouse, John Hosinski is a freelance writer and a former Fulbright scholar (Poland), with extensive travel and work experience in Central and Eastern Europe. John currently lives in Zagreb, Croatia with his wife Elizabeth and two-year old son JP. Zagreb is their first post.

Driving You Crazy: Lessons Missing from Driver's Education

by Claudette Friedman

Driving in foreign countries is not a problem ... as long as you genuinely love driving, don't mind lots of erratic traffic, and have excellent reflexes. If, however, you are more like I am, and actually like enforced traffic laws to ensure "fairness" on the road, you may feel tense while adjusting to the driving patterns at many overseas posts.

Operating a vehicle on unfamiliar roads requires a different set of skills from finding one's way around a new city. Some brave souls have no fear and plunge right into traffic, no matter how frightening. Many others need a constant navigator. Others simply hire taxis or their very own personal driver. Some people enjoy mass transit in countries where it is safe and reliable, and they leave their cars parked at home to avoid the stress.

Adapting to driving on the left in places like Australia and Brunei is a whole separate challenge, especially if you import a vehicle with the steering wheel on the "wrong" side. It can take weeks or months to unlearn the habits of checking to the left for oncoming traffic. This adaptation is possible, I am told, but there will always be the odd, surreal moments: a spouse in Trinidad reports glancing instinctively to the left side of an oncoming truck's windshield to check that the driver had seen her—and being greeted by the grinning face of a large, shaggy dog.

Operating the vehicle

Not all roads in the United States are marvelous (I grew up in Maine, once notorious for its potholes). Anyone who has spent time in the Washington, DC area knows that bad driving is ubiquitous there. However, poor roads and poor road manners just seem more prevalent elsewhere.

I had taken for granted the quality of road construction in the U.S. until we went bumping along a Ukrainian "highway" in the mid-1990s at a bone-rattling 45 mph. In cities such as Kiev and Zagreb, the patch-fill (but not smoothed over) method of fixing potholes creates bumps that are as bad as speed bumps. In many developing nations, dirt roads are still the norm. In countries such as Mongolia, it is possible for a driver not to use a formal road at all, but to forge across an empty steppe in the general direction of his or her destination.

My husband contends that people who learn to drive in Europe on narrow streets with narrow lanes have a better sense of the size of their cars—they can happily zoom along with only a rear-view mirror's width between themselves and the rows of parked cars. Americans, who (for the most part) learn how to drive on wider roads—or even in huge, empty mall parking lots after hours—aren't as instinctively aware of the size of our cars. Therefore, we aren't very good at judging how to get through tight European streets, especially with our large vehicles. Some roads that are narrow enough to be one-lane, one-way in the U.S. are used as two-directional—plus parking on both sides!—in Zagreb, Croatia.

On occasion, when meandering through the old hill roads of Zagreb—and I'm betting this is true in other quaint, hilly towns—one encounters former footpaths now used as roads; if you meet another car, one of you will have to back up and pull entirely out of the road in order for the other car to pass. Try that with a Dodge Grand Caravan. Therefore, if a street is very narrow but fairly short, you may want to go very fast down the middle and hope that you can get to the end before meeting another car, which would require tiresome maneuvering.

Incidentally, the problems of a large vehicle are exacerbated when trying to park. We're glad to have our minivan for the family trips and occasional carpools, but for everyday errands, it is ludicrous (as is the gas mileage, not a small concern since gasoline prices in many other parts of the world are much higher than in the U.S.). No wonder there are a few brands of cars available here in Europe that make a golf cart look spacious; they can park anywhere! Creative parking solutions in Croatia include simply leaving the car in the middle lane of a street. I have developed a new skill: parallel parking up a 6" curbed sidewalk. This is normal here. We are fortunate to have a few very modern parking garages, but the tight design can cause even locals to scrape the sides of their cars on the support beams.

Of course, a large, solid vehicle may be recommended in volatile places, where colleagues are also warned against driving out of the city limits or at night because of safety issues such as bandits and terrorists. Some people also simply prefer to be surrounded by a lot of heavy metal that sits high up off the road.

Road manners

Post-Soviet countries went through a dramatic boom of private vehicle ownership in the 1990s, which meant that a huge new group of inexperienced drivers began operating under lax traffic laws. Beware small vehicles with toy-sized engines that can easily slip in and cut you off but then cannot get up to speed on a slight rise, so you have to slam on the brakes of your much more powerful vehicle. Be aware that in some countries, such as Turkey, many drivers lean on their horns in what seems like an attempt to make a red light change to green more rapidly.

In diverse areas of the world, it seems that the more expensive the car, the less courteous the driver is expected to be. Do not be surprised if such a vehicle passes you when you are stopped in line at a traffic light so that it can be the first car at the intersection.

American drivers generally adhere to the one lane/one car concept. Other countries find this a waste of time and space, and try to fit as many cars side-by-side as possible within one lane. In parts of Europe, a red light turns yellow to indicate that it will soon turn green, just as the green turns yellow to warn of an impending red light. People tend to jump the gun a bit on both sides (see photo of a major Kiev street at midday; this is not a parking lot, nor an accident site: it is an ordinary traffic jam in the mid-1990s with all cars in motion; none are parked).

Speed limits, when posted, may be recommendations only. Other challenges include baby carriages being pushed on the street-side of parked cars, stray dogs, cars suddenly pulling out of driveways, double-parked delivery vans obstructing the view, and pedestrians with no fear (perhaps never having driven a car themselves) who start walking across the street without checking for oncoming cars, or walk down the middle of a pitch-black rural road at night.

In cities such as Bangkok or Mexico City, the sheer volume of cars creates havoc (grains of sand can go through an hourglass only so fast).

In Cairo, donkey carts are added to the mix. A military family member recently told me that in Yaounde, Camaroon, she feels a fear-for-her-life sensation starting up along with the car's engine because of the aggressive, merciless drivers there.

The good news is that certain road signs, such as a red octagonal "Stop," seem to be universal. Of course, it is important to remember that many people consider this merely a suggestion. Also bear in mind that what appears to be an obvious right-of-way may be nothing of the sort. Many Americans assume that if they are going "straight" through an intersection, they will have the right-of-way. This is not necessarily true overseas. Here is one of my favorite road signs in Croatia:

This indicates that the right-of-way curves at least at a 90° angle. I approach such intersections with caution because this information is not necessarily posted on the other streets. In some places, cars approaching from the right have the right-of-way (unless otherwise posted), even if the streets they are emerging from appear to be secondary to the main road.

Getting around

When learning your way around a strange new place, do not expect to get there on the first try. Long roads may change their names every few traffic lights (as they do in Northern Virginia back home). Some streets may have barricaded access. Many times I have consulted a map, carefully plotted my route and set out with (relative) confidence, only to be dismayed to find that the street I wanted was a one-way in the wrong direction. Street maps can be unreliable: I had to throw out a Zagreb tourist bureau map that incorrectly indicated such an important landmark as a hospital. Asking local people (especially those who walk everywhere) for directions may lead to colloquial names not listed on the map, or streets that are pedestrian-only.

In Croatia, it took me two or three tries to fully comprehend that a road marked "stube" ends in a staircase that does indeed connect to the required street, but I would not attempt this even with a Ford Explorer. Not speaking the local language is an obvious disadvantage. Here it seems that half the street names begin with V or P, contain at least four syllables and end in ska, čka, čeva or ova. At least this language uses the familiar Latin alphabet.

When riding with someone else, I try to pay attention to landmarks. I discovered one of my favorite back routes out of my neighborhood thanks to a savvy taxi driver. Alternative routes are important for those occasions when road construction crews block the street with no advance warning. Other valuable information might be: which streets are one-way? On tram tracks? No left turn allowed? Seven blocks until the next opportunity to turn around? Are there parts of town to avoid for reasons of safety, rush hour traffic, or potential loss of muffler? Transportation challenges can certainly add to the adventures (or frustrations) of living abroad—unless, of course, you really like driving.

Claudette Cyr Friedman has been living the Foreign Service life for 11 years. She has followed her FSO husband to Kiev, Ukraine with one child, Ottawa, Canada with two children, Washington, D.C., and Zagreb,

Croatia with three. The family's next assignment is Bandar Seri Begawan, Brunei. When Claudette first wrote this article and mentioned Brunei in passing, she had no idea she would end up there!

The Fourth of July Overseas:
Not Always a Picnic

by Susie Csorsz Brown

Independence Day is the epitome of Americana. More than just a holiday, it's a tradition. And this tradition is carried out by U.S. missions around the world, from Australia with hundreds of official Americans in the embassy, thousands of U.S. businesses and tens of thousands of American expatriates, to Zambia, with under 20 official Americans and a few hundred expats.

Foreign Service folks plan for months for the Fourth of July. They shop online and from catalogs, ordering everything imaginable in red, white and blue. They arrange, they schedule, and when they finally finish, they have created a little piece of America in their host country's backyard. It's ironic, really, that the celebration of our country's day of independence—an informal occasion for picnics and parades in the States—becomes a major logistical challenge at Embassies and Consulates abroad, requiring Foreign Service officers (FSOs), their families, and local staff to plan and prepare for months ahead of time.

Official versus unofficial

Overseas, Foreign Service celebrations of the Fourth of July fall into two basic categories: official and unofficial. Official events are parties given by the embassy for the host country. This event is formal and elaborate—and included as part of the embassy's budget. The purpose of the official event is to share a notable ceremony with the mission's most important contacts in the host country.

The unofficial event is given by the embassy for the embassy community itself. It often includes the entire local staff of the mission as well as the wider American community living in the host country. No money is included in the embassy's budget for this event. The unofficial Fourth of July party must be funded with entry fees and tickets, voluntary contributions, and/or donations solicited from the community (usually from American businesses). The unofficial event can be a much larger event than the official reception, involving many more guests.

Both celebrations can be organizational headaches. The planning begins early, sometimes as early as July 5th of the preceding year, and, in some cases, may not end until the last star-spangled balloon is popped. Depending on the country, the events may not even be scheduled in July; for instance, it may be the middle of the rainy season in the host country.

Organization of the official event generally falls to the Public Diplomacy section of the embassy. Good Public Diplomacy offices have copious notes filled with "lessons learned" files from previous years. The Front Office is also very involved in the preparations for this event, as this is their opportunity to represent America and throw an all-American party for host country officials.

The list of invitees for the official event is very important. It includes all of the important contacts for all of the offices in the mission. Unfortunately, space (and sometimes budgetary) constraints at some posts may mean that not all personnel or their spouses can be included.

One Foreign Service spouse, who was excluded from an Independence Day event, comments:

> *We were in Sydney and the Consul General and the American Chamber of Commerce hosted a July 4th cocktail reception for Americans in the area. Though there were only seven of us, consulate spouses were not invited. The only spouse included was the Consul General's wife. I couldn't help thinking that I, too, was an American living in Sydney,*

so why wasn't I included? It was my Independence Day, too! July 4th is the only American event held where those of us overseas can gather to embrace and affirm our "American-ness" and have a chance to display our pride in our country and our contributions in service to our country.

Those who are on the guest list sometimes have a different opinion. One FSO states:

It's sad. The Fourth of July used to be one of my favorite holidays. Unlike Christmas, it's not really commercial, and unlike Thanksgiving, you don't have to worry about a Martha Stewart menu—just hotdogs, hamburgers and the whole family together for fun in the sun. I would trade one month's paycheck to miss a Fourth event. I still aspire to the good old days of fun Fourths—perhaps after I've retired!

The official celebration can actually encompass a series of events. In Uruguay, the official observances went on for weeks, starting before July. One FSO related her surprise at a tasking shortly after arriving at post: she was given the monumental assignment of organizing all of the official Fourth of July events, even though she was a first-time junior officer.

First, the embassy hosted an essay/coloring contest for host country youth, with entries focusing on a different theme each year (e.g. "The U. S. Constitution versus the Constitution of Uruguay" and "How to be a Good Citizen in a Democracy"). The contest was announced months in advance, a committee was formed to choose the winners and prizes were awarded in an elaborate ceremony. At the insistence of the Ambassador, each of the business leaders who made significant contributions for the year's celebrations had a speaking role in the ceremony—not an easy event for a first-tour officer to orchestrate.

Another celebration required the Ambassador to present a floral arrangement and give a speech honoring soldiers. This involved a great amount of work and time to make arrangements with city officials.

Finally, there was a formal reception hosted by the Ambassador with specific requirements that had to be met. With July falling in the middle of winter, space heaters had to be set up, run safely, and concealed adequately without becoming fire hazards. Since the Ambassador was Jewish, the meal had to be completely kosher. The junior officer devoted five months of her time to arranging the countless details, from all aspects of the menu planning, to flower arrangements, to the hanging of country flags in the same order as the vehicles in the motorcade. The officer had the foresight to create a binder filled with records of each event for the next year's organizers. This was a smart move. For the following Fourth of July, she was tasked with organizing all of the same events again!

Organizing and hosting unofficial events generally fall to the Management section. The General Service and Community Liaison offices are deeply involved, as is everyone else at post, whether they are employed at the mission or not.

The unofficial celebration more closely resembles the casual, family-fun event that is customary in the U.S. In many cases, it presents an opportunity to introduce host-country staff and their families to the traditional carnival games we grew up with in the United States. One favorite is the dunking booth. When living overseas, it can take months to design and build one of these. Most Americans are familiar with these booths at Stateside fairs and carnivals, but it can take a lot of miming and stick-figure drawing to explain the concept to the host country's maintenance staff, especially if they have never seen one before. Once built, though, it is normally a big hit, especially if senior-level members of the mission are the "dunkees."

One of the most challenging parts of organizing events is finding a sufficient number of volunteers to make things happen. It is simply not possible to pay all of these helping hands for their services, so organizers must ask for volunteers. Though volunteers usually have the best of intentions, they also are attending the event to have a good time rather than to work, so some may not feel compelled to follow directions, or even stay their allotted time.

Fortunately, this is not always the case. Depending on the size of the post and the closeness of the mission community, getting volunteers can be somewhat easier. In hardship posts, the community members tend to be closer and much more supportive of mission events. One Foreign Service spouse observed,

> *One thing I have noticed, the more of a hardship the post is, the more the community gets involved in the event, and, in the end, the more fun everyone seems to have. One of the best Fourth of July parties I've ever been to was in Niger, a true African hardship post. The post was so small that everybody got involved in the planning and we had such a good time. The relay games got everyone soaked; the food was good; and we even had a cookie bake-off that provided friendly competition and dessert! It was a great afternoon—one my family and I will never forget.*

The menu

Trying to recreate the traditional Fourth of July menu overseas can be a challenge. For example, it is more difficult to find a can of baked beans in Dar es Salaam than in Dallas. Fried chicken may not come out "crispy on the outside, tender and juicy on the inside" in countries where chickens are kept alive as long as possible before consumption in order to get the most egg-producing years out of them. Then there are times when the foods we know and love are complete mysteries to the host-country invitees. One Community Liaison Office coordinator (CLO) told of an event that featured a line of grills with people cooking up hamburgers. The committee had worked for weeks getting the seasonings for the meat just right and had pre-formed the patties to simplify the grilling. Guests filed through, got their bun and patty, and then moved on to the fixings. However, most of the people from the host country were not familiar with American hamburgers, so they placed the bun on one side of the plate, heaped the fixings up next to it as a salad, and placed the meat alongside. The CLO had to quickly find a spare volunteer or two to help with the assembly process of the burgers, so that guests could enjoy an American-style burger instead of eating each food separately.

In addition to making the decision on what to serve, it is just as difficult to figure out how much to serve. The official event is a little easier to plan because the events are generally catered and guests are expected to RSVP. The caterer then figures out the rest.

For the unofficial event, however, there are more uncertainties. The guest list may include the entire mission (direct hire employees, locally employed staff, and all of their families), as well as all Americans in country. The number can vary by the hundreds depending on where the event falls in the school year, the entry fee involved, and the success (or failure) of the previous year's event. The challenge is to figure out how to feed a group of anywhere from 200 to 2,000 guests without running out of food or having large amounts left over. One American Club manager suggests,

> *We always do the food for the unofficial event. We serve chicken, burgers, and hotdogs hot off the grill. The embassy cafeteria is also our domain, so we can keep the prepped foods (precooked chicken, preformed burger patties, and hotdogs) in the cafeteria's fridge, bringing it out as we need it, and finishing them on the grill. Anything left over can then be "recycled" into meals from the cafeteria later in the week—chicken pot pie, anyone? Once we hit upon this solution, everyone was happy. Guests could enjoy hot and fresh food without long lines, we didn't run out of food, and the Club didn't lose a lot of money from waste and spoilage, especially if the turnout wasn't as good as expected.*

Decorations

Making any area look patriotic is simple—just decorate it with red, white, and blue! Finding decorations deemed appropriate and tasteful can be more problematic. The decorations for the official event are more sedate and traditional, presenting a very conservative image of Independence Day.

The setting for the unofficial function, however, is more casual with all things red, white, and blue hung from any non-moving object (and even some moving ones). Every good CLO and GSO knows the best suppliers of balloons, crepe paper, flags and other patriotic decorations. At the event, one can always identify the members of the decorating committee by their sore cheeks from blowing up balloons, and by their inability to lift their arms, due to hours spent taping up crepe paper streamers, fan-like paper bells, stars made from tissue paper and Tiki lanterns.

Fireworks

Like everything else related to Independence Day celebrations overseas, obtaining fireworks can be challenging. Normal shipping methods for ordering supplies from the U.S. is not an option, because flammable items are prohibited in the diplomatic pouch. Organizers must use other sources.

One possibility is to begin the process very early and import the fireworks from a nearby country. This can take months, however, and involves trying to convince various local country ministries that the supplies are for a celebratory display, not for any form of violence or criminal acts. Unfortunately, this also means trusting unknown vendors and buying sight-unseen, possibly resulting in an order of old fireworks that do not explode in the end. The best bet is to find another local group that uses fireworks frequently and go through their supplier. It always pays to ask your friends!

There is always the previously-recorded-and-projected-onto-screens approach, but that can be a bit of a letdown. In the end, the displays generally go off without a hitch, but the list of "what ifs" can be daunting.

It is ironic that a casual, fun, family-oriented holiday celebrated in the U.S. requires so much time, money, hard work, and extra effort to put together when serving at a U.S. mission overseas. That is not to say that all the hard work does not pay off in the end. Though hosting Fourth of July celebrations overseas requires lots of effort and energy, everything usually comes together and people feel that the party was worth it. As one CLO stated,

> *It is hard to get in the spirit of things when you are spending your time worrying about the banners, if the hats will arrive in time, if the Front Office will be happy with the final outcome, and then working on the "big day." But, that said, this is a celebration of our nation's history and the chance to show our host countries that in many ways we are just like them—proud of our history and culture.*

Susie Csorsz Brown is working on her sixth unofficial Independence Day celebration in yet another country. She and her husband have served in Niger, Tanzania and are now in Cambodia, collecting pets and kids along the way (one dog, two cats and a son, Lucca).

Who Am I Now? The Identity Question for Foreign Service Spouses

by Debra R. Bryson

As a Foreign Service spouse, I wasn't quite prepared for the profound effect moving overseas would have on me. I wanted to move overseas just as much as my husband did. We were both excited when we discovered that we would have the opportunity to move to Bangkok, Thailand, to live and work overseas, and to experience a foreign culture together. It was something we had both dreamed about and planned for.

Shortly after arriving in Bangkok, as I attempted to settle into my new surroundings, I felt like my internal world had been turned upside down. I experienced conflicting thoughts and feelings which made no sense to me. At one moment I felt excited about living in a foreign country and culture. I was fascinated with the Thai people and their ways of life. I enjoyed the warmth of the tropical climate and I relished basking in the sun by the pool below my new apartment. I found the unique smells of the spices used in cooking enticing, and I savored meal time. Even though I spoke the language clumsily, the Thai people encouraged me to speak more, which motivated me to improve my language skills. I enjoyed being a part of the diplomatic and expatriate communities and I liked meeting new people, attending embassy functions, and exploring Bangkok.

Then, at other times, I questioned why I had ever agreed to such a move. I cried easily and I felt overwhelmed, irritable, angry, and lonely.

In private, in the presence of my husband, I would rant and rave about everything I missed in what I called "my former life" in Washington, DC. It seemed like I missed everything—my home, job, friends, activities, familiar foods, and my family (even though they lived in the Midwest). I felt an emptiness inside that I didn't understand. Although I would remind myself that I had wanted the move, I found little comfort in this. I longed to jog and ride my bike through our former neighborhood, as I used to do after work. I reminisced about "little things" I missed, like being able to get my own mail. I resented having to rely on my husband to collect our mail at the embassy and bring it home. I felt embarrassed by my outbursts and I was confused by my thoughts and feelings. I was sure something was wrong with me.

At first I attributed my inner turmoil to culture shock and cultural adjustment, which I had read about before the move. I tried to reassure myself that in time, I would adjust. Others I met suggested that I fill my time with activities, and said that eventually I would be just fine. However, I wasn't confident that time or their suggestions would be the healer I wanted and needed. I suspected that something else was occurring deep within me, although I didn't know what.

I also discovered during this time that I was prohibited from working in Thailand because of my diplomatic status. I have a master's degree in Clinical Social Work with a specialization in mental health counseling, and I had looked forward to continuing my career overseas. I was devastated because I was told prior to the move that although there was not a formal bilateral work agreement with Thailand, spouses of embassy employees routinely worked on the local economy.

I was already experiencing many conflicting thoughts and feelings about the move when I discovered that I was prohibited from working in my profession. I was miserable, and at one point, I even considered packing my bags and returning to the States so I could work and resume my former life. But, after a lot of self-reflection, I made a commitment to myself to remain in Thailand for the duration of my husband's tour and try to regain my equilibrium. I also became a primary

advocate for spousal employment issues at the U.S. Embassy. Fortunately, after about six months, the culmination of my efforts and the
efforts of key individuals at the embassy were rewarded. The Thai government allowed me to work legally in Thailand, which paved the way
for other spouses to work as well.

It was while I was employed as a counselor at the Community Services of Bangkok (CSB), an organization that provided counseling services to the expatriate community, that I met Charise M. Hoge, a
military spouse and a counselor. Talking about our personal experiences following our husbands overseas for their careers, we discovered
that although our experiences were different, there were many similari-
ties and common themes. We decided to collaborate to develop an in-
depth understanding about what happens to a woman's identity when
she moves overseas primarily to support her husband's career. Our collaboration led to writing the book *A Portable Identity: A Woman's
Guide to Maintaining a Sense of Self While Moving Overseas*. Although
the book and our work primarily focused on women who trail their
husband's careers, we believe that a lot of what we have learned about
this topic applies to the male accompanying spouse as well.

The conflicting thoughts, feelings, and behaviors I experienced after
moving to Bangkok, Thailand are examples of what many spouses go
through when they move overseas in support of their partners' careers.
I share this story with you because as the spouse of a Foreign Service
officer (whether you are a female or male accompanying spouse, new to
the Foreign Service, have already moved one or more times, or your
partner is considering a career in the Foreign Service) it is important
for you to understand that an overseas move will have a profound
effect on *you,* your own sense of self, and your identity. It is also crucial
for you to understand how your identity is affected at each stage of an
overseas move, so that you can be prepared for the effect when it occurs
and make choices that support a successful experience overseas.

In the remainder of this chapter, I will provide you with our defini-
tion of identity and discuss how your identity as a spouse is affected

during three key stages of an overseas move, and how the changes and losses to your identity at each of these stages results in an identity in transition. Lastly, I will discuss how you can take charge of the changes that occur to your identity as a result of the move, so that you can successfully adjust to expatriate life and have a more meaningful experience overseas.

The importance of understanding your pre-move identity

As a Foreign Service spouse, it is essential that you have a clear understanding about your pre-move identity, (or, if you have already moved, how you defined yourself prior to moving overseas), so that you can use this as a baseline to understand what happens to your identity during several key stages of an overseas move.

In our book, we define identity as a composite of four main facets: internal view (how you view yourself); external factors (how others view you); roles; and relationships. These are reference points that help you look at the multitude of components that make you unique. The significance of each facet of identity will be different for each person. For example, the internal part of your identity includes your self-perceptions; your beliefs, values, and attitudes; your likes and dislikes; and your gender and how you feel about being female or male. External factors affecting your identity include the importance to you of others' opinions about you; societal influences; and the impact of the community and culture in which you live. Your identity, in part, is also comprised of the roles you occupy (e.g., spouse, parent, child, sibling, employee, student, volunteer); the importance of these roles to you; and how these roles affect your self-esteem. Finally, your identity also includes the relationships you have with others and the significance of these relationships to you.

To get an idea of your pre-move identity, look at the descriptions that follow each of the four facets of identity in the previous paragraph and consider how they apply to you. Depending on where you are in the move, you may apply these descriptions to the present time or in retrospect. For example, if you are in the pre-departure stage of the move, your response to these descriptions will be in the present and be a reflection of your current identity. If you have already moved, you will be looking back at your identity before your move, and your response to each description will be a reflection of your identity at that point in time. The descriptions can also be used to help you look at your identity between one overseas posting and another and during repatriation.

Your identity is affected during three key stages of an overseas move

There are three key stages during an overseas move where identity is noticeably affected: after the decision to move is made, during the departure period, and once you arrive overseas, when you are confronted with the foreign culture and new roles and relationships are added to your life. Let's look at these stages individually.

Stage 1: The effect of the decision to move overseas

When you move overseas in support of your partner's career, each of the four facets of your identity (internal view, external factors, roles and relationships) will be affected, starting at the moment of your decision to move. For example, your internal view begins to shift as you think about yourself in light of the changes that will occur in your life as a result of being a spouse of a diplomat in a foreign country. As you think about the differences between the community and culture in which you live and where you will move to, external factors that support your identity are beginning to be affected. As you prepare to leave familiar roles, such as a job or an established routine, and start to bring projects to a close, the process of letting go of these key components of your identity begins. When you withdraw membership or participation in various groups, and as you tell others that you will be moving, your relationships begin to change, especially if people don't want you to move or if they are envious. You may also find yourself starting to pull away from key relationships that have been supportive for you. As the move draws closer, your time and attention shifts away from activities that have been central to your identity, and toward completing tasks associated with the move. During this time, you are faced with the reality that you will be leaving everything that is familiar to you. As these changes in identity begin to occur internally, you may react in a variety of ways. For example, you may have twinges of anxiety that you don't fully understand; you may feel overwhelmed by all the tasks involved with preparing for your overseas move; or you may feel sad as you begin to say goodbye. You may also feel resentment toward your partner and/or the Foreign Service if you don't want to move, or you may feel excitement and joy if you are looking forward to the move.

Stage 2: The effect of the departure

The effect of the overseas move on your identity may be most visibly apparent to you when you physically leave your home country. You are instantly devoid of most of the major components that comprise your identity—including your roles, relationships, community and culture.

For example, when you move, if you have had your own career, you may be without the role of work (at least temporarily, or for the duration of your posting if you move to a country where it is difficult or impossible for you to work) and the meaning it has had in your life (for instance, a sense of accomplishment, connection, security, and/or independence).

Your relationships will also change when you move. When you leave friends and family behind, you also leave the support and companionship they have provided. Although they may still be available via phone or e-mail, you will have to figure out new ways to maintain the relationships from abroad. Some relationships may become strained or severed with the move due to the geographic distance. When you leave your home country, you also leave the familiarity of your community and culture and intuitively knowing "how to be" and "how to operate on a daily basis" within your environment.

The effect of the departure on these facets of your identity will depend on how you defined yourself before the move, how you feel about leaving those aspects of your identity behind, and how you feel about the move in general. For example, you may be aware of everything you are leaving behind and feel a tremendous loss. Or, it may be a relief to let go of certain aspects of your identity, such as a role that no longer fits. Alternatively, you may only be marginally aware of how the move is affecting your identity at this time because you are so focused on the move and your upcoming arrival in the foreign country.

Stage 3: The effect of the foreign culture and the addition of new roles and relationships

When you arrive overseas, you have just left behind many important relationships and key aspects of your life. Simultaneously, you are confronted with the unique value system of the foreign culture, which may include behaviors, values, and beliefs that are very different from your own. As a Foreign Service spouse, you also immediately take on new roles, such as "foreigner," "diplomatic passport holder" and "dependent spouse." This can be a very vulnerable time for a spouse, because you are expected to immediately start navigating through your new environment without any structure or framework in place (such as a job, home, or community). You must create a new structure for your life, which is an enormous task. This can be extremely overwhelming because you are expected to start re-building a framework before you have had time to figure out what kind of framework or structure you need for yourself in this new and foreign land.

As an accompanying spouse, it is important for you to know the importance of relationships, and the role of work, to your identity, as the absence of either one or both of these at this stage can make the move even more challenging. If relationships are central to your identity, until you can form new relationships overseas, you must manage the task of creating a new structure *on your own*. If work is central to your identity and you are prohibited from working overseas, or if you are not able to work in your chosen career overseas, being without this structure or framework in your life may be extremely difficult for you.

Identity in transition

At each stage of the move, from the time you make the decision to move overseas, to your actual departure, to landing on foreign soil, your identity is affected. It is normal for this to occur, as it is a major life change. The changes and losses you experience in each facet of your identity throughout the move result in your identity being in a state of transition. This, too, is normal. Your identity is in transition between what it was before the move and what it is becoming in your new environment. Each time you move with the Foreign Service, your identity will be in transition again.

While your identity is in transition, you are in a very vulnerable place. This vulnerability may cause you to question yourself or to doubt who you are. You may experience a range of feelings, emotions, and behaviors that are often associated with changes in identity. Some of these feelings and emotions you may experience include irritability, anxiousness, anger, frustration, resentment, hopelessness, impulsivity, and depression. Some of the behaviors may include tearfulness, changes in appetite, increased alcohol use, shopping excessively, fantasizing, withdrawing from others, criticizing the country to which you have moved, and strained relationships. While your identity is in transition, it's important for you to understand that within the context of so much change, it's normal for you to experience some of these emotions, feelings, and/or behaviors to some degree. (However, people who find themselves unable to manage these feelings, emotions, or behaviors on their own; find that their ability to function on a daily basis is significantly impaired; or continue to experience these reactions beyond what seems normal for the situation should seek professional help.)

The period during which identity is in transition is a critical juncture for the spouse and other family members because there is the potential for a positive or negative outcome from this phase. If the spouse does not understand what is happening to her/his identity, she or he may be tempted to pack her/his bags and go home. However, when a spouse understands that the transition period for identity is a normal phase, she or he can be prepared for it and steer the course of change toward a positive outcome.

Spouses can take charge of change for a successful overseas experience

As a Foreign Service spouse, it is crucial for your success overseas to view loss of identity as a temporary state, and know that you can take charge of your experience overseas and successfully resolve this state of transition. This will help you avoid the negative outcome of loss of identity, where you can become stuck in this state of transition, or be dissatisfied with your experience overseas, or abruptly return home.

In order to reconstruct your identity in a way that is meaningful to you within the foreign culture, you will need to take three steps. (These steps are part of a model called The Wheel, which is explained in greater detail in the book *A Portable Identity*.)

First, you will need to make a commitment to yourself to take charge of the changes in identity that occur when you move overseas. This commitment to yourself is vital to your success overseas because it serves as the foundation of all your actions and propels you toward meeting your goals. Your commitment will also keep you focused on what you want and need, and help you prioritize the steps you need to take to reconstruct your identity.

Second, you will need to access your personal resources. Personal resources are your innate abilities or skills that you can tap into to reconstruct your identity. Your personal resources include the following: ability to let go, ability for self-knowledge, ability to manage stress, ability to access supports, and ability to be open-minded. Self-reflection can help you gain an understanding about how well you access each of your personal resources. You may find that it is easier for you to access certain ones more than others. This is important to know because you may discover that you may need to strengthen a particular personal resource in order to reconstruct your identity.

And third, you will need to pick up and use tools for change. Tools help you identify what is missing, or out of balance in your life overseas, and help you take action to put those missing components of your identity back into place in some *modified or new* way within the foreign culture to which you have moved. There are seven tools: re-establishment of a sense of stability and security, communication with the self, communication with others, re-establishment of a support network, seeking out internal activities, seeking out external activities, and acceptance. How you decide to use each tool will be unique to your situation. There is also overlap between the tools, and you may use several tools at once in the process of reconstructing your identity.

Let's look at an example of how these steps work together. For example, once you settle into your new home overseas, you may miss the daily or frequent contact you had with friends you left behind when you moved. You are also aware that you don't have any close friends overseas. Without the closeness to others that you are used to, you feel that you are floundering in your new environment. You decide that you need to do something about the lack of friendships in your life. When you make this decision, you are taking the first step to reconstruct your identity, because you are making a commitment to take charge of a change that has occurred to a facet of your identity (your relationships) as a result of your move.

As you access your ability for self-knowledge (a personal resource), you discover that having close friends is central to your identity. You also discover that you are having trouble accessing your ability to let go (another personal resource). When you reconstruct your identity, this does not mean that you have to let go of the friends you left behind. Instead it may mean that you are having difficulty letting go of your friendships *as you have known them.* This may also be preventing you from allowing yourself to be open to new friendships, because you want the friendships that you left behind to remain the same even after you move, and this is not possible. To continue with our example, in order to reconstruct your identity, you may find that you need to strengthen your ability to let go. The tool of acceptance may also help you. By accepting that the friendships you left behind are not available to you in the same way, you are then able to use another tool, communication with others, to explore other ways to maintain these key friendships back home (e.g., by deciding to e-mail daily or several times a week, or to schedule regular phone calls) while simultaneously you can take risks to find and develop friendships with people in your new environment with interests similar to yours. As you make new friends overseas, you will also be using another tool, re-establishing a support network.

In the process of reconstructing your identity, if you determine that what is missing in your life overseas is unavailable or unattainable in the foreign culture to which you have moved, you can still use these three steps to make a decision about what you want or need to do. For example, if you determine that work is central to your identity and you have moved to a country that prohibits spouses from working, you may desire to return home so you can continue your career. However, as you work through the steps, you may identify other options for you to consider as well; such as staying in the foreign country and becoming an advocate for spousal employment issues, or staying in the foreign country and focusing your time and energy on exploring other facets of your identity (such as a particular skill, interest, or passion) that you haven't had time to concentrate on or develop in the past because your attention has been directed primarily towards work. By engaging the three steps, you will be actively involved in making choices that will determine which of these options is right for you.

For a Foreign Service spouse, moving overseas is inevitable and change is a given. Your identity will be affected each time you move and at each stage of the move. You will experience a wide range of feelings and thoughts that are normal when your identity is in transition. When you decide to take charge of the changes in identity that you experience, and make a commitment to yourself to actively take the steps necessary to reconstruct your identity within a foreign culture, you will thrive. You will be in charge of *you*, and how you define yourself and your role within the Foreign Service.

Debra R. Bryson, MSW, LCSW, is co-author with Charise Hoge, MSW, LGSW, of A Portable Identity: A Woman's Guide to Maintaining a Sense of Self While Moving Overseas, *Revised Edition, 2005, and co-founder of* www.aportableidentity.com, *which includes book order information, links, a chat group, and other content aimed at supporting accompanying spouses during an international relocation. Debra has dedicated her career to helping others reach their full potential, and has counseled clients, including expatriates, in a variety of multicultural settings. As a Foreign Service spouse, Debra helped successfully advocate for spouses of embassy employees to be able to work legally in Thailand. She has relocated over fifteen times, and currently resides in Austin, Texas, with her husband and two daughters.*

Looking at Foreign Service Life Through the FLO Prism

by Faye G. Barnes
Family Liaison Office Director, 1998–2005

Why do we have a Family Liaison Office (FLO), and has this office made a positive difference for employees, families, and children who are part of the mobile Foreign Service lifestyle? How much progress has been made in the almost 30 years of FLO's existence?

Reflecting on more than 20 years of living overseas as part of a Foreign Service family, seven years working inside FLO, and almost nine years as a Community Liaison Office coordinator (CLO), I often ask myself how much progress we have really made since 1978. While we have not fully resolved the basic issues identified in the tumultuous 1970s—the goals of quality schooling for all dependent children and meaningful employment for all spouses who desire it remain elusive—we have made progress on many fronts.

On the positive side, one of the biggest success stories has been the growth and development of the Community Liaison Office (CLO) program. It is hard to remember what life was like overseas before CLOs. There are now nearly 200 CLO positions worldwide. CLOs are paid employees who serve as relocation counselors, community advocates, active listeners, catalysts for good morale, and acclaimed trip and tour organizers—yet they do not have U.S. government funding for their programs. Communities expect organized events, trips and outings, but these cost money up front. During CLO training, it was always a revelation to those of us in the Family Liaison Office to learn how many CLOs front their own money for the community and often do not get that money back. If there is no employee or recreation organization at post to provide a source of funding, CLOs will sometimes use their own credit cards to purchase party supplies or rent buses for organized tours that the community expects. And when there are no-shows, the CLO picks up the loss.

We like to think that CLOs who have received training paid for with U.S. government funds will go on to serve at more than one post. There is a cadre of dedicated spouses who do this, but there is also a high burnout rate. Adding financial losses to this makes it even harder to recruit what I have affectionately termed "repeat offenders."

I often refer to family member employment as the Achilles heel of the Foreign Service. The Foreign Service Act gives the Family Liaison Office authority to assist spouses with locating employment. It also allows the Foreign Service Institute to train spouses prospectively, providing them with skills that will help them find employment. This includes language skills and functional training for potentially available embassy positions. While we have made progress, I have scratched my head in frustration many times with some of the roadblocks that we face inside the bureaucracy.

What are the obstacles, often referred to irreverently as "the enemy within"? Why haven't we reached optimal employment levels for those spouses who wish to work or to volunteer in substantive programs? An insider's perspective is this: having the authority to assist spouses, but lacking adequate funding or ultimate policy responsibility, makes it difficult to reach our employment goals. Family member employment policy resides with another human resources office, and training falls under the Foreign Service Institute management. There are also many factors related to employment that we cannot control, including spouses' educational and skill levels, their language facility, local salary levels and work permit issues in the host country.

Spouses have voiced concern about the level of the positions available in our overseas missions, yet they will often opt for a mission job over one in their field at the local salary level. This may be because they are more comfortable working in a U.S. environment, and mission jobs do have their benefits! However, increasing employment opportunities for spouses in the mission to keep pace with the rising number of spouses has been a serious challenge. The Diplomatic Readiness Initiative (DRI) brought in about one-third of our current officers since 2001, rounding out a hollowed Foreign Service. However, it also brought in more spouses, including more male spouses. At the same time, opportunities such as Professional Associate and Consular Associate positions (where spouses worked in unfilled junior officer positions or carried out the duties of a consular officer) have declined due to increased security requirements.

The lack of a serious commitment from the State Department to increase employment opportunities inside U.S. missions, along with a growing number of spouses with aspirations for a professional career, were key in FLO's decision to look outside the mission for employment opportunities. This led to the development and growth of the Strategic Network Assistance Program (SNAP), a groundbreaking and high-risk program for a U.S. government entity.

The SNAP program, while not successful at every post, demonstrates that targeted employment assistance works. The Local Employment Advisor (LEA)—hired at post to assist spouses with resumes and interviewing tips, provide employment workshops and counseling, and help line up employment contacts for spouses—has been a major morale boost. Similar to the development of the CLO program, but with an employment focus, the LEA provides a valuable service to spouses and, in turn, to the retention of employees. The SNAP concept has increased the number of spouses employed locally and has catered to the professional needs of spouses. I personally hope that this program will become as institutionalized as the CLO program has.

New developments in online training for entrepreneurial spouses wishing to set up Internet-based businesses, as well as the development of a pilot program offering fellowships or stipends for spouses at hardship posts, are also promising. There is no "one-size-fits-all" in employment, and that is why FLO keeps adding new opportunities, trying to provide a menu of options for spouses.

Unaccompanied tours and service overseas without families has added another layer of stress and concern to Foreign Service life. Evacuations have become almost routine, but the needs of employees and families who are uprooted and displaced still require individual attention. With FLO advocacy, benefits have improved tremendously, and employees fare much better financially today then they did back in 1998, when FLO began working to make these changes. But separation is inevitably stressful, and divorces and familial discord are not uncommon after a long separation. Keeping families united over a three- to six-month evacuation is not as difficult as it is for a one-year unaccompanied tour at a very dangerous and/or isolated post. This is the newest challenge for the Foreign Service and for FLO. With the addition of a part-time employee to the FLO staff to a develop a program and address those needs, I am confident that FLO will rise to the occasion and provide the necessary support for separated families.

So, what do you think? I leave it to Foreign Service employees and family members to decide. Has the Family Liaison Office made a difference? As a former "insider," I am aware of all the attempts made to resolve a wide range of concerns and issues. Many of these never made it out of the building ... but advocacy means never saying "I give up!"

Canadian-born Faye Barnes shelved the white lab coat from her first career in food product development for the role of accompanying Foreign Service spouse and advocate and has never looked back. She and her Foreign Agricultural Service husband and two daughters have lived in London, Mexico City, Bonn, Lima, Madrid and Caracas. During her last three overseas tours, Faye served as Community Liaison Office Coordinator. Among many other activities, she has also worked in public relations at the National Press Club, served as President of American women's groups overseas, and organized and taught cooking classes in Madrid, Lima and

Bonn. Faye was Director of the U.S. Department of State's Family Liaison Office from 1998 to 2005.

Foreign Service Highlights

by Michelle Flannigan

1. Sipping *guaraná* soda with the children of a local orphanage after a long day painting their home.

2. Checking in at the airport with a black diplomatic passport.

3. Shopping for shoes with visiting U.S. Senators.

4. Taking advantage of every three-day weekend to discover a new pocket of the world, such as Buenos Aires, Argentina and Gyeongju, South Korea.

5. Learning to eat with chopsticks.

6. Opening my change purse to find Euros, reais, pesos, won, and quarters.

7. Exploring a new neighborhood each time we move.

8. Discovering forgotten possessions every few years when we unpack our boxes again.

9. Learning to cook foreign cuisine like Brazilian *fejoada*.

10. Dressing up for the Marine Corps Ball.

11. Receiving phone calls from home after my family opens our exotic Christmas presents.

12. Growing tired of the "ordinary" wildlife: monkeys in Brazil, llamas in Bolivia, cuckoos in Korea.

13. People-watching on public transportation.

14. Speaking gibberish to the locals, who actually understand me.

15. Finding the Irish pubs in every city.

16. Growing to appreciate my husband, the only friend I take with me from post to post.

17. Buying novelties like Dr. Pepper and salsa from the embassy commissary.

18. Filling our home with furnishings from diverse cultures.

19. Swapping adventure stories with other diplomats.

20. Helping to improve the perception of the United States, one taxi driver at a time.

Michelle Flannigan is a Foreign Service spouse whose family has been posted in Rio de Janeiro, Brazil, and Seoul, South Korea.

PART II
Practicalities of Foreign Service Life

To Have or Have Not:
What to Pack for the Rest of
Your Life in the Foreign Service

by Dawn Sewell McKeever

"What to pack?" All travelers face the open suitcase and ask themselves the same question before each trip. Taking into account the country and culture to be visited, the length of the trip, weight restrictions, weather, medical needs, personality traits, comfort levels, and previous traveling experience, we make our choices. The competing forces of "Will I need this?" versus "Do I want to lug this around with me?" often come into play. While everyone who travels makes these decisions before departure, the open suitcase takes on a different dimension for Foreign Service families deciding what to take with them for the next two to twenty years overseas.

"As a Foreign Service family, we try to make a conscious decision to pack the kinds of things that symbolize traditions for our girls. We realize we can't give them the same kind of 'roots' as normal families, so we use the 'potted plant' analogy that we are carrying our roots with us. We therefore are heavy on Christmas decorations, Halloween items and other decorations that will help them to build memories wherever we are," says Colette Marcellin.

"To make the moves and transitions easier on my children, I have always brought all my holiday decorations, and my son recently thanked me for doing this," says Kris Orth. Randall Budden states, "We make more of an effort to celebrate religious and secular holidays abroad than we do at home. I always have a Christmas tree and it goes up earlier and stays up longer than it would in the U.S. We participate in embassy and expat community celebrations, even of holidays we don't observe in the U.S. I've never been Santa Claus in the U.S. but I've been Father Christmas in Mexico."

Maintaining connections with home and preserving family traditions, even if somewhat altered to fit existing conditions, is very important to most Foreign Service families. Dot Blocker, a veteran of many African tours, says, "I only have two absolutes in what I bring to post: my cast-iron skillet and a bag of cornmeal, because I think food is a comfort, especially something from home. I make cornbread, because it's from my home in the South and also because I want my kids, who didn't grow up there, to have a connection to the South."

For many families, food is an important part of their holiday traditions. Every Foreign Service family has holiday stories about the holiday gone wrong or the holiday that "was strange, but fun because we made the best of it," which becomes part of the family lore. Ours include a whole Thanksgiving turkey cooked on the "barbie" and served poolside by Australian friends trying to help us to feel at home. Another time, Aussie friends served prawns and salads for Christmas dinner before we all went off to the beach together. It just didn't feel like Christmas that year, but it was fun nonetheless. Many an administrative officer or Community Liaison Office coordinator has spent countless hours trying to find suitable turkeys for Thanksgiving and Christmas in places much less likely to have turkeys than Australia, all so that we can say "it certainly feels like Christmas," even when it's 110 degrees Fahrenheit outside.

In addition to preserving family traditions, food can be another way to encounter the new culture. Says one spouse who counts Turkey and Vietnam among her many postings, "I always take an English-language cookbook of the country to which I'm going so I can try local recipes with the readily available local ingredients."

In the Foreign Service (FS), we often judge countries and postings by what is, and is not, available on the local economy, especially food-wise. Among the first questions we ask are: What can't you get there? What should I bring with me?" I remember one spouse grousing about the lack of capers in the stores of Niger, which is sometimes listed as the poorest country in the world. "How can one cook without capers?" she wondered. Inside I was laughing because I was sure I'd never even thought about buying or cooking with capers in any country I'd ever lived in.

The list of what each family considers essential is varied and fun to read. Besides capers, different families listed the following as their want-to-have foods: brownie mix, pancake mix and maple syrup, marshmallows, Miracle Whip, salsa, taco shells and tortilla chips, Pop Tarts, Ranch dressing packets, peanut butter, Hershey's syrup, chocolate and butterscotch chips, nutmeg, allspice, molasses, cinnamon, microwave popcorn, pumpkin pie filling, cranberry sauce and items needed to make and decorate Christmas cookies.

Advances in computer capabilities and Internet connections, even in developing countries, are making it easier for Foreign Service families to get a taste of home. "With Netgrocer available, there is little need to pack comfort foods any longer," states Makila James. The downside may be that this hampers families' incentives to adjust and explore their new environment. My Moroccan vet recently chastised me for buying cat deworming medicine while in the U.S., at $25 for 3 doses, by stating, "Trips home are not for doing your daily shopping, Madame! You could have gotten that medicine here for three or four dollars." True, but I can more easily explain exactly what I'm looking for in my own language.

One can not underestimate how much Internet shopping has eased the stress of worrying that we have to get everything now or else go without for two or three years. "If we find we really need it and we're really desperate, we can get it on the Internet," my husband told me when I fretted that we hadn't gotten everything on our list during our last trip home. However, shipping fees can be expensive and liquid items (such as contact lens solutions) are prohibited in diplomatic mail pouches. At most posts, we are not allowed to ship boxes home, and so we cannot return items that don't fit or aren't exactly what we thought they were when we ordered them. Although I know people who do it, I think it would be very hard to buy shoes over the Internet without trying them on first.

Every Foreign Service spouse I know keeps a running list of needs and wants. For each U.S. visit, I have a three- or four-page typed list of what we need or want. I try to anticipate what the kids' clothes and shoe sizes will be for the next two or three years; what they might like for birthday or Christmas presents; how much and what type of medicines and hygiene products we'll need for two years; what school and art supplies to get; what household items need replacing; and what books, CDs or DVDs we might enjoy. Every time we do this I wonder what life lessons my children are learning from this binge style two-month shopping spree done every two or three years while we're on home leave.

Helene DeJong says, "We don't overdo it. We have learned to live off the local economies and do well, and we don't need much 'stuff' to make a place feel like home. I'm proud to say I lived through three hardship posts without ever once ordering from Netgrocer."

Sally Womble agrees. "We have learned to use what we bring and enjoy it until it is gone, and not to fret or mourn or obsess over what we have not, because they are only extras, not needs. Now I focus on emotional things like special holiday foods, birthday surprises ... and items that we really cannot get in Africa."

Part of what makes Foreign Service packing different from regular packing, even though some of the stress has been reduced by the Internet, is the fear that we'll have to live without something important for years. If we make the wrong decisions about our household items, such as furniture, toys or musical instruments, we really do have to live with the consequences for years.

After four years in DC, we packed out for our posting to Sydney, Australia. It was our third overseas tour in the Foreign Service, and none were the African tours we'd requested and for which my husband had prepared academically. All his books on Africa went into storage, where they remained while we moved on from Sydney to live in Niger, Uganda (where he had regional responsibility for ten African countries) and Morocco. In the end, we found that several of those stored books would have been a tremendous help to us.

Debbie Cavin describes leaving the piano her parents had struggled to buy with a cousin, thinking it would be safer than in storage and having been warned by the Department that "pianos are often ruined in the tropics, and should probably be left behind." She says "it was a cruel and, in hindsight, stupid deprivation, considering that in those pre-VCR (and in our case, pre-children) days, there were many week-nights when I'd have loved to pour out my emotions or assuage my boredom on the keyboard, and weekends when it would have been fun to gather around the piano as we entertained." Ironically, when her cousin moved, the piano was dropped and one of its legs broken. "I've learned that a piano is not a valuable to be left behind and protected. It's a solid possession that we need to take with us: a memory-maker. Not 'consumables' but soul food."

While it is technically possible to obtain access to your storage during moves by requesting the specific box number containing the needed items, I can't imagine any family knowing exactly which box contains which items, either in storage or in the regular household effects (HHE) shipment. It is not possible to watch several packers in different rooms and note exactly which items go into each and every box, and it is not unusual for a typical family of four to have 250 boxes in an ordinary move. Even packout days that go relatively smoothly are still confusing and stressful.

Many families learn this lesson and deal with it in different ways. Some become packrats, keeping everything because they never know when it'll come in handy and they'll be in a place where they can't get it. Others become like Arab traders in the *ancienne medina*, buying and selling everything from cars, household furniture and appliances to children's toys and leftover consumables at yard sales at the end of every tour. One administrative officer admits that "selling the TVs and stereos you have to 'those in need' is the best excuse for buying the latest models."

On the other hand, we have a multi-system TV that we bought in 1990 that is still going strong and works fine with the newest DVD and satellite technology. "For most of us it depends on the tour. We tailor our packing with what the immediate surroundings offer in terms of lifestyle. In Barbados we brought snorkeling equipment and a windsurfer and sold it all when we left. In Paris we brought lots of camping equipment and bikes because we camped all over France," says Marcellin.

It's important to ask questions and get information about each post, though that can be difficult or confusing. Sometimes one doesn't even know which questions to ask until arrival in country, and by then it's too late to repack or re-do your consumables order. Post reports are often outdated, like the one that told us to bring spices to Jamaica. It was our first posting so we dutifully did as advised, only to find any spice we could ever want in the local supermarket at half the U.S. prices.

Advice is often contradictory. Should you bring your pet? "Leave behind your dogs and other animals; they are everywhere and you can get them relatively cheaply" vs. "Definitely bring your pets because they are family." DeJong says: "We left our dog behind when we moved to India, our first post. Our daughters cried for weeks about leaving that dog! We brought our dog on our most recent move, and it did help with the transition." Ahni Turner's tours in Korea and Niger led her to agree. "The only thing we ever left behind and regretted were our pets. Our kids are older now and more attached to their pet. I would go to great lengths to make sure the pet moved with us."

Foreign Service families do just that as they jump through entry and exit regulation hoops and fight with airline personnel who often don't even know their own companies' policies on animal travel. And what do you do with pets during training and home leave? Marcellin says, "The first thing we worry about packing are the pets—in our case, two cats. We choose posts where the cats can travel because we believe that pets are even more important to Foreign Service children than to non-Foreign Service kids. It's hard enough to ask children to leave their friends behind, but to leave their pets, too? I think many a Foreign Service child confides in their pet and holds their pet extra close in the first weeks at post when loneliness can be an big issue."

Should we bring family keepsakes or put them in storage? "What's the use of having it if you never see/use it" competes with "Don't bring anything irreplaceable or of great value." For our first tour, I put most of our belongings in storage and didn't bring much to post. I felt like I'd made the right decision when I met a more experienced spouse who said she'd lost all her wedding china and gifts going to their first posting in Asia. But then it seemed ridiculous to have all these things and not be using them. When the children came along, I thought about how certain family keepsakes wouldn't mean anything to them if they didn't grow up with them.

On the other hand, Herb Treger states: "I never take any of the family keepsakes. [They stay] in storage. Probably the most important item I'd never want to lose is the one of least value—it's a battered green canvas trunk covered with baggage labels that tells the exact date my grandparents immigrated to the United States and went through the Port of Entry at Niagara Falls, New York. For me, it's priceless."

Like the list of comfort foods, what each person or family doesn't want to lose is interesting to read, and the things that people have lost are heartbreaking. David Newell, a self-described book fiend, leaves his rare first edition and autographed copies of *To Kill A Mockingbird* behind. Tanya Anderson wishes she'd left behind the silver her grandmother had left her; it was stolen from her shipment as it was leaving the Philippines. "I'm not a materialistic person; however, I am very sentimental, so I was deeply hurt by this loss. Not only was the silver valuable, but the box it was in was handmade by my grandfather for my grandmother, so it was particularly precious to me."

Cavin adds, "I think the only things I might leave home nowadays, in light of experience, are things I feel aren't really mine, but which I hold in trust. I should not have taken the originals of the letters my great-great-grandfather wrote to his wife during the Civil War before he was killed at Gettysburg. I feel incredibly guilty, because those letters represent 'touchable' family history for my many cousins and their children, not just for me and mine."

Every family has heard the horror stories of rushed evacuations and ships sinking. In the end, most families learn by trial and error, and learn to live with the consequences. Thomas Daughton writes in his April 2005 *Foreign Service Journal* article "Cause and (Household) Effects" about the results of losing most of his HHE during his transfer from Gabon to Malaysia: "From now on, I really will understand what the risk of losing my belongings means. I'll probably still opt to take them with me overseas, but the things themselves are going to mean a lot less to me." Daughton was told that his was the "largest loss sustained by a Department employee in 2003."

The one thing that everyone agrees is important to bring, no matter where the posting, are family photos, if not the family photo albums. "I feel strongest about family photos since they are the window to our past and our heritage. Since the kids don't get to see grandparents, great-grandparents, or even cousins, I feel having their images around the house keeps them connected to family," says Blocker. DeJong adds, "I bring photos of friends and family in our carry-on bags. We tape these photos on doors and closets to bring some familiarity to a new and bare home." Susie Brown says with a smile, "We want to have the pictures so we can recognize the people picking us up at the airport during home leave."

As an avid photographer and scrapbooker, I have agonized for years over the photo decision every time we've moved, and prayed we won't be evacuated. When my father died and left the family photos to me I spent hundreds of dollars having negatives and copies made; the copies to take with us, the originals and negatives to be kept in the safety deposit box. With the recent advances in digital photography, photos can be saved more easily, and much less expensively, by burning an extra CD for the safety deposit box.

For those who scrapbook, making color copies of scrapbook pages to take with you means you can leave the scrapbooks in a safe place. Scrapbook pages can also be digitally photographed and burned onto CDs. For those, like me, who still prefer film, I figured out a solution: at the end of each tour I hand-carry the negatives and contact print sheets from that tour home for placement into the safety deposit box. Rachel Ehrendrich agrees, "The only thing I keep in storage are negatives. If the ship does go down or we are evacuated, I will be able to replace the family photos, at least."

"Our goal has been to create a home for ourselves and our children. We want to be comfortable inside our home and be able to relax. So, we brought the whole house and did not leave anything in storage," states Womble. Making each house or apartment seem like home is extremely important. "When we go overseas, the first things I think about taking are hanging pictures and lamps. Having familiar pictures hanging on the walls makes me feel less disconnected, less far away from family and friends. We bring lamps because the FS never supplies enough and I hate overhead lights!" says Cristin Springet.

"After 27 years in the FS, I still love to hang in each successive home a framed piece of needlepoint my aunt stitched for me long ago, which says 'Memories are our only solid possessions,'" says Cavin. She adds, "With that mindset, I stopped over-insuring things we take with us. We've lost a few I had really enjoyed—an antique map; some jewelry that recalled people and places—to thieves along the way, and I have a tinge of sadness if I think of those things, but I figure that's the price we pay for the pleasure of roaming. We have so much 'stuff' that we can easily afford to give some of it away when we leave."

Makila James makes a point of bringing things with her for just that purpose. "When going to Africa—where most cultures value family life highly and where poverty is a concern—I always pack lots of gifts for local children (books, pens, crayons, trucks, dolls, etc.). When I travel to rural areas I give them out. I also bring children's clothes that my son has outgrown and then encourage relatives to send me nice stuff from their kids, too, for me to give away. I buy cosmetics and hair products from discount stores; these are sometimes hard to find or can cost a lot in some countries. I also bring books to give to colleagues and local friends; I pick them up cheaply at local U.S. libraries' sales, or at yard sales. It goes a long way in building goodwill and friendships with Foreign Service Nationals and locals."

Most of us agree that we usually end up bringing too much. Newell says the first of his postings to Sarajevo taught him the importance of culling his possessions and "made one realize what was really important to have at post." Restricted to 400 pounds of air freight for the entire tour, he took his clothes, TV, VCR and Sky1 Decoder. "I may not have had running water, but, by God, I could watch Sky Movies and Sky Sports!"

Problems can arise, however, when different members of a family have a different take on how to resolve this problem of culling. "We fall into the 'bring everything you own with you' category, but to do so we are constantly weeding stuff out. I'm much better at discarding stuff I don't want anymore, and go at this with a vengeance every time moving day approaches," says Audrey Huon-Dumentat. "My daughter is definitely the keep-everything type. I have to throw things away when she is not around, even half-finished drawings! The day before she was born I bought her a stuffed Nala (Lion King) toy. We took pictures of Nala on my huge stomach, one of which features prominently in her baby book. Unfortunately, for the first five years of her life, she couldn't care less about Nala. I don't think I ever saw her pick Nala up, so when I was doing my give/sell binge before moving from Niger I gave Nala away. She went to a happy family. I felt good about that until Melea started to pine for Nala. How could we give away the first toy we ever bought her? She would look at her baby book with sadness for her long-lost friend. So guess what we bought her for her ninth birthday? We had to search high and low, but we found one."

While culling is important, taking whatever one needs to pursue a hobby, or to give comfort or continuity, is also very important. Doing something enjoyable not only relieves stress, but can also help with meeting new people in the host country. Carol Jenkins states, "for me, taking art supplies is … essential, since good quality art supplies are difficult to find in some countries. I try to connect with local artists, which allows for an immediate connection to the host country and allows me to make friends outside the embassy community, as well as to connect the embassy community to the local art scene. I recently organized a printmaking workshop taught by a well known Ugandan artist and Fulbright scholar which was attended by … other embassy employees and spouses. We all had our work exhibited in a local show and some of us sold pieces."

Family and friends in the U.S. will often say to us, "You all must be old pros at this moving business by now. You know just what to take and what to leave behind." In some ways we've gotten better with each move, but in other ways, it's as if each move is the first move. We're moving *from* a place we've never moved from before, and we're moving *to* a place we've never moved to before. The children are at different stages and have different needs, and we're at different life stages, too. At times I feel like the Hindu destined to keep re-living this one stage, packing and unpacking, until I get it right.

Some places we're okay with leaving and don't really miss much when we go, even though the tour was a successful one. With other tours we need a period of grieving as part of the moving process as we mourn the people we may never see again, and the lives, and lifestyles, we've left behind. Says Linda Lipinski, "Every move I leave behind a small piece of myself, hoping I've made a positive difference in at least one person's life."

Those pieces of ourselves, and our family and friends in the U.S. and at various postings, become the most important of the possessions left behind. "We are not there for the milestones," the weddings, funerals, graduations, baby showers, birthdays, reunions and other events, "good and bad, that shape and glue families and friends together," notes Budden. As a result, we quickly realize that it is not the things we leave behind, or the things we bring that are most important. Rather it is how we maintain those long-distance relationships and how we adjust to our new surroundings that become the stabilizing factors in our transient lifestyle. While we may take everything with us but the kitchen sink, "it's really important to take your patience and flexibility with you," states Elisa Greene. Janet Fitzgerald adds that "my son and my sense of humor" are what she most needs to bring with her to post. Budden makes sure to always pack his "hope and a spirit of adventure." Hope, patience, flexibility, sense of humor and adventure—it's the packing of these things that make or break any trip, whether it is for two weeks or a lifetime of overseas service to the United States of America.

Ms. McKeever is married to Foreign Service officer Matthew McKeever and has accompanied him on tours to Kingston, Jamaica; Paris, France; Sydney, Australia; Niamey, Niger; Kampala, Uganda; and Casablanca, Morocco. With Helene DeJong, she was awarded the Avis Bohlen Award for Volunteerism in 2004 for their work promoting literacy and libraries in Uganda. In 2002, Ms. McKeever was given a certificate of appreciation by the mayor of Niamey, Niger, for her volunteer work with various orphanages and village schools. The McKeevers have two daughters, one son, one grandson, and four cats.

You Want to Go Where? Tips on Putting Together a Bid List

by Gwen Simmons

Bidding is a very stressful but exciting time. I am always champing at the bit when I am waiting for the bid list to come out, curious about all of the possibilities. Many people, such as those in my family, are in the Foreign Service not only for the great career that it offers, but for the chance that it gives you to explore the world. Bidding is a time to consider places that you might never have thought about, and also a time to rule out places that might have seemed ideal for your circumstances before. I see it as a chance to further my knowledge about the various countries around the world, such as finally figuring out where Ouagadougou is (Burkina Faso!). Below are my tips on putting together a bid list. The most important things are to be realistic and to have fun exploring the possibilities.

Research, research, research

With the Internet, countless resources are at your fingertips. Websites on every country let you review what is available there. A great website for unadulterated comments is **www.talesmag.com**. Foreign Service officers (FSOs) and other expats who have lived in just about every place imaginable have posted their comments on this website. It structures the submissions with a questionnaire (health, schools, cost of living, etc.) which results in continuity among the answers. Another website, **www.expatexpert.com**, is maintained by Robin Pascoe, a Canadian diplomatic spouse and the author of numerous books, including *A Mov-*

able Marriage, Homeward Bound, and *Culture Shock! Successful Living Abroad: A Wife's Guide.* Her website offers a lot of great articles, covering topics such as culture shock, relocation issues, dealing with being a trailing spouse, and much more.

The Associates of the American Foreign Service Worldwide (AAFSW), publisher of this book, offers a helpful website at **www.aafsw.org**. Most important for those in the bidding process may be its e-mail group for the Foreign Service community, Livelines, whose members show a great willingness to share their experiences at posts around the world.

The State Department website offers a lot of great resources, such as the official Post Reports, the Family Member Employment Report (FAMER), and the bidding tool. Keep in mind that many documents can only be accessed via the workplace intranet. Another great resource is the Community Liaison Office coordinator (CLO) at post. CLOs are accustomed to being asked about their post, and don't mind receiving inquiries. Their finger is on the pulse of the embassy, and they have more information at their disposal than you can imagine.

Contact the incumbent in the position. They will give you a good idea of the amount of work involved, the day to day living, and the general morale at post. Finally, don't be afraid to network among your colleagues, and find out who knows someone who has been to the post that you are considering, and would it be okay to contact them. Most FSOs are willing to answer questions about a former or current post, regardless of whether their experience was good or bad. The Overseas Briefing Center at the National Foreign Affairs Training Center (NFATC) also maintains a list of returnees who are willing to be contacted with questions.

Don't mess with MED

If you or any member of your family has been given a limited health clearance by the Medical Department, do not try to circumvent the system. The Medical Department, fondly referred to as "Med," is not there to make your life miserable. In fact, they generally try as hard as they can to see if a post will fit for a family. I have seen it happen first-hand. There have been many instances that I am personally aware of, in which the State employee does whatever he/she can to get a desired post. However, the children arrive at post not being able to go to school, or not having the medical facilities that they need, and the family has to curtail. Not only is this unfortunate for the family members who have been put through such unnecessary upheaval, but it will also leave a bad taste in the mouth of the post. Keep in mind that there are many beautiful posts in Europe that have the medical and educational facilities for about any disability. Some people would kill to spend their entire careers moving around Europe. You still get the overseas experience, but without harming your family's mental well-being or health.

Location, location, location

Let's take Maputo, Mozambique, for example. Maputo, at the time of this writing, is a post with a 25 percent pay differential, an authorized shipment of consumables (food and household supplies), a 2-year assignment length and one authorized rest and recreation (R&R) trip. Looking at a map of Africa, you can see that Mozambique is located on the southeastern coast and is bordered by Tanzania to the north, South Africa and Swaziland to the south, Zimbabwe to the west and Zambia and Malawi to the northwest. The real hidden gem near Maputo is Madagascar, and the Seychelles are off the coast of Mozambique. For anyone who is into SCUBA diving or wildlife, this is a perfect location. South Africa, Swaziland, Zambia, Madagascar and the Seychelles have some of the best animal life in all of Africa. Something to think about.

Just because it's a great vacation spot doesn't mean you want to live there

There are many countries in the world that people would give their left eye to visit on vacation, but that does not mean that these countries are great places to live. To the ordinary citizen, that might not make sense. However, there are numerous things to consider when moving versus taking a vacation. Cost of living is a big factor, with many "vacation countries" receiving a cost of living adjustment of as much as 75 percent. Do you want a housekeeper or nanny? Is the housing furnished or unfurnished, and will it be a large house or a small apartment? What are the employment opportunities for your significant other? What are the schooling options? What is the weather like? These are all things to seriously consider before bidding.

The great balancing act

OK, the country's beautiful, the housing is swank, the cuisine to-die-for and the schools outstanding. But what about the job? Accompanying spouses need to remember that a great deal of your family's happiness will depend on the job satisfaction of the officer spouse (and vice versa). Some important considerations include post morale, physical facilities, work requirements, and career aspirations. Keep abreast of the ever-changing evaluation and promotion precepts, and be sure you're not short-changing your career for the sake of excellent local brews or beaches.

It is not always possible to make everyone happy. For single FSOs, taking into account only their own wants and needs can be a great advantage. For FSOs with family, different needs come into play and must be considered as much as possible. Keep in mind that many "trailing spouses" gave up successful careers to pursue the dream of the FSO, and quite possibly, to pursue their own dream of traveling around the world. If the family is dead set against going to two French-speaking posts in a row, and there are other viable options available, try and adjust your bid list accordingly. I am not saying that you should jeopardize your career. It is just that it's better for everyone to be happy about the decision, whenever possible. The spouse and children need to know that their opinions count.

There is a reason for the differential

Posts with high pay differentials tend to have some of the best housing in the Foreign Service, as it is assumed that you will be spending a lot of time in your home. Differentials are determined based on a range of factors, including the crime rate and other dangers, pollution, high altitude, the availability of basic supplies, the ability to travel around the country on your own, the ability to drive your own vehicle, and the lack of restaurants and entertainment. I have a friend who specifically filled her list with posts that did not have a McDonald's. Before deciding to bid on or reject a high-differential post, look at the latest post report and contact the Community Liaison Office coordinator at post, or the incumbent of the job you are considering, to find out what the reasons are for the differential. Some hardships may matter more than others to you. Keep in mind that there are "fair-share" regulations requiring officers to take their turns serving at hardship posts, which are posts with at least a 15 percent differential.

Do not put any post on your list that you would not be willing to go to

Since bid lists must include several posts and a certain amount of geographical diversity, bidders sometimes "pad" their lists with posts they really would not want, but think they are unlikely to get. Inevitably, they are extremely disappointed when their Career Development Officer (CDO) sees that they placed XYZ on their list and immediately assigns it to them. Having the chance to move around the world is a wonderful thing. Make it as easy on yourself as possible by only including posts that you really would be okay with going to. Of course, there are going to be some posts that you would rather go to than others; however, not everyone can go to Paris or Sydney, so be realistic. There should be a few things about the post that you are happy with; otherwise, do not list it. You may just get it!

Gwen's philosophy:

No matter what post you go to, there is always going to be at least one food item, and one cultural aspect, that you are going to love. It may be that the post has the best tomatoes that you have ever tasted. It may be that post has really inexpensive gold. It may be that the post is in a perfect location for travel. Whatever it is, if you focus on it when times get rough, you can get through and enjoy your time. After all, it's only two or three years of your life—not a very long time in the grand scheme of things. Besides, think of the stories you can tell your friends and family, not to mention the shock factor when you tell them where you are moving to!

When she wrote this article, Gwen Simmons was serving as Community Liaison Office coordinator in San Jose, Costa Rica. In 2006, she moved to Chennai, India with her husband Brian and their two young children. She has also lived in Manila, Philippines and Manama, Bahrain. As the "trailing spouse," Gwen has been able to complete her MBA online.

Making Your Foreign Service House a Home

by Kelly B. Midura

Foreign Service life poses many challenges, not the least of which is making generic embassy housing into a home. We all want to personalize our living spaces, and yet we are constantly faced not only with repeated transfers, but with bland, traditional décor and furniture that we didn't choose. Though that distinctive State Department style is likely to be serving overseas longer than we are, we don't have to put up with living in what feels like a hotel room! Here are some ways that you can turn your embassy quarters into a welcoming home for your family.

A little background for the uninitiated: the State Department, through the General Services Administration (GSA), offers renewable contracts to private companies in the U.S. to supply furniture for embassy housing overseas. In recent years, that supplier has been Drexel. Furniture is ordered in sets by the Administrative section of the State Department with input from overseas posts, the Family Liaison Office, and so on. This process, the goal of which is to please the most people for the least money, is the reason that nearly all posts have the same furniture, regardless of the size or style of the houses, and that the colors and styles are usually very mainstream, to say the least.

Houses typically are outfitted with large dining room sets, including tables to seat 10–12 people, china hutches and sideboards; formal living room suites with lots of coffee and end tables, and two large matching bookcases; and formal bedroom sets with either queen or twin beds (king size beds or bunkbeds are generally not available). Other pieces may or may not be supplied by individual posts: for example, small computer desks, entertainment centers, kitchen tables, patio furniture, and so on. In keeping with the generic theme, all embassy-owned housing interiors, to my knowledge, are painted white.

In short, if you wish to impose your personal style on an embassy house, you have your work cut out for you. So, let's get started!

Do the research

It is always a good idea to find out as much as possible about your new quarters before you start packing. Just because your family size indicates that you are entitled to four bedrooms, for example, doesn't mean that you are going to get them. You'll want to know in advance if the house is small, so that you can give away or store some items before packing out. Furniture inventories vary as well: some posts may be overflowing with furniture, generously supplying rare items like computer desks, while others may be scrounging for sofas and bookshelves. While you may not be able to get information about your particular house before you pack out from the previous post, you should at least be able to get some sense of what you are likely to end up with. If you are lucky, you may even be able to contact the current occupant of your next house and see e-mailed photos of it, as I was on my way to Prague.

Get out the paint!

If you've had it with trying to scrub little finger and paw prints off flat white walls, or even if you haven't, consider painting. If you'd rather not devote a great deal of time to the project, try painting just one wall in your living room, and see how much warmer and inviting it becomes. Surprise your visitors by painting a small room such as the foyer or powder room. Or jazz up your kids' room by painting a rainbow on the wall.

In high-traffic areas (anywhere that kids are likely to be), use latex paint in an eggshell or satin finish for easy cleaning. Stick-on borders are also an option, as is stenciling. Just remove, or prime over, anything you do to the walls when you leave. While I have found that most General Service Officers (GSOs) do not require this, as the house must be repainted between occupants anyway, you are still technically (and morally) obliged to bring the house back to its original condition and should at least offer to do so upon your departure from post.

Cover it up!

Not only may embassy furniture be unappealing to you, but it may be well-used by the time you inherit it. The quickest solution to either of these problems is to cover it up. If you live in one of the many countries where handmade tablecloths, hangings, pillows and other textiles are cheap and colorful, buy a big stack for current and future use. My ponderous dining tables were covered with Bolivian carrying cloths for years. Mexican shawls covered the sofas, and Guatemalan table linens were thrown over end tables and coffee tables. I made inexpensive hand-woven placemats into snazzy throw pillows that have adorned numerous sofas and lasted for over a decade. Living rooms that were once intolerably stuffy to me acquired a lively ethnic look that my family was more comfortable with. I've seen other houses with inexpensive carpets thrown over everything. Usually, these textiles are practically indestructible: after all, they were made to be cleaned by scrubbing on rocks in the river! (If you do not live in a country blessed with a rich textile heritage, or if you lack sewing skills, you might try shopping for some interesting weavings, batiks, table linens, or throw pillows at online auction sites.)

If you are a serious decorator, note that those embassy sofas, no matter what the upholstery (one of mine had large orange and brown flowers on it), come in just one shape and two sizes. There are only a couple of types of chairs as well. So, consider investing in slipcovers from an online outlet, or, if you live in a country where upholstering is inexpensive, have slipcovers made to order, as one of my friends did in San Salvador. It's a small investment for two to four years of use, and the chances are very good that you will be able to use them again in your next post. Slipcovers are also an excellent way to protect those white damask sofas that are always mysteriously allocated to families with small children.

If they don't supply it, bring it with you!

There are several items that are rarely, if ever, included with embassy furnishings. I have never, for example, personally seen an embassy entertainment center, though I'm told they do exist in some places. If you are not lucky enough to get one, consider buying one or having one made to be shipped from post to post. Our television and stereo sat in a messy pile of cords atop a dresser until we had a large entertainment cabinet custom-made and painted with folk art in San Salvador. Ten years and several posts later, it still occupies a place of honor in our living room as one of the best, most useful, purchases we ever made.

As for bookshelves, there is a general consensus in the Foreign Service community that there simply aren't enough to go around, especially for such a book-loving bunch of people. Furthermore, heavy, seven-foot bookshelves are inappropriate, and even potentially dangerous, for children's rooms. Most Foreign Service families that I know ship bookshelves for their children at the very least, and usually ship one or two lightweight bookshelves for their own books.

If you have, or plan to have, a baby during your tour, you should also expect to ship your own crib and changing table, as these are not part of regular inventory. A rocking chair is also an excellent idea. Since embassy furniture is so very big, other child-sized furniture is also very useful, such as a low table and small chairs for finger painting and tea parties, or a comfy little chair for watching television.

As for home offices, twenty years after the advent of the personal computer into American homes, desks designed for computers are still uncommon in embassy inventories. Foreign Service family members everywhere sit in Queen Anne dining chairs answering their e-mail on computers perched atop "escritoires" and wondering why their backs hurt. So, my advice is to bring at least one computer desk and ergonomic desk chair wherever you go. If you plan to operate a home business, consider bringing other items that may be unavailable at post, such as file cabinets made to fit American folders, work tables, a printer stand, and so on.

If they do supply it, and you just don't like it, bring it with you!

State Department lamps tend to the large, brass, and colonial, gobbling up table space and posing hazards to curious children and pets. You may wish to bring a few of your own. Even if you like brass, it wouldn't hurt to bring a few task lights such as desk lamps or nightlights. Most lamps will work just fine on either 110 or 220 volts, with an appropriate plug adapter and local light bulb.

And then there are those polyester curtains. If your new home is afflicted with baby blue polyester drapes, as my most recent quarters were, I suggest that you stash them in the attic or garage for the duration. You probably won't be able to replace all of the drapes in your house, but it might be worthwhile to do so a couple of rooms. Or just take them down to let the sun shine in. This is another potential use for the textile collection that I mentioned previously: with the addition of inexpensive drapery clips, any fabric you like can become a curtain. No sewing required!

Collect "ethnoplunder"

Here's a top diplomatic secret: the real reason that many Foreign Service spouses shop so much is not boredom. It is part of a master plan to compensate for their furniture. Any experienced diplomatic spouse knows that there is nothing like the biggest African basket you can buy sitting on a table to distract attention from the table itself. Interesting artwork on the walls of your dining room draws attention away from the plain white paint and clunky dining set. Filling a dowdy china cabinet with colorful ceramics will make the cabinet itself seem to disappear. The old-fashioned, somewhat cluttered, British Colonial look is very big in the Foreign Service community, and always will be. Experienced spouses and officers alike have learned to enjoy the challenge of combining their artwork and collectibles with embassy furniture in an endless variety of ways. (They may as well, since they have no alternative.)

Plant something

It can be hard to get motivated to develop or improve a garden in what is essentially a rental property. After all, unlike furniture, plants can't be taken with you when you move. But if you get started within a few months of your arrival at post, you can derive considerable enjoyment for the remainder of your tour from an investment of very little money and just a few hours of work.

If you live in a temperate climate, plant a few bulbs in the fall. Sit back and enjoy them the next spring, and the next, and maybe even the next. When I arrived in Prague to face an utterly bland and unimproved former cow pasture in a new subdivision, I took the time to plant daffodils and tulips in my front yard. Was I ever happy to see those flowers a few months later, at the end of the seemingly endless Czech winter! So were my European neighbors. As a matter of fact, I consider those tulips to be one of my personal contributions to American diplomacy.

In more tropical climes, it's even easier to put down roots, and not just because hiring a gardener is often quite affordable. Plants that are annuals in most parts of the U.S. bloom year-round in warmer climates. We enjoyed a perpetual herb garden of basil, oregano and rosemary in San Salvador, along with a nice patch of four o'clocks grown from seed from my mother's garden. In Lusaka we grew impatiens under shady jacaranda trees, and pumpkins just for fun. Apartment dwellers can grow herb gardens and flowers on balconies and in window boxes. There is nothing that makes a place feel more like home than a garden, no matter how small.

A few house plants also add a homey touch as well as oxygen to your surroundings. They are an especially cheerful touch in northern countries. You don't have to buy new pots and plants every time: invest in a few nice ones, and give the plants to friends in plastic bags or disposable pots when you leave post. Clean out the pots for packing (allow time for them to thoroughly dry) and fill them with potting soil at your next post. Ask your co-workers or neighbors for a few cuttings to start your plant collection. It's not only practical, but a great conversation starter!

Store it! (Or get rid of it!)

Depending on the post, and the available housing inventory, you may be assigned a house that is too large for your family, with outbuildings and unused bedrooms, as we were in Lusaka. Or you may be assigned a house that is much smaller than you are theoretically entitled to, as we were in Prague. In either case, it is unlikely that you will find storage furniture when you arrive, such as garage shelving. Don't subject yourself to teetering stacks of moving boxes for the next two to four years. Invest in collapsible storage shelving, either before moving or after your arrival, depending on the post. You may also be able to buy used shelves from the previous occupant of the property—don't be afraid to ask! One creative spouse faced with storage issues in Havana even hired local carpenters to make shelves out the remains of her wooden packing crates.

Because Americans have so much stuff, the U.S. is without question the best place to stock up on storage solutions of all kinds. A few large plastic tubs can be worth their weight in gold in some climates, and many will be too bulky to order via APO or pouch once you get to post (I have learned this the hard way!).

You may be assigned furnishings that you either have no room for, or simply can't stand. Despite protestations to the contrary, I've found that most Embassies will come pick up items and return them to the warehouse. A certain pink and green paisley carpet made such a journey within a week of my arrival in Prague, along with a loveseat that had been loved a little too much by the previous owner's dog. To date, I have never encountered much resistance to returning items like these.

But, if you are unable to convince GSO to come get their stuff out of YOUR home, store it in the garage, attic, or some other place that won't inconvenience you. We stored half of our 12 dining chairs and two of our dining table leaves in the garage of our tiny house in Prague. Some have been driven to extremes by their furniture, such as the spouse in Lusaka who simply shoved everything she didn't like under the carport and told GSO that, as far as she was concerned, it was stored. You probably won't be forced to take such measures, but if faced with items that are truly unacceptable—damaged by earlier residents' pets or children, or by a local upholsterer with an affinity for aqua floral brocade—don't be afraid to take photos, a stained sofa cushion, or what have you to the desk of the person in charge. There is nothing in the FS contract that states that you have to live with furniture that rightfully belongs at the curb.

With all the moving around that Foreign Service families do, it is easy to think of each house or apartment as merely a way station. It's hard sometimes to sum up the energy to make a house your home when you know you will be leaving in a couple of years. But I have found that it is well worth the effort. I don't regret a minute that I have spent painting my children's bedrooms, tending to flowers, putting together shelves or unpacking "extra" lamps, pillows and throws. No matter where in the world we are, we should all be able to live in a house that is truly a home.

Kelly Bembry Midura is a writer, website designer, at-home parent and longtime Foreign Service spouse. She accompanied her Foreign Service officer husband, Chris, to Bolivia, Guatemala, Zambia, El Salvador and the Czech Republic before settling in Reston, Virginia. You can read more of her articles at www.aafsw.org, *or visit her business web page at* http://www.midurafamily.org/design.htm.

The Foreign Service-Mobile

by Anne Allen Sullivan

Ahh! The perfect Foreign Service-mobile: a big 4x4 with all the accessories—because, while you know you'll be off-roading, you still want some of the comforts of home. You've submitted your bid list. You're chomping at the bit. You're ready to go … to … Tokyo. Oops! The big off-roader is now faced with narrow, winding city streets and parking spaces that accommodate only the driver's half. (Do you think the General Services Officer might approve two parking spaces side by side?) Time to downsize.

We had friends who were lucky. Bob and Lilia[*] bought their dream car when they entered A-100: an impressive Pathfinder 4x4 with all of the amenities. It could go anywhere, they claimed, and they could sleep comfortably in the cargo area when they went camping. They got Zimbabwe. It was a perfect match.

We originally had such dreams for our POV (Personally Owned Vehicle). We envied Bob and Lilia's car. While it would be a huge expense, wouldn't it be worth it? Then those dreams were overtaken by fears. What if the automatic windows broke in the "open" position? What if the automatic locks wouldn't lock? We'll get the basic, no-frills, stick-shift model, we decided. No power anything!

---

[*]   Names were changed for privacy.

As she wrote this article, Anne Allen Sullivan, her FSO husband John, and their two daughters were car shopping in preparation for their current posting to Kiev, Ukraine. The family has lived in Honduras, Guatemala, Chile, and Korea, but they found driving in the Washington, DC area as challenging as at any other post.

Have you ever tried to engage a stick shift on a dirt road, going uphill, after an emergency stop, in the rainy season, only to find that the Detroit engineer decided to equip the car with a foot-operated parking brake instead of a hand brake? Okay, my husband assured me, next time we'll have an automatic.

Tom wasn't as lucky as Bob and Lilia. He, too, bought his Foreign Service car upon entering the A-100 training course. He got his assignment, Abu Dhabi, and was thrilled, until he looked at the regulations. No tinted windows. That's right, no tinted windows were permitted at all. He had to have clear windows custom-made for his brand-new car, or put it in storage.

He opted to place his car in storage, at government expense, and purchase a smaller car without window tinting. Once he got to post, he noticed how many others had gone with the custom windows option for their cars. Of course, as is typical of Foreign Service experiences, the host government repealed the tinted windows ban shortly afterward, but several other posts continue to impose window tint restrictions.

Fortunately for Tom, his navy blue second car was fine for Abu Dhabi, but there are colors that may not be permitted everywhere. For example, in some countries, only taxis may be yellow. During our car search, the only basic, stick shift, 4x4's on the lot were red or champagne. Yes, cherry red! How patriotic! But maybe a bit too ostentatious. Doesn't it come in black? Would black be too aggressive? We settled on the champagne, which ended up being exactly the same color of the Honduran dirt roads, so we didn't have to wash our car every day, or even every month. It looked the same no matter what we did, and it didn't have any of the frills that could break down. We were set.

I soon stopped seeing power locks as mere frivolity. If I had any back-seat passengers, I had to do the door dance, which is fine if you combine it with the around-the-car security sweep RSOs suggest you do at some posts, but is otherwise inconvenient at best, or even dangerous. I had to open the passenger door, reach around to unlock the back door, lock the front door, shut the front door and open the back door, all while my passenger was left standing on the sidewalk. I also quickly learned about the benefits of power windows.

Mary was visiting her daughter and son-in-law at their new post. They had gone to dinner and were driving home in the balmy evening. The car windows were open, and the warm sea breezes blew gently across their faces. They had completely let their guard down. Then, an arm came from nowhere and grabbed Mary's purse from her lap. Everything—her ID, traveler's checks, glasses, prescription medicine, even her camera—was gone!

I kept this in mind whenever I drove. Since our first car had no air conditioning, I had grown accustomed to driving with open windows. Now, if my windows were open, I had to be constantly vigilant for anyone who might try to grab my purse, who might try to get in the car, or who might try to throw something in the car (like the snakes we heard about in one country). There was nothing very diplomatic or subtle in the way I had to lean across the entire front seat to roll up the passenger-side window. I either had to stop at a corner with no pedestrians, or attempt to smile at their inquisitive stares as I performed this feat. I learned to rely on the air conditioning.

Now that we have children, power locks and windows make even more sense. I can control everything from the driver's seat, discreetly. If the rear window is open, and I notice someone sauntering toward it, I can close it without drawing undue attention.

Aside from windows, power locks, and engine/vehicle size, there are a few other issues to consider. In some countries, such as the United Arab Emirates, pick-up trucks are not permitted. When we were in Central America, pick-up truck drivers were obligated to carry any passengers who jumped onboard while the truck was stopped at a red light or stop sign. They would jump off when they had gotten close enough to their destination. Likewise, tossing groceries in the back of your pick-up isn't such a good idea overseas. In fact, having a pick-up truck isn't such a good idea overseas, unless you like providing transportation (and groceries) for half of a small town.

Then, there's the carjacking issue. We were in Guatemala during a spate of carjackings and owned an SUV. Even though it was small by SUV standards, and the color of dirt, we were told that its model was the preferred carjacking target. Fortunately, we needn't have worried. The FIRST day we drove our car, we were in an accident. Nothing interfered with the operation of the vehicle; the damage was all cosmetic, but it looked nasty. There was a dent the size of a rhinoceros on the driver's side of the car, fitting precisely between the driver's door and the rear wheel, as if it had been planned. Any would-be carjackers were immediately deterred once they pulled alongside us. We never did get that dent fixed.

The driving culture will vary drastically from one country to another. In Korea, the lane lines are merely suggestions, and there are few street signs. During rush hour, a four-lane street would have seven lanes of vehicles snaking through the city. (Slow, yes, but you can get delicious hot pastries delivered to your car window in the winter.) Depending upon where you are, taxis may be seen driving in reverse on the sidewalk, and cars may frequently make left-hand turns from the right lane—across six lanes of traffic.

In Honduras, be very cautious if you see a small branch or palm frond in the road. Branches are placed over *large* potholes as a courtesy to other drivers. Our accident in Guatemala happened while crossing a one-way street that was not marked because "everyone knows it's one-way." These are just some of the differences among countries that drive on the right; now imagine trying to learn this while driving on the left side of the road! The basic rule of thumb is, when driving in a new country, keep alert, expect anything unexpected, and go with the flow. Just when you think it's just like driving at home, you'll see something you never thought possible.

Getting a driver's license sounds like it should be a big problem. It's not. Check with GSO at your new post to see whether you need a valid

U.S. license or an International Driver's Permit. Then, the embassy will take care of any other licensing needs once you arrive at post. The same goes for your vehicle license plates.

What is a family to do if they need two cars, and the government will only ship one (as is the case with non-tandem couples)? Many families opt for taking their best choice for the country, then purchasing another car in-country if they decide they need it. That's how Janet, posted to the Bahamas, ended up with her Hyundai, a model never sold in the U.S. One caveat: ensure you have proper documentation from the seller, as sales of stolen vehicles are common in some countries.

"Having a second car just did not fit into our one-car, Foreign Service mindset," Janet says, so she and her husband, finding a second car a necessity, decided to spend as little money as possible. They bought an ancient vehicle from a missionary and named the car "Aunt Ethel," apropos to the car's vintage.

"Aunt Ethel had a plant growing out of a rust hole on the side (it died in a drought), and let water in through holes almost big enough to qualify her as a Flintstones car!" reports Janet. "After a big rain I would park her on an incline so that all the water in the car would run to the side and I could bail it out with a plastic bucket." That said, Aunt Ethel navigated the island streets and was already weathered from the salt air, so Janet didn't have to worry about depreciation. Aunt Ethel was reliable enough, she served her purpose, and Janet eventually donated her to a public high school that was starting their first driver's education program. Janet adds, "Fortunately, the school also features a shop where the kids learn car repair!"

For many in the Foreign Service, even one car doesn't fit into their mindset. Suzanne wasn't sure if she would need a car. She was going to Paris, so why would she? She could walk to the embassy, rent a car for weekend getaways, and take public transportation the rest of the time. So she didn't ship a car. But those weekend car rentals never happened because they seemed like too much trouble and expense. She did go on a couple of embassy-sponsored trips, but aside from that, she felt a bit stuck.

Bob, on the other hand, a native New Yorker, believes fervently in relying on public transportation. He says there has not been a post yet where he hasn't been able to obtain transportation for himself and his family (yes, he has kids), whenever he has needed it. I, a native of California, have a hard time imagining how one could get family and gear home from a remote cloud forest picnic, but he assures me that there are ways. Agreed; in Japan, a "personally owned vehicle is not absolutely essential" because of the excellent public transportation system, according to the Post Report. Yet, in Armenia, while "several travel agencies plan regular tours, and a car can be hired to get you where you need to go," the Post Report cautions that hired cars have "varying quality" and "a low level of safety." This is true at many other posts, as well.

Therefore, when faced with the car dilemma, seasoned Foreign Service professionals always … dread making a decision. Nevertheless, there are a few things they consider when preparing to send their Foreign Service-Mobile to a new post. Answers to these and other questions may be found in the Post Report, the Real Post Reports at www.talesmag.com, and by contacting someone at post, like the CLO, GSO, or your sponsor:

• How old may the car be? Some countries only allow new cars; others specify a certain age range.

• What other restrictions are there? Check for limitations on window tinting, engine size, placement of the steering wheel (i.e. right- or left-hand drive) or paint color; requirements for brake lights (some countries require the addition of a third light in the rear window) or child safety seats, and even more strict emissions controls than in the U.S. (such as those in Iceland). There may also be limits on the purchase price. For example, in Argentina, attachés and vice consuls may only import a car that was purchased for under $30,000.

- Are there types of vehicles that should be avoided for security reasons? (You can probably leave the Lamborghini at home.)

- What will the driving conditions be like? Do you really need that off-road package? What about snow tires? Is air conditioning essential? How much clearance is recommended? Does the undercarriage need to be rust-proofed?

- What type of fuel is available? Does the catalytic converter need to be removed to accommodate leaded gasoline? (Note: if your auto uses diesel fuel, attach a note stating "DIESEL ONLY" to the ignition key before shipment.)

- Are replacement parts readily available? If not, what parts should be sent in your household effects (HHE) shipment? (Check with your insurance company before shipping motor oil, as some policies will not cover HHE shipments if motor oil is included.) Alternately, would a car with local or European specifications be better for your next post?

- What makes of cars can be serviced?

- Do you need a micro air filtration system? Some newer cars now have these. They might very well be worth the additional expense if you are going to a post with very dusty roads or high-particulate smog.

- Where will the vehicle be parked at night? Do you need a security system? Are there other parking considerations?

- How, and to whom, may the car be sold at the end of the tour? For example, in Ukraine, cars more than five years old may only be sold to other diplomats. Therefore, many officers take cars less than three years old for a two-year posting to avoid this restriction. In other countries, vehicles must be in-country a minimum time before they may be sold. In Japan, for example, a POV may be sold tax-free only if it has been registered with the Ministry of Foreign Affairs for at least two years, and it may not be sold by proxy.

Some countries with a high tax on vehicles may allow diplomats to sell without paying the tax. This may put you in the position of being able to sell your POV for the full purchase price, even though it may be several years old. Cyril took his car to three different Latin American countries, then sold this now-4-year-old car for its original purchase price—and the buyer was happy to get it. Anti-profiteering laws do not permit you to make a profit on the sale (although the excess can be donated to an approved charity), and interest paid on the loan can not be included in the sale price. However, spare parts or after-market accessories can be included at their original purchase price. One note of caution: don't count on the tax structure remaining the same during your tenure. Tax laws can be reformed, leaving you unable to sell your car at a price you are willing to accept. So, consider it a benefit if you can sell your car for its purchase price, but be prepared to take it to your next post if the market for diplomats' cars changes.

• What types of vehicles are available for sale locally? Is anyone departing the embassy selling a car? (Check with the Community Liaison Office and read the post newsletter, often available in PDF format.) Are there duty-free import options from a third country?

• How long will it take to ship the car to post? Will you need it more here, or once you get there?

• What insurance coverage is required, and do you want more? For example, in Israel, if your car is stolen in transit, you will will have to pay the customs tax, which can be $10,000–$30,000, depending upon the car's value. Some local policies say they cover this, but they don't always do so. Is there additional coverage needed while the car is in transit? Does your insurance company cover travel to areas outside the post city or to other countries?

- And by all means, check with GSO at post BEFORE you make a car purchase to see if the information in the Post Report has changed.

Getting and shipping the perfect Foreign Service-Mobile may seem like a daunting task, but it is well worth the effort and expense. Even if you are wary of driving in some countries, you may be able to hire a driver for your car (a car you know is safe), and if you just drive on your days off, you will still enjoy the freedom to go where you want, when you want to. Finding the right car is always a challenge, but in what other profession could my husband and I boast of driving from Honduras to Guatemala on winding dirt paths, fording three rivers, visiting remote Mayan ruins, and photographing spider mon-keys—with the family cat on my lap? (Yes, this is all true.) There's an adventure out there waiting for you, too.

I Shop, Therefore I Am … in the Foreign Service

by Leslie Ashby

I have always said that I agreed to join the Foreign Service for the shopping. Let others worry about diplomacy; I was in it for the spoils, the thrill of the hunt, the amazing finds at exotic bazaars around the world! While not everyone in the Foreign Service (FS) shares my zeal, we all have shopping in common. Love it or hate it, no matter where we are in the world, we all must shop to fulfill our basic needs, and in my case, not-so-basic needs.

To learn more about how shopping figures into the Foreign Service lifestyle, I informally surveyed friends and colleagues. These active duty and retired FS employees, spouses, tandem couples, singles, males and females offered plenty of insights and anecdotes. Many agreed that exploring flea markets, antique shops, handicraft bazaars, and farmers' markets are excellent ways to get to know the culture and history of a place and use the local language. Even more agreed that shopping sprees on R&R (rest and recreation) trips, mission commissaries, online shopping, and consumable shipments from the United States and other Western countries are vital to their happiness at post. It seems that shopping in the American Foreign Service is as much an *American* experience as it is a *foreign* one.

To boldly shop where no tourist has shopped before

Let's face it; most of us do not join the Foreign Service community for its ease and predictability. We chose this lifestyle to understand and appreciate the uniqueness of a place like no tourist ever could. Each post is different, but wherever the Foreign Service takes us, an effective way to learn the local sights, sounds, faces, and places is to go shopping. A trip to the area market is not just about buying bread; it is a window on the host country.

Mette Beecroft, a 35-year veteran Foreign Service (FS) spouse, agrees. "Shopping … gives you a feel for how people deal with each other, what the farmers produce, what people consume as food, how much or how little they have to spend, what people consider to be luxury, what handicrafts are produced, how skilled people are, and even what people believe." Shopping often figures into a newcomer's orientation at post, as FS spouse Julie Johnson experienced in Chennai, India, where she was introduced to the city with a tour of stores and shopping areas. That initial tour helped her navigate the city and recognize what it had to offer.

Many of us delight in using our foreign language skills in the market. According to Rachel Cooke, a Foreign Service officer who served in Bishkek, Kyrgyzstan, "It is great to chat with the nut seller to learn the difference between the five different varieties of pistachios he sells." Others, like Foreign Service spouse and mother Francesca Kelly, have found shopping to be a great motivator for her children to practice the local language. "You would be surprised how quickly the kids learned to ask for all the ice cream flavors they wanted in Italian!"

In many countries, bargaining is an essential part of commerce and another opportunity to tap into the local culture and language. Trying to negotiate a good deal with a shrewd merchant is a new and intimidating experience for some of us, and we Westerners often end up paying much more than locals. Yet even as we bicker over the price of tomatoes or discuss the finer points of hand-painted pottery, we can appreciate how bargaining humanizes commerce. "Buyers and sellers are obligated to communicate and build a rapport, even if it is, at times, adversarial," observes Stephen Ashby, a Foreign Service officer who enjoys shopping almost as much as his wife does. Whether we develop a talent for haggling or not, bargaining can lend a bit of sport and exoticism to shopping overseas and often provides entertaining stories for the folks back home.

So how are we in the Foreign Service spending our euros, yen, and pesos? We search antique shops, auction houses, flea markets, and craft bazaars for treasures like hand-woven textiles, original paintings, and common household items from the host country that are reborn as *objets d'art* in the Foreign Service home. "To this day," says Mette, "we can walk around the house and think about where we were and what we were doing when we acquired a given object." As the years and the tours go by, this collection of "ethnoplunder" can get rather eclectic: antique doors from Morocco, a rusty grappling hook from Nova Scotia, an ox yoke from Turkey. You name it; someone in the Foreign Service has bought it.

Many of us also happily pay for big-ticket items, like crystal, jewelry, and furniture that can be found more cheaply overseas. During a trip in Ashgabat, Turkmenistan, Rachel was shocked to find that "Persian carpets that would cost $15,000 at home were $500!" She and her husband had to buy extra luggage to get all their carpets home. When the deals are especially good, even the most adamant non-shoppers among us will buy in quantity and dole out the loot as gifts to friends and family.

Mishaps and mistakes

Shopping overseas is hardly idyllic. How do you know if it is okay to handle the produce or inquire about a price without being forced into a sale? In Paris, you would be a reprobate to squeeze the lemons; in Tashkent, you would be a fool not to. Language barriers, cultural differences, and basic math can get the better of us and lead to misunderstandings, embarrassment, and plain old frustration.

In many parts of the world, we in the Foreign Service are viewed as "rich Americans" who can easily pay double the "local" price or more on just about anything. In countries where the cost of living is extremely low, this is certainly true, but for those of us looking for a bargain, the idea of paying the "foreigner" price or being forced to barter well above what any local would pay seems undemocratic. It may not be fair, but "we learned to take it easy and accept whatever the outcome," says Foreign Service spouse June Williamson of their time in Indonesia. She and her husband got a lesson in price rigging when they sent their driver to purchase coconuts on their behalf. The transaction was almost complete when the shopkeeper realized he was actually selling to foreigners. He immediately raised the price—to which June and her husband agreed—but then suddenly decided not to sell them any at all. June believes the shopkeeper decided that no sale was better than accommodating dubious foreigners, who are often resented for their relative prosperity.

Despite our best efforts in language training, many of us trip over our tongues once in the field. Carol Quade, a Foreign Service spouse of Korean descent who was posted in Seoul, remembers asking the price on a piece of pottery, but slipping up on her pronunciation. "Since I look Asian, the shopkeeper mistook me for a Japanese tourist and answered my inquiry in Yen. I, of course, didn't understand a word he said in Japanese and assumed that the price was so outrageously high that we hadn't even learned the number in class."

John Hosinski, a first-tour spouse in Zagreb, Croatia, admits to buying massive amounts of produce due to language mistakes and a habit of ordering in kilogram or half-kilogram quantities. "I forget a kilo of apples is not the same as a kilo of green beans," he says. "I've purchased major quantities of Brussels sprouts, beans, cheeses, and lettuce. I've even found myself eating the evidence to save myself from having to explain, yet again, to my wife that I bought, say, all of the olives on this side of the Adriatic."

In addition to the metric system, currency conversions can make the Foreign Service head spin and pocketbook hurt. While on R&R in Istanbul, Sara S. Villarreal Bishop and her husband bought a bathing suit for their two year-old son. "As we came out of the store, I saw my husband looking at the receipt and counting '5, 6, 7,'" recalls Sara. "When I asked what he was doing, he said 'I thought I paid 24 million lira, but I paid 240! There are *seven* zeros here!' We'd just paid $80 for a toddler swimming suit."

United Shoppers of America

Foreign Service people are global nomads, explorers, and adventurers, but we are also Americans who crave the simple things from home like peanut butter sandwiches and affordable, quality footwear wherever we are in the world. We shop online and with mail order catalogs; we order massive consumables shipments; we even beg friends and family back home to send those things without which we just cannot live.

Before heading to post, many of us talk tough about living off the local economy, but once on the ground, we can have a change of heart. Amy Kennedy-Penuel, a spouse in Beijing, China, confesses, "I was determined not to be one of those Americans who orders everything from the States ... but just because it's made in China does not mean you can buy it in China." Like many before her, Amy came to the conclusion that some items are better purchased from home. For her, it was children's clothing. Others bring or order children and adult shoes, adult clothing, wine and other libations, paper products, household cleaning supplies, personal hygiene products, medications, pet products, toys, books, movies, music, plastic storage containers, and specialty food items from the U.S.

Those of us within reach of a commissary or military Post Exchange tend to take advantage of the relatively low prices and consistent supply of coveted American products like maple syrup and tortilla chips. Others of us at more remote posts have to keep our eyes open for American products to pop up around town—and buy them when we see them, even if the need is not urgent. Just because a store has Haagen-Dazs ice cream today does not mean it will have it tomorrow.

At hardship posts, consumable shipments are another way to get goods from home, but always in bulk. It can be a bit painful to spend

$1,000 or more at once on dry goods and household supplies, but that huge supply of toilet paper can last all tour or longer. My family is still using cotton swabs and aluminum foil we purchased before going to our first hardship post over four years ago. This propensity to over-purchase and hoard can be a tough habit to break, as one Foreign Service family fresh from a hardship post has experienced in Canada. With less than two miles separating them from a wholesale club, three grocery stores, and numerous convenience shops, they still fight the knee-jerk reaction to buy a lifetime supply of paper napkins or olive oil on each shopping trip.

At most posts, American goods can be mail-ordered and shipped through the diplomatic pouch or military mail service. Whether we are at hardship posts or not, we order American stuff on the Internet for the convenience, price, availability, brand recognition, and expectation of quality. Amazon.com, LandsEnd.com, NetGrocer.com, and other online stores attract significant Foreign Service business from all over the globe. "Shopping, specifically via the Internet, is part of what keeps us from feeling adrift. I have a regular NetGrocer order for those comfort foods." says Sara. Old-timers may reminisce about simpler, more adventurous Foreign Service days before the Internet, but few would go back. Shopping on the Internet offers Foreign Service families tangible, and often indispensable, links back to the U.S. and the comforts of home.

It is not just pancake mix and polo shirts we pine for; those of us with strong ties to other countries also seek out items that make us feel at home. Foreign-born spouse Euhna Krost makes a point of finding a Korean restaurant whenever she arrives at post. There she can be sure to find information on Korean grocery stores and get connected to the local Korean community. Julie, who is originally from Australia, admits that she cannot live without Vegemite on her toast every morning. "When I first moved to the U.S. over ten years ago," she says, "my mother used to send me boxes with carefully wrapped jars of Vegemite inside. Nowadays, I can order it directly on the Internet myself."

Of course, it is impossible to duplicate an American life overseas, and who in the FS would want to? Even with all our consumables, Internet shipments, and catalog orders, most of us in the FS thrive on experiencing local life at post. We mostly do our shopping at local markets where choices are fewer and stock is seasonal, but where produce is often fresher and organic. We learn to find acceptable substitutes for items that are not available, use certain expired goods, or simply do without. At our first post with no Bisquick in sight, I learned that (gasp) I can make pancakes from scratch. Others learn to bake fresh bread, toss homemade pizzas, and even butcher the unwieldy chunks of meat often sold at markets into recognizable cuts. There is a certain freedom in knowing we are not completely dependent on prepackaged goods.

Living off the land, so to speak, not only puts us in touch with our surroundings and its people, it is also humbling. "Overseas, I see a lot of people who live just making ends meet … I think that we Americans sometimes take our high standard of living for granted," observes John. "I also see how people make do with less, and it helps me be more resourceful." Foreign Service officer Carrie Muntean adds, "Being in the FS has made us less brand conscious, less choosy … and far less fussy. Shopping in Angola really drove home how difficult the regular Angolans' life was."

Return of the native

"Life in the Foreign Service has changed how I shop in the U.S., as my shopping there tends to be when I am on R&R or home leave, so I am very focused about what I need to take back to post with me," says Julie. For many of us, trips to the U.S. between or during postings can turn into one long shopping (and shipping) spree.

Some shop with purpose. Kids need shoes and clothes in several sizes to get them through the year. Easter, Halloween, Christmas, and other decorations must be bought for use back at post (good luck finding them all in July). Gifts must be purchased for birthdays that are months away. A trip to the department store is necessary to try on shoes, undergarments, cosmetics, and other items that cannot easily be purchased sight unseen through catalogs or on the Internet. Hitting the sale racks is also a popular way to stock up on inexpensive clothing that may be out of season in snowy Boston but perfect for sunny Bogota.

Others shop for pleasure. I look forward to visiting my favorite gourmet kitchen supply store where the helpful sales people smile and I can browse the thoughtfully displayed wares at leisure pretending I am Julia Child, another Foreign Service spouse. "Living overseas has made me appreciate all the little things so much more about home, says Laura Veprek, a Foreign Service spouse who lived in Yaounde, Cameroon. "We're extremely lucky to have good roads and nice cars to take us to nice malls and shops to buy whatever we want whenever we want." A slight variation on this sentiment comes from Foreign Service spouse Kelly Midura, who loves second-hand shopping in the U.S. "It reminds me of the thrill of the hunt in the developing world. It was a big deal to find strawberries in Lusaka or the best bargain on weavings in Guatemala, and it's equally fun to find cheap jeans at a thrift store."

When coming in from the field, however, the onslaught of American consumerism can overwhelm even the most diehard Foreign Service shopper. Many of us have had the experience of being completely dumbfounded by our first trip to a grocery store or mall. "After our tour in Lusaka, I actually froze up in the middle of the food court when we went to our first mall on home leave," says Kelly. "I was so unused to any kind of sensory overload and having any kind of choice, my husband had to pick out lunch for me. I had been looking forward to shopping after a year in Africa, and I found myself unable to buy anything that day."

Living far from American mega-marts and commercial TV can give us some perspective on American consumerism. "Many of us have been posted to countries that are extremely poor or have suffered some sort of upheaval. We have seen people get by with very little," comments Mette. "I have no problem with having some nice things or wanting to bring home souvenirs … however, I do have a problem with a value system that seems to encourage buying more and more, always needing new things, and outdoing one's peers."

Others are a little less philosophical. "Having lived in places where Christmas is more of a novelty, more religious than commercial, or on a totally different day, I can't stand the [American] Theme Park Christmas … I avoid it online even," states Sara. "I really appreciate the dorky [AFN public service announcements] on TV overseas because my son isn't constantly begging to go see the latest movie or buy the newest video game," says Susan Cheatham, a spouse in Surabaya, Indonesia. "I love American shopping malls because you can get everything in one place, but I also hate them because every single one is the same soulless place as the next," adds Francesca. Perhaps a unique benefit of the Foreign Service is to be able to "get in and get out" of the American consumer whirlwind as we see fit. Some of us eagerly await the delivery of fashion magazines and catalogs to keep up with the latest crazes at home, while others spend hours in cyberspace filling their virtual shopping carts, and still others leave it all behind and live off the economy.

Shopping and bidding

Even a devoted shopper like me does not bid on a post solely because of the shopping opportunities (or lack thereof); however, the question is ever present in my mind, especially once assigned. Is this a consumables post? Is there a commissary or military exchange? If the post is really "out there," are goods like clothing and pet food available? According to the State Department's Overseas Briefing Center (OBC), the top three bidding considerations are housing, schooling, and spouse employment, followed closely by health and security concerns. Shopping may not make or break a bid list, but the OBC routinely provides information on purchasing consumables, cars, and 220-volt appliances, and their Personal Post Insight reviews offer advice from people at post on what goods are available locally and what you should bring with you from the U.S. Bidders can also contact the Community Liaison Office coordinator (CLO) at post and access **www.tales-mag.com** to find out what life is really like in Quito, Cairo, or anywhere else we serve.

Whether shopping plays a role in our bidding process or not, many of us agree that shopping influences how we feel about our posts. For Carol, shopping is how she gauges the accessibility of a post. "If the shopping is easy and convenient, then the post is. I don't mind trying new products and food, but if the stores are difficult to get to and I can't communicate easily with the clerks, then I feel frustrated ... Life is much easier when shopping can be a pleasant experience." It can take months to figure out the best places to shop for the freshest produce, American items, or household goods at a new post, but the rewards are increased confidence and comfort in your new surroundings and a sense of adventure as you explore.

Others enjoy—or at least fondly recall—posts for the exact opposite reason. In certain far-flung places in Asia or Africa where even the most basic foodstuffs are scarce, shopping can turn a diplomatic mission on its ear. Tandem couple Bill and Carrie Muntean roughed it in Angola for two years where "... the embassy was only open half-days on Fridays, partly because it took at least half the day to do grocery shopping and the stores were better stocked than on the weekends." Moreover, when Embassy Angola's consumables shipment would arrive from South Africa with frozen meat and other treats, a call would go out over the emergency frequency of their handheld radios. As Carrie recalls, "it was accepted that all officers, from the Ambassador on down, would stop what they were doing to get their goodies home. An interesting use of the emergency frequency, for sure!"

There is also a dark side to shopping in the Foreign Service that can rear its ugly head when we experience depression, boredom, loneliness, isolation, and homesickness. Excessive shopping, either in person or online, has been known to affect Foreign Service spouses especially, but with no empirical data from the State Department or other resources, it is hard to gauge just how prevalent this problem is. Nonetheless, several Foreign Service spouses interviewed, including Carol, confided that "during the winter in a foreign post, it can be difficult to get outside, so shopping is an easy and safe way to spend the day practicing your language skills or just browsing and people-watching. Otherwise, one could start to feel very isolated." She added, "I know some women can shop compulsively as a way to fight homesickness ... It depends on what other outlets there are for spouses and mothers at post. For example, a playgroup can be a positive support group for you and your family."

And the total is ...

Shopping in the Foreign Service is a huge subject, and the ideas expressed herein may not represent everyone's experiences or inclinations. Lest anyone get upset, it is important to remember that shopping in the Foreign Service is also a small subject compared to the critical work of diplomatic missions and the difficult situations of many FS families. Shopping can be a morale booster when it is plentiful and interesting, or a morale buster when it is not, but as Sara puts it so well, "Living somewhere where you could conceivably have to leave it all behind drives home the idea that it is 'just stuff.'"

That said, I still love to shop. It is more than a task; shopping is an integral part of the entire FS continuum. It is present when we prepare for post, live at post, leave post, and remember post. It can influence how we feel about a foreign country and also our own country. It can delight us, fill us with dread, frustrate us, and calm our nerves. I, for one, am glad to have the opportunity to know firsthand the highs and the lows of commerce around the world. Shopping in the FS may impoverish us—but won't the experience be enriching!

Leslie Ashby is a mother, freelance writer and editor, member of the Associates of the American Foreign Service Worldwide (AAFSW) and Foreign

Service spouse who has lived in Bishkek, Kyrgyzstan; Montreal, Canada; and Manila, Philippines. When not shopping, Leslie enjoys dabbling in arts and crafts, cooking, and sipping wine with her Foreign Service officer husband, Stephen.

Taking the Home out of Your House: Tips on Renting Out Your Property

by Jan Fischer Bachman

Although it may seem a daunting prospect, renting out your U.S. home is often one of the best moves you can make while overseas. Some homeowners have enjoyed phenomenal equity gains—perhaps one of the only legal ways a government employee can make so much extra money tax-free. And having someone else pay your mortgage while you are posted abroad is, as Foreign Commercial Service spouse Chris Robinson* says, "one of the best deals in our compensation package."

Cynthia Jones,* State Department spouse, adds, "It has been terrific to have [our house] because it has given us the illusion of roots and a yearly break on our taxes. We know, and our kids know, that if our Foreign Service career ended tomorrow, we would have a place to go."

How can Foreign Service families benefit from the financial and psychological advantages of owning property while minimizing the problems of being an absentee landlord? Sail the three "C"s: consider, convert, and communicate.

Consider

Location, location, location.

There are two initial questions to consider. First, which is the best location for a Foreign Service rental property? The former pat answer was the Washington, DC metropolitan area, specifically, near a Metro line, in a good school district, and/or close to a military facility. Current wisdom: anywhere you can afford something more than a broom closet!

"We've owned a house in New Jersey nearly all of our married life," says tandem officer Linda Cunningham*. "Since it is a property in a beach town, we are able to rent it for the summer season only. Renters can't possibly do as much damage to a property in three months as they can in a full year."

Cynthia Jones' home is in Charlottesville, Virginia, "not a place we will live in during our Foreign Service career, but a place we would like to retire to."

"College kids are good renters for some people," State Dept. spouse Kristi Streiffert points out. "We've camped out in our rental on R&R and home leave because our tenants are college kids in a college town. For two years we've had the lease written so that we get to have the house in the summer. We use lawn chairs and loungers to sit in and inflate-a-beds to sleep on. We keep everything in our (rather large) SUV stored over the winter, including a set of basic cooking and eating utensils. This is not for everyone, I'm sure, but we love staying in our house!"

If you are able to swing a purchase in the DC area, take rental prices into consideration. For instance, when we purchased our first home in Fairfax, VA, we could afford a three-level townhouse or a small, one-bathroom single family home. I soon discovered that townhouses were renting for $300 per month more than equivalently priced ramblers. That piece of information made our decision—and helped us to rent our place at a slight profit while we were overseas.

Chris Robinson advises, "It is helpful to have property managers look at the property before you buy it if possible." Experienced property managers should know the market well enough to help you avoid expensive mistakes, such as purchasing a condo that cannot be legally rented or a large house that will sit empty for months on end.

Investigate neighborhoods, consider supply and demand of rental properties in the area, look at rental prices, ask a property manager—and then consider following your heart, since quite possibly the market could change no matter how reasoned and logical your decision.

Who's in charge?

The second basic question to consider is, "Should we hire a property manager?" What does a property management firm do? Teta Moehs, a second-tour officer, replies, "They advertise the house, determine the rent, screen and interview tenants, do careful inventories of our house, collect the rent and pay us our share, track what repairs need to be done and use their network of repair people to make sure everything runs. Between tenants, they suggest what work might need to be performed to maintain the value of our home. At the end of the year we get the documents we need for our taxes, plus a CD of photos. In short, they do everything so we don't have to be bothered, and that's how we like it."

Spouse Evelyn Wilson* says, "I attended an Overseas Briefing Center seminar on renting property, and the property managers there made the liability and housing laws sound difficult to master. After getting multiple recommendations, we chose a company that promised to be meticulous with our home, a townhouse in Fairfax. The property manager found a tenant immediately. I would describe the situation as fairly problem-free while we were overseas: the company collected the rent and sent us a quarterly report. If a repair was required, we would get an e-mail asking for approval. Unfortunately, when we returned, we had a number of problems, including trash left in the yard, six-foot weeds, very dirty walls, a water stain on the ceiling that was the fault of the tenants, and more. I would use a property manager again, because it is SO easy to have someone else in charge of everything, but I would definitely stay on top of things more, especially when returning. I would also make a point of having someone directly in touch with the tenants, even if the company told me not to (as they did)."

Foreign Service spouse Lynn Markham* says, "We didn't use a property manager. Our house was simple and rather run-down when we started, so we figured not much could happen to it. We also thought the fees were too high.

"We found our first tenant through the Pentagon bulletin board, and then when they were ready to move, we offered them one month's rent bonus to find the next people. This worked through several tenants. The one time it didn't work, we paid a Foreign Service friend who was posted in DC to find a tenant for us.

"For repairs, we asked the tenants to take care of things themselves, send us the receipts and deduct the work from the rent. This worked pretty well. One tenant even refinished our wood floors himself and charged us only for the materials. Unfortunately, our last tenant was a rather dysfunctional family and they didn't bother to make repairs, even though we would have paid for them.

"The tenants would mail the rent to our local bank in Virginia or go through the drive-through and deposit it into our account. The rent was late a few times, but it never became a problem. Any receipts (for deducted repairs) were mailed to us. The tenants also had the number of local friends to call if they needed immediate help.

"We were lucky that we didn't face a serious problem (tenant refusing to pay rent, major destruction of property), but I think we could have appointed someone as our agent locally and paid them to handle it if this had happened."

Situations change

Even after making the initial decision about whether to hire a property manager, changing circumstances may require alterations to your plan. Cynthia Jones says, "We rented our house to friends for our first seven years of ownership, under an informal, no-lease arrangement. When they moved out three years ago, we contracted with a property management company that has found renters for us and looked after maintenance. We chose our property manager based on background research, recommendations and a personal meeting, and we believe all three steps are the minimum necessary to find someone who matches your expectations. We are, after all, entrusting her with the most valuable piece of our financial portfolio. We have found our property manager to be as responsive and responsible as we could hope for."

Why don't we name names?

When you read a positive or negative experience, you might wish that we had listed the property management companies praised or panned. However, we have not found consistent recommendations. Here are two different takes on the same company:

"I cannot recommend strongly enough NOT to use Company X. During my meeting with them, I was explicit on my requirements: $2000 a month in rent, 80% of the hardwoods covered with rugs, and HVAC filters (provided by me) changed every three months. They then proceeded to sign a lease for less than $2000 a month with the person THEY thought was the best candidate. Worse than that was that I was told by a neighbor that someone was moving in. The company never told me they had signed a lease, let alone for less than I had agreed to. On top of that, they never wrote in the instructions I had asked for into the lease. Then, when I began to question them, the company owner wrote, 'Please feel free to seek another property manager at your earliest convenience.' It boils my blood whenever I think about this."

—*Josh Weisman*

"Company X did a really great job for us. We were constantly kept in the loop by monthly statements and e-mails from the actual property managers. The service was super. Whenever we returned home on leave (or whatever), a simple e-mail would ensure that we'd have access to inspect our houses. Whenever the manager thought something ought to be done for maintenance, we'd get an e-mail with several estimates.

> "The owner of the company acted as our realtor for the sale of one of our properties last year, doing all that was necessary to make it look beautiful for the market and then showing it for us. She was super."
>
> —*Jeff and Susan Garrison, tandem couple*
>
> Choosing a "good" property management firm does not seem to guarantee a successful rental outcome; therefore, we have chosen not to make specific recommendations.

Don't try this at home

Experienced Foreign Service homeowners make strong cases both for using a property management firm and for going it alone. Having a non-professional acquaintance manage the property seems to be the all-around least satisfactory option.

Before going overseas with her Diplomatic Security husband, Sheri Mestan Bochantin rented out a condo in Arlington, paying a neighbor to manage it. "I don't know that I'd do that again," Sheri says. The neighbor was unresponsive—to the extent that she did not notify the Bochantins, by then out of the country, when the tenant moved out!

The military approach

Renting to military families and asking them to manage the property was the option receiving the most rave reviews.

"We strongly feel that, if your place is anywhere near a military facility that's the way to go," emphasizes Sheri. "Our second time around, we only advertised at the Pentagon. We were going to hire a property manager, but the tenant said, 'I'm a homeowner, too. If you're willing to trust me, I'll take care of it for us.' We split the difference in the rent, dividing the property management fees. When we needed a new dishwasher, he comparison-shopped, asked what we wanted, and gave us three choices. We would do it again in a heartbeat."

"I HIGHLY recommend military families," Foreign Service spouse Sandi Parker* agrees. "They make excellent tenants. They know that if they don't live up to the agreement all you have to do is tell their superior officer. Also, when you write your own lease you can put in every detail that matters to you. I have never heard of a bad story."

How to Find a Property Management Firm

Ask for recommendations; however, be aware that service seems to vary more by specific manager than by company. In getting referrals, include questions on how repairs were handled, how often the firm communicated, what condition the property was in when tenants vacated, how often the property manager changed, and anything specific to your property (a beautiful garden that needs upkeep, new hardwood floors—will they be willing and able to deal with it?)

When interviewing a company, consider the following questions:

- What fees do they charge? (standard seems to be 8% of the monthly rent plus one month's rent for finding a tenant—but fees for other services vary)

- How much money do they require on deposit to cover expenses?

- What is their procedure for handling repairs? Which companies do they use, and do they get multiple bids? Are tenants required to contribute to any repairs?

- What does the company do if one repair does not solve the problem? (note: they should have the same vendor come back or contact you regarding a purchase rather than getting a second company to try to fix the problem)

- What qualifications do individual property managers have? What is the turnover rate? How long do most property managers stay with the company?

- What recourse do you have if you are not happy with the service your specific property manager provides?

- What is their procedure for notifying you if your property manager is going to change?

- How does the company verify the initial condition of the property?

- How often do they inspect (not just a drive-by)?

- Will you be allowed to visit the property?

- What reports will you receive and how often?

- When will you be notified if a tenant is moving out?

- Are they agreeable to allowing an outside representative for you come to the final walk-through?

- What do they consider "normal" wear and tear?

- What does the company do if there is a gap between tenants in terms of maintenance and safety?

Convert

Once you have considered where to buy a residence and whether to use a property manager, it is time to mentally convert your home to a business. This transition might be easy, if you purchased the place simply as an investment. Emotional ties could make it much more difficult if the property has been your home after years of moving.

"Some people who've had bad experiences seem really nervous and personally involved with their houses," Chris Robinson notes. She advises, "You are going into this whole thing as a winner: the tax law favors you, so relax and consider the property manager an ally. They will make mistakes, they will present you with expenses—but it's a business."

A personal ceremony can help you make the break. For the religiously minded, the book *For Everything A Season: 75 Blessings for Daily Life* by the Nilsen family includes a beautifully written reflection and ritual for moving out and moving on. Among other ideas, the book suggests lighting a candle and moving from room to room remembering what has happened there, saying goodbye, and speaking a blessing for those who will live there in future.

I found that preparing our townhouse helped break the immediate attachment: after cleaning, painting, having windows repaired, putting in a new dishwasher, and doing what seemed like an endless list of things, I was relieved to leave! However, two years later, when the renters had moved out, I was devastated to see the state of "my" home. A more formal transition process might have made the situation much less painful.

Whatever the mechanism, your property should now form part of your financial portfolio rather than your heart. As with any investment, your earnings may go up or down as market circumstances dictate. Taking certain steps, such as those that follow, will make a positive outcome more likely.

Look for support

First, line up your back-up team, even if you have hired a property manager. "Our house is in a small town," Linda Cunningham says, "so we developed a good working relationship with the local realtor who handles most of the summer rentals. One of us gets back there at least once a year to check on the place, arrange for repairs and visit the realtor. In between our visits, we have family members who check the house for us. And we have really great neighbors who keep an eye on it. Keep in touch with your neighbors and show them your appreciation."

"The friends who used to live in our house moved to a home only a few streets away, and it's fair to say they are even more attached to the place than we are," Cynthia says. "They drive by now and then, have introduced themselves to all of our tenants, and e-mail us if there's anything they notice about the house. They are a great back-up source of information. For example, a sublet situation came up, which our property manager neglected to e-mail us about until we wrote her to say that our friends noticed a sign out front."

Chris Robinson adds, "Use your old neighborhood as a resource. When I needed new windows, the property management firm was saying that they could only find expensive ones. I called the homeowner's association and got a referral from a homeowner who had windows done recently."

Sometimes it is even worth hiring someone. Sheri paid a neighbor to do the final walk-through for her. The neighbor found dirty walls and carpet, so the tenants contacted a cleaning company. When the Bochantins returned, Sheri says, "We were impressed with how good it looked."

Make a list

Next, compile contact information for local companies providing services your property might need. When our property management firm said that we had to have a toilet replaced, they gave us a price and two style options. I called my favorite plumber, who quoted a similar cost. That gave me peace of mind that the company was not charging us too much. I also carried in my files the name of the vendor I wanted to use if we needed to have the (elderly) furnace replaced. Other Foreign Service families recommend packing a local phone directory for easy reference.

Prove it!

Finally, make sure you document the condition of your home. Betty Snow, a veteran State Department spouse, says, "Regardless of whom you get as property manager, you and they—along with the renter, if selected—might like to take a video of the property, along with narration. Thus, there will be no doubt about conditions of screens, walls, floors, carpet, and so on. You might find there are priority items or care instructions you wish to mention and otherwise might have forgotten."

Communicate

While you might breathe a sigh of relief upon handing over the keys to your property, you will still need to stay in frequent communication with your property management company or tenants. "I wish this had been branded on the top of my head," Kristi Streiffert exclaims. "I think that it is the biggest key to a successful situation." She advises, "Call the property manager every six months if nothing is going on—every month if you or the house is in a transition period. We just had a situation that cost us $600, all because I thought that *they* would call *me*."

When our family returned to the U.S., we found that our property manager had changed twice without any notification. Then the renters moved out early and the walk-through was completed without us knowing it. By the time we saw the place, it was too late to ask the tenants to do more cleaning, especially since they had moved nearby (and the children ended up in the same Brownie troop as my daughter!). We really needed to communicate more frequently—and with clearer expectations—during the handover process.

Regularly checking on your property is also part of staying in touch. "We make it a point to visit the house once a year with our property manager, even if only for fifteen minutes, in order to take a firsthand look at it," Cynthia says.

Don't be afraid to go higher if you aren't satisfied with your manager. Chris Stuebner (State) says, "For better or for worse, we've stuck with one property management company. My husband knew the husband of the founder's daughter very well from work. Whenever we've had a hassle on the property management side, we've copied her on the e-mail, and she's generally done whatever prodding was necessary. Bottom-line: having a proactive property manager at the working level is a blessing. As not all the working level folks have been equally resourceful, it's been real helpful to have the personal relationship with someone much further up the chain of command."

Chris Robinson agrees. "In 2000 our property manager told us that our property would probably be vacant for up to six months. We had asked the head of the property management company to look at the place for us before we bought it, so we knew it was an excellent rental property. As it happens, we were making an emergency trip home anyway, so we had the company head and the property manager meet us in the house. The company head "lit a fire" under the property manager and the place rented in two and a half weeks. The property manager just had too much work to do and didn't want to take on the rental."

The financial low-down

Rent revenue is taxable income, reported on the IRS 1040 form, Schedule E. You can deduct many expenses, including depreciation, repairs, mortgage payments, real estate taxes, and operating costs, such as property management fees. IRS publication 527, Residential Rental Property, covers many details, while publication 946 explains more about depreciation.

A recent tax law change allows property owners to exempt up to $250,000 per person ($500,000 per couple) from the sale of a home, as long as they have lived there for two out of the past five years. The five-year period may be suspended for up to ten years for those people on qualified extended duty in the Armed Services or Foreign Service. Qualified extended duty means being stationed at least 50 miles from the residence sold or residing under orders in government housing. Details currently can be found at: **http://www.irs.gov/taxtopics/tc701.html** .

Tax Traps

Certified Financial Planner Barry B. De Marr lists three common Foreign Service tax mistakes. First, many people consider their home a personal residence and so do not claim depreciation. However, if the property is later sold, depreciation for the rental period is taxed, even if it was never claimed in the first place (strange but true). There are slightly complicated ways to "play catch up" if you have not depreciated the property, by filing to change your method of accounting or adjusting prior claims. Consult your tax advisor for details. A second common mistake is including the land cost in the basis for depreciation: land does not depreciate. Thirdly, problems occur when taxpayers claim interest and real estate taxes on both schedule A and schedule E; the deductions cannot be duplicated.

If you have been away from your property too long to qualify for the new exemption, you can still avoid capital gains taxes through making what is known as a 1031 or Starker exchange, in which you sell one rental property and purchase another of "like kind." Personal residences are considered like kind, even if they differ in value. After the new property has been rented for a time, you can return to live in it without penalty. The IRS has not defined the length of time you must rent the property, but most accountants suggest six to twelve months. In other words, if you would like to buy a different place for your next DC posting, sell the old property in a 1031 exchange long enough before your return that the new home can be rented out for a time before you move in. As of October 22, 2004, you have to hold on to the new place for five years before you qualify for the tax exemption, although you only need to live in it for a total of 24 months over that time period.

Jeff Garrison, an officer with State, describes the process: "We did a 1031 exchange this year. The deal went beautifully. To do this right you need to do a few things. First, get good advice from a tax accountant or attorney. Next, pick an 'intermediary' with whom you're comfortable. The intermediary will handle the proceeds of the sale and will 'purchase' the new property for you with the proceeds of the sale of the old property; you aren't permitted to get any cash until the transaction, both sale and purchase, are complete. It helps if you know the property you want to buy up front, because the tax law has tight timelines for you to identify and purchase the new property."

The replacement property must be designated within 45 days of the sale and the transaction must be completed within 180 days. If you fail to meet the deadlines, you are liable for capital gains tax; there is no additional grace period. If the new place costs less than the old, you have to pay capital gains tax on the excess amount, known as the "boot." This normally amounts to 15% or 25% on any depreciation that must be recaptured. For more information, search for "like-kind exchange" or "1031" at **www.irs.gov**.

The bottom line

Cynthia Jones says, "After paying the mortgage and all the repair expenses, with the tax benefit the house costs us on average between $100 and 200 per month. Not a bad monthly price to pay on a fifteen-year mortgage."

While the actual figures may vary, having help paying the mortgage while posted overseas should prove a financial advantage—and rising equity can lead to substantial gains. Carefully **consider** where you should buy and whether you should use a property manager. Take the time to **convert** your home into a business, and communicate, communicate, **communicate**. By sailing the three "C"s you can cross an ocean and still have confidence that your primary investment remains afloat.

*Some names have been changed for reasons of security and privacy.

Jan Fischer Bachman is a writer, editor, web content manager, violinist, mother, and Foreign Service spouse. She has lived and worked in Spain, Ecuador, the U.K., China, Mexico, the Dominican Republic, the Bahamas, and the U.S.

Resources

Barry B. De Marr, CFP, EA can be reached at 703–289–1167 or **finfore@aol.com** .

The Transition Center presents a program once a year called "Managing Rental Property from Overseas." A videotape of this program is available for loan at the Overseas Briefing Center on Arlington Boulevard.

The National Association of Independent Landlords offers credit reports, background checks, rent collection, monthly reports to credit bureaus and more. There is a $60/year membership fee, as well as additional fees for certain services, but the organization could theoretically save hassles for a solo landlord. **http://www.nail-usa.com/**

There are many online resources for getting credit reports on tenants. Prices vary; check more than one website before choosing.

A variety of property management software is also available; use a search engine to find the one most relevant for you.

Books

Complete Idiot's Guide to Being a Smart Landlord by Brian F. Edwards, Casey Edwards, and Susannah Craig

Every Landlord's Legal Guide by Marcia Stewart, Ralph Warner, Janet Portman, Nolo, Ralph E. Warner

Property Management for Dummies by Robert Griswold

The Everything Landlording Book: An All-in-one Guide to Property Management by Judy Tremore

Undercover in Washington

by Francesca Huemer Kelly

You're happily browsing in a suburban Borders bookstore, getting a good dose of home-leave Americana, when you spot her: that friend from four posts back whom you stopped trading holiday letters with more than two years ago.

What do you do? (choose one):

1. Hide in the romance novels aisle and hope her tastes run to military history;

2. Try to sneak quietly out of the store, forgetting you have unpaid-for books, and setting off the store alarm; or, most likely,

3. March up to her and say, "Paulette! How great to see you! What are you doing these days? And here's Dave, too! Oh, I'm sorry, yes, it's Dan. How GREAT to see you both! We're leaving Washington in (look at watch), God, in about 3 hours! Must run! Let's keep in touch!"

And as you scurry away, you hear her whispering to her husband, "God! What is that woman's name again? Didn't we know her in Belgrade? I thought I was going to die when she saw me ..."

Francesca Huemer Kelly, a trained singer, freelance writer and the mother of four children, is Founding Editor of Tales from a Small Planet, www.talesmag.com . With her husband, Foreign Service officer Ian Kelly, she has lived in Milan, St. Petersburg, Moscow, Belgrade, Vienna, Washington, Ankara, Rome and now Brussels, where she works as a counselor for high school students.

PART III
Family and Relationships

The Family and the Foreign Service

by Kristi Streiffert

Few career choices impact families more than Foreign Service life. Both parents and children are changed profoundly by the experience, and sometime in the future you might be tempted to ask yourself how your family would have turned out if you hadn't joined the Foreign Service. Would your kids have done better if they remained in the same school system through high school? Has moving so often handicapped your kids when it comes to making friends or making commitments? Did you spend too much time at the embassy while your children were young? Were your teens more, or less, rebellious because they grew up abroad? Did the poverty in Brazil, or the malaria in Africa, place such stress on your family members that their characters have been shaped by it?

Questions like these deserve reflection—but the key is to consider the issues they raise before you go abroad, not during retirement. Having realistic expectations and acknowledging that this lifestyle does not come cost-free will go a long way in making your overseas family life rewarding and satisfying to each member of your family. In order to enjoy the benefits of this rich, complex, stressful lifestyle, families must plan ahead, be flexible and put a lot of effort into details that most "normal" parents seldom need to bother with.

First, step back and think about how you define a happy family, and how you define success as a parent. Parents who are working for the Foreign Service or considering the job often take a idealistic view of an overseas family life, assuming that the advantages of international

115

travel will make up for all the upheaval and moves, and that if the parents are following their dreams, then their family can only be enriched. Others take the opposite view and carry a lot of guilt because they chose a lifestyle that requires frequent international moves: "My kids didn't choose this, and so I must make it work for them." Sometimes, this attitude can lead Foreign Service officers (FSOs) to bend over backward trying to accommodate what might actually be unjustifiable demands by their kids. Successful Foreign Service parents seem to fall somewhere in the middle on a spectrum between these two viewpoints and to do their best to balance them.

On a most basic level, nearly all parents will feel they have succeeded if they assure that every member of their family feels *safe* and *nurtured*. In my opinion, life abroad presents challenges to these foundational concepts because of constant moves, school changes and disorienting cultural adjustments.

Parents, with the help of the security offices in the American embassies overseas, naturally do all they can to make sure their kids are as safe as possible, but the next step is assisting your children to *feel* safe in a foreign setting. Your children will have broader experience than their stateside cousins and friends, and they really will, in many senses, have more to fear—and they know it. It is a big scary world out there, and they are "out there."

In an essay in the book *Unrooted Childhoods: Memoirs of Growing Up Global*, Sarah Mansfield Taber tells of developing a sudden bedtime fear of kidnappers as she adjusted as best a nine-year-old can to a new life in Holland. She was only reassured when her parents inspected each nook and cranny of her room each night, sometimes more than once. "It was as though my body remembered, even if my mind did not, that change, though rhythmic and regular, is still a ransacking and still a threat." That is why parents should have a routine for addressing fears, both rational and those that pop up unexpectedly at certain stages of development. Patience and loving, reassuring routines can alleviate fears, but never quickly—it takes time and patience to make a child feel safe in a new environment.

Foreign Service (FS) life requires you to have more patience with your children than you otherwise would, as well as more patience with yourself and your spouse. Give everyone lots of leeway for stress-related insecurities and adaptations.

It will also take time for both parents and children to feel socially "safe" in each new environment. Take reasonable steps to help each other through difficult times. Anne Reese, a social worker for the U.S. State Department counseling office (called the Employee Consultation Service) says: "up until they reach adolescence, a child's adjustment to each move will depend almost entirely on the parents." Parents' good attitudes about a place will communicate to the child that he or she will also be happy there. Reese says that when a parent calls her and says their six-year-old can't stand their new post, she can be sure that the parents haven't found a way to make it work for themselves yet, either. That is why parents must support each other and help each other find ways to settle down in each new location and make a life for themselves.

"Even for an adolescent, when it gets harder to make conditions right for the child, a lot still depends on the parents," she continues. Some posts are really hard on teenagers, but parents can communicate to their children that "we are sympathetic, and we realize that Foreign Service life is not perfect, and we don't love every minute of it, but we still believe that it is valuable."

Reese counsels never to diminish or minimize a child's adjustment problems (no matter what their age) and suggests that parents take action to gain as much information as possible about the place long before arrival. "Be in contact with as many people as you can before you get to post and talk to people who have made a life for themselves, who are happy there." She suggests talking to the Community Liaison Office coordinator (CLO) at a new post both by telephone and e-mail and gathering as many contacts as possible. Compile a list of children and parents that you can e-mail and start to get to know before you arrive. Smoothing the way for the kids will smooth the way for you, too. The older your children get, the more information and contacts you will need. Younger kids make friends much more quickly and easily than preteens and adolescents.

With each move, introducing strange new foods will be another challenge you'll face in helping kids feel "safe." This may seem like a minor issue, but moms and dads the world over will assure you it is not. Unfamiliar food makes kids feel lost. One FS mom says that food was always a concern with her kids. "So many meals were left uneaten!" she says. "Children have a hard time realizing that their favorite foods just can't easily be had. And then, they had to change their eating habits again with the next move. The foods we learned to enjoy in one country just couldn't be found or duplicated in another."

Eventually, children learn (mostly from their friends at school) to eat things they've never heard of or imagined, and many grow up with a much more tolerant, wide-ranging palate. It is an amazing thing to see an 8-year-old gasp in shock (and pain) at Mexican spicy chili-flavored candy when she first arrives, and then see how much she misses it two years later when the family moves on to a country that specializes in—"yuck!"—candied fruits. One trick on introducing new foods is merely to serve them at mealtime regularly alongside old favorites. Don't even invite the children to eat them. Just seeing the parents eat them will make the new foods familiar, and therefore more likely to eventually be accepted and enjoyed. Many parents living abroad find that their children not only pick up new eating habits at school, but are then eager to introduce their parents to new foods.

The idea of *nurturing* has been defined as creating "a soft place to fall" for each family member. The family is a space where kids (and moms and dads) can try and fail and try again, and never be betrayed: a place where they are always accepted and loved and welcomed with joy. Children of FS employees may need this "space" even more urgently than other kids. Your children may be gawked at because of their skin color or for some other reason that makes them obviously different in appearance from the people of your host country.

Many times this attention will make your family members feel special, but there may be times when the locals are not especially friendly. In another essay in *Unrooted Childhoods*, Anora Egan tells of her experience as a white child in China: "Sometimes soaking in the attention feels good ... But more often the looks do not nourish, do not reach out with a smile or a welcome." My daughter was accustomed to the warm curiosity of Mexico, but in our next country, the stares she drew from the poverty-stricken locals felt hostile to her. She also noticed that at age 13 she got much more attention from both adolescent boys and adult men (whistles, pointed stares and comments) than she did when she was in the United States, and I had to explain to her certain aspects of local culture (for instance, the fact that many girls of 13 were already married there). Other FS parents report that their daughters have had to cope with different cultural and sexual mores. One blond-haired American teenager in Cairo had to put up with men making sexually explicit comments to her on the street, and her family pointed out to her that these men had gotten a certain impression of "white women" from American movies and pornography.

Even if it is not so extreme, there will be times when your children will see your home as a haven from the too-different world outside, and sometimes they will just need to hide and process their experiences. (You know how children process such things, right? According to my daughter, the only acceptable method is to eat popcorn and watch SpongeBob videos.) Consider ways to make your home always be a safe place for your family members, even if that sometimes means having fewer outside social interactions than you might like.

In her book *The Heart of a Family*, Meg Cox says that childhood is just like being an adult in a foreign country, "where you don't know your way around or speak the language fluently. Everything feels a little chaotic, tentative, even scary." It is good to keep in mind that your children are not only navigating the foreign land of childhood but also the added context of a real foreign country. That is why Meg Cox's advice to create nurturing family rituals resounds for me. "With children," she says, "ritual is an anchor, a home base." She suggests daily rituals like mealtime blessings, daily chores, special evening study breaks and a bedtime story. She also suggests weekly routines such as "taco night" or "family movie night." Of course, the flow of the seasons goes more easily for children if they can look forward to many enjoyable seasonal rituals as well (like Chinese food every Christmas Eve). Rituals that are specific to your family—and that *everyone* enjoys—are best.

One FS spouse, now living in the Washington area, says "How about just making a big point of having dinner together every night? That is our ritual." In my family, we have a routine that encourages staying home in the evenings on school nights: Monday evening through Thursday, we seldom shop, socialize or go out for entertainment. This has brought our family closer just because we spend that much more time together, and there are many times when our evenings are spent talking about and working through the adjustments to life in a new country.

The reward of this lifestyle is that many families feel exceptionally bonded by their shared overseas experience. Karen Evans, who raised her family in Botswana, Poland and Singapore, says that she thinks this is one of the best benefits of the FS life. "Through twenty years of traveling, we tried to keep our focus as a family—that we were doing this together. I believe it created a brotherly bond that will draw my sons together in the future."

Other parents agree—as one put it: "Now that we are back in the States we feel kind of like a four-person private club who share the experiences of traveling in Tuscany, visiting Dutch cheese museums, and so on. This keeps our teenage daughter close to us as she grows up—she needs us because we are the only ones who really understand where she's been."

Marcia Bosshardt, mom to twins and wife in a tandem couple who have served in Madagascar, Costa Rica and other posts, says that not only does this bonding offer the entire family a richer experience, it can also give children a more protected environment to grow up in. "I think my children are more innocent compared to my nephews in the U.S. I think FS kids can stay younger longer, and not have to cultivate a consumer mentality, for example, so early."

Bosshardt also notes that the embassy community can provide an instant closeness and a set of "aunts and uncles." "This is something we've really enjoyed—the small town atmosphere and instant community we have after we move."

But Bosshardt points out there can be an insensitive side to this instant community. She notes that a lack of privacy and the FS's "suck it up" culture made a difficult time in her family even worse. Years ago, when she and her husband Mark Cullinane decided to try to start a family, they struggled with infertility problems and then faced life-threatening complications during a pregnancy. Bosshardt says, "We felt like we didn't want to tell a lot of people about our issues because it could affect our jobs. Plus, there is this stoic atmosphere in the Foreign Service, where you suffer in silence." Looking back, she says she would advise parents to be aggressive and creative when they are having problems. "We didn't avail ourselves of all the resources that were available to us, and I ended up being separated [by an ocean, not estrangement] from Mark during a very difficult recovery process after the babies were born because we just didn't really communicate to co-workers and bosses that we were in major crisis."

Bosshardt's excellent advice to "be aggressive and creative" works well for many aspects of FS family life—especially the bane of all: moving time. Even as your family bonds grow, you will still find the family exceptionally challenged when you move. Moving time is the crucible for family stress.

Each family deals with moving in different ways, but those who plan proactively and creatively usually come through more easily than those who let the chaos of moving day arrive unexpectedly. One thing to keep in mind is that at least one person in your family is paid a good salary and excellent benefits to move. If the State Department employee takes full responsibility for the move during working hours, the family pays a much lower price in stress than they would otherwise. Some employees even take mercy on their families and send them off to grandmother's house a week or so before the moving van arrives. After all, single FSOs handle solo moves all the time.

Bosshardt says that their last move, from Costa Rica to Nicaragua, worked out well because she arranged to arrive at post a week or so before the rest of the family, and she was able to get the household set up for the twin second-graders and the rest of her family in advance.

Once you've planned your logistics to make everything flow as smoothly as possible, it is a good time to remind each other that frequent moves can be a gift. Everyone gets to start anew. Everyone has the freedom to reinvent themselves. Yes, we must acknowledge the losses for ourselves and our kids. But moving really does give us opportunities—so be on the lookout for them. Don't let each other forget that Foreign Service families have the world as their playground; we can collect overseas experiences the way children collect seashells. And since each capital city around the world is filled with diplomatic families from other nations, we can increase our exposure to other cultures exponentially. We've never been to Switzerland, Peru or Korea, but we now have friends and neighbors from those countries.

As a family, we share the joys of these experiences with each other daily—and we will always have these memories together. When Karen Evans recently visited her college-aged son, they spent some time reminiscing about the payback for FS families. "My son and I talked about not only the benefits we received from living in another country, but the advantages of travel throughout the host country and the surrounding countries." Her son has his own view of the benefits of FS life: "My brothers and I are more open-minded and have a more realistic view of the world," he told his mom.

Kristi Streiffert is a freelance writer, covering topics ranging from family travel to environmental issues. Her work has been published around the world, including Central America, Singapore, Israel, the Netherlands and the United States. She and her FSO husband have been married for 24 years, and they have a teenage daughter. They have lived in the U.S., Mexico, Nicaragua, and now Cyprus. Kristi loves birding, hiking, canoeing and exploring new ecosystems wherever she lands.

Employee Consultation Service, located at Main State, telephone: 202–663–1815.

Feeling overwhelmed? Have some counseling needs, but don't want an official appointment with a mental health professional? Many FS families would like to speak to their post Medical Officer about stress-related issues, but they fear that it might affect their medical clearance. Fortunately, those stressed-out by a recent move, suffering marriage problems or facing difficult issues with their kids have a confidential resource available. Employee Consultation Service social workers can be contacted by phone, in person, or via e-mail, all in complete confidentiality. Anne Reese says that she and her colleagues never write in medical records or share information in any way without the permission of the person who has contacted them. "There are no State Department regulations that lead us to ever violate confidentiality, unless someone is a danger to themselves or others. You can talk to us without risk."

I asked Reese what her most common phone call sounds like. "The exciting career of an FSO sometimes gets in the way of family happiness," Reese says. "It is not uncommon for me to get a phone call from a spouse telling me that his wife or her husband is completely happy, working 80 hours a week, and the rest of the family is utterly miserable." The FS employee is putting his or her job first, and this is not uncommon in the work world, she says, but when you have your family in a foreign land, and you are not addressing the fact that they haven't yet adjusted well, your family is going to get very angry. "If I can, I talk to the employee and tell them," Reese says, "you are in this boat together. If your family feels lonely, trapped and miserable, you need to start figuring out some solutions—together."

The Perpetual Foreign Exchange Student

by Jaimee Macanas Neel

Typical fourth grade classroom, 10:00 a.m., in the United States:

"Hey, what's for lunch today?"
"I don't know ... probably fish sticks, tater tots, and Jell-o."
"I just hope it's not the mystery mush from last week."

Typical fourth grade classroom, 10:00 a.m., in Sao Paulo, Brazil:

"Hey, what's for lunch today?"
"I don't know ... but I saw them loading sacks of fresh potatoes into the cafeteria."
"It's probably mashed potatoes, pot roast, and passionfruit mousse."

There are some definite perks to living overseas. Nevertheless, as with other aspects of Foreign Service life, schooling abroad comes with its ups and downs. Perhaps nothing is more worrisome for Foreign Service families than having to constantly transition children into new schools—especially *new overseas schools*. The list of concerns seems endless. Families never know how different a new overseas school will be until they arrive. Even a simple change to freshly prepared school lunches can surprise someone on the first day. Each time children transition to a new school, they face new challenges and opportunities. The following views from former and current overseas students address the pros and cons of being a perpetual foreign exchange student. Whether it is the first overseas school or the fourth, becoming an overseas student is the beginning of an unpredictable and amazing life experience.

Studying overseas is normal

"What is normal anyway? For me, taking a sixteen-hour Russian train ride through Siberia to Helsinki every month—just to get my braces tightened—was normal!"

—Ralna, former overseas student

Parents often wonder if their children will still be "normal" after studying overseas. While Ralna's experience was unique, it highlights the fact that Foreign Service students still deal with the "normal" fears and issues common in all school experiences: getting braces, being the new kid, cliquishness, etc. Although the scenery may be different, the issues are the same. Foreign Service students are simply normal kids studying overseas.

Moving to a new school overseas is just like moving to a new school anywhere else. Whether moving from Taipei, to Helsinki, or moving to a new school across town, the "new kid" phenomenon is universal, regardless of locale. However, being the new kid takes its toll on Foreign Service children because the experience repeats itself every few years. In this regard, Foreign Service kids need to be reminded that they are not alone! Children of expatriate businesspeople, military families, and religious and humanitarian workers also move every few years. Changing schools is not an "abnormal" experience. Whether it's moving to a new city or moving into a new house in the same town, kids commonly change schools while growing up. While the transient Foreign Service lifestyle can be stressful, most Foreign Service kids agree that moving from Manama to Manila is more exciting than moving from Iowa to Idaho. Foreign Service parents can find success in emphasizing that changing schools is a normal event for many—while the exotic scenery makes for wonderful opportunities.

During our tour in Brazil, I had the opportunity to meet three grown-up Foreign Service kids: Ralna, Christian, and Patrick. Each had a distinctive Foreign Service childhood. One witnessed the Soviet coup that ousted Gorbachev. Another grew up in the heart of Africa. The other was evacuated from Yemen. Their tales are filled with exotic peoples and distant lands. Like many Foreign Service kids, it was their school years that have forever connected them to Pakistan, Abu Dhabi, Mexico, Yemen, and so on. Overseas schooling helped shape them into the adults they are today. They each speak several languages, they are lifetime learners, and they are not afraid to experience new things. Every overseas student has the opportunity to acquire these qualities, while at the same time gaining a unique perspective on the world and its diversity.

The challenge of studying overseas

While Foreign Service students deal with normal issues, overseas schooling is not without difficulties. In a new school, there is always an adjustment to a new routine. In a new country, there is the added challenge of a new culture and new language. New schools, like new countries, can be disorienting, especially for young children.

Foreign Service kids find themselves in a new school with no friends over and over again. This repeated cycle can be very taxing. Making new friends is not always easy, particularly for shy children. However, even outgoing children are hesitant to make new friends because the situation, like before, is temporary and will not last more than a few years.

Easing the transition

By researching the school ahead of time, parents can ease the anxieties associated with changing schools. Depending on the age of the child, some factors will be more heavily emphasized. For teenagers, one could stress the possibility of exciting extracurricular activities and academic prospects. Highlighting the benefits of this unique opportunity will not only provide security, but also create the anticipation that the new overseas school will be a positive experience. While it is important to accentuate the positive, it is equally important to establish realistic expectations.

Other ways to ease the transition include asking the prospective school for a list of parents to contact prior to arriving at post; initiating a dialog with international school personnel by asking education counselors, at present and potential schools, for information and advice; and tapping into resources available through the Family Liaison Office at Department of State headquarters in Washington, DC.

Overseas schooling options

The educational philosophy and language of instruction are key features to take into account when considering schooling options. At post, there will usually be at least one international school serving the expatriate community. In major cities, there are often American, British, German, and French modeled schools in addition to faith-based institutions. Parents and students need to determine the type of school system that provides the best fit.

Experts caution parents about alternating between different school systems (e.g., moving a student back and forth between British and American systems) as there are differences in curricula. Experts further counsel that, when possible, parents should keep students in a unified system throughout the high school years. Some schools offer full English instruction, and some schools, such as those available in Mexico City, may offer half English instruction, with the other half in the language of the host country. At most international schools, the language of the host country may be offered as an elective or mandatory course, in addition to other foreign languages. Each of these issues comes into play when deciding which school best meets student goals and interests.

The overseas school experience

Overseas schooling can be a very rewarding and satisfying experience. Academics, extracurricular activities, social interaction, and college preparation are all emphasized overseas. In most ways, the overseas experience reflects opportunities offered domestically, with the added backdrop of foreign cultures and exotic landscapes. While the cycle of pack/move/adjust presents challenges, Foreign Service students gain educational experiences unmatched anywhere else. When studying overseas, Foreign Service students can expect high academic expectations, unique extracurricular activities, and an appreciation for cultural diversity.

High academic expectations

"My school is very academically oriented. Kids talk to each other on online groups about projects and homework assignments. When I went home to the U. S. this summer, my friends were talking about who they wanted to take to the Halloween dance—still three months away. I couldn't believe it! In the hallways in São Paulo, I hear people talking about the causes of World War II!"

—Jennifer, a senior at the Escola Graduada, the American school in São Paulo, Brazil

Often, academics in overseas schools are more intense than expected. Many Foreign Service students find schooling abroad to be more challenging than U. S. public schools. In addition, overseas schools place high emphasis on college preparation. Coursework is consistently above grade level. Many students find their coursework more advanced compared to what their peers are studying in the U. S. Laura, a high school sophomore in Guatemala City states, "There is no comparison—most juniors are doing college-level math." She describes her overseas courses as "more challenging, more advanced, and more work."

The experience of studying overseas helps foster a college-bound mentality because students are placed in an independent learning environment. They rotate classes and colleagues every semester and are given high expectations for independent study and research, just as in college. Also, international schools tend to have extremely well-qualified, well-educated teachers, with many teachers holding advanced degrees. This affects students in two ways. First, they are consistently exposed to teachers and role models who place a premium on university training. Second, teachers with advanced training prefer more advanced material.

Unlike college, however, parents find that many international schools emphasize individualized teaching. This is aided by extremely favorable teacher-to-student ratios found at most overseas schools. With fewer students per class, teachers can give more attention to each student. Parents often find that although pushed academically, their children are still taught with their individual strengths and weaknesses in mind.

In a recent comparison of 2004 mean S.A.T. (Standardized Achievement Test) scores, the College Board determined that, compared to the national average, U. S. citizens in overseas schools scored 75 points higher on the verbal test and 65 points higher on the math test. In all S.A.T. subject tests in U. S. history, world history, math, biology, chemistry, physics, French, and Spanish, overseas students scored higher than the national average. English writing was the only area in which overseas students scored lower than the national average. Foreign Service students, therefore, often require extra emphasis on English composition to be competitive in this area.

Unique extracurricular activities

As a high school student in Pakistan, Ralna was involved in several extracurricular sports. Throughout her high school years, she partici-

pated in volleyball, field hockey, soccer, and basketball. Being on a sports team in Pakistan was the same as in the U. S. She was required to keep high grades, she attended practice after school, and she learned to appreciate teamwork and healthy competition. However, instead of hopping on a school bus and heading across town for a tournament, her team traveled throughout Pakistan, India, Bangladesh, and Sri Lanka! Her travel with school teams took her to entirely different countries—and just for a sports event!

Each new country opens doors to explore new cultures. Likewise, each school has unique extracurricular activities to offer. Many posts have an impressive variety of extracurricular opportunities available. James, a high school sophomore, praises the technology at the Escola Graduada in São Paulo: "I have a film editing class that I absolutely love. My school has invested enormous amounts of money in computers, software, and film programs. There are very few schools (even colleges) where I could have a class like this with such professional equipment."

In Yemen, Christian participated in various after school activities: sports, natural history, science projects, and arts and crafts. His favorite field trips were visiting ruins, caves, and historical sites. Even twenty years later, after having lived in South Africa, Belgium, Germany, and Brazil, Christian still remembers Yemen as "the neatest place on earth" because of opportunities to experience the Yemeni culture and people through after-school activities.

Having an open mind is key to extracurricular success. Since a smaller student body results in less competition, many students are thrilled to find they can participate in everything their school offers. On the other hand, students sometimes become frustrated with the lack of competitiveness and find the quality of the activities wanting. Often, parents and students simply have to make the best of what is available and try their hardest to enjoy the experience.

Once again, as part of the bidding process, parents and students should do their homework on the availability of extracurricular activities and elective classes. This allows families to set realistic expectations prior to arriving at post. This will help reduce frustration in the long run. If a student is especially interested in a particular club (e.g. drama) or a particular sport (e.g. baseball), not having it at a new school may cause resentment—even in later years. Not all American sports are offered everywhere, and this can be frustrating for students set on basketball or American football. Additionally, parents and students must understand that just as in the United States, not all schools are funded equally.

Rigorous academics also place limitations on which extracurricular activities a student may be able to participate in without sacrificing grades. Just like students "back home," Foreign Service kids find themselves balancing schoolwork and playtime. Also, some posts, especially in big cities, have limited after school activities due to heavy traffic and the significant amount of time needed for commuting.

At certain hardship and danger posts, extracurricular activities can be limited for security reasons. However, this is not always the case. Patrick found that his school in Kinshasa offered drama, speech, debate, chess, a student newspaper, a yearbook committee, and several sports. He admits he was surprised that a school in Africa boasted more extracurricular offerings than his school in Mexico City. Sometimes this may reflect on the availability of activities in the community. If more activities are offered locally, then schools may not have as many extracurricular opportunities. Conversely, if few extracurricular outlets are available in the community (as in hardship posts), then activities will often revolve around the school. In a very real sense, the school becomes the community. At hardship posts, school can be much more than a place to study; it becomes the entire focus of student social life.

Appreciating cultural diversity

One of my favorite childhood memories was celebrating United Nations Day in our school. Each student would dress up in the traditional attire of their home country—turbans, sarongs, burkas, etc. We would each share about our cultures and our home countries. We'd get to try new cultural foods and enjoy the differences between us."

—*Ralna, former overseas student*

Being an ethnic, religious, or national minority is a "real life" lesson in diversity. At international schools, the American students will frequently be outnumbered. One of the big advantages touted by parents and students alike is that overseas students make friends from all over the world.

The nature of the student body at an international school is such that many students have had the experience of being "the new kid." This engenders what one Foreign Service dad calls "a wonderful sense of empathy," making it easier for newly arrived Foreign Service kids to assimilate. Since students are constantly moving in and out, teachers and classmates tend to be especially understanding and helpful.

Making friends with students from different backgrounds and cultures gives Foreign Service kids a better sense of what the world offers. The world becomes smaller each time Foreign Service students meet someone from a different culture; their understanding and appreciation of diversity naturally increases. Laura, a Foreign Service mom in Pretoria, was very pleased with the social atmosphere her children were enjoying in South Africa. She writes: "I was very impressed with the knowledge and acceptance of other kids from all over the world. Not only have my kids felt this, but they have been involved in treating others who may speak differently or believe differently with acceptance."

One fear Foreign Service parents have is that their kids will be unable to make life-long friends due to distance. Once a child leaves post, will former friendships merely fade into memory? Traditionally, these friendships last because of the common bond shared between internationally mobile students. They understand the challenges of learning new languages, adjusting to culture shock, and having to constantly adjust to a new home. Moreover, friends can communicate using e-mail, instant messaging and webcams from anywhere in the world.

Additionally, programs such as Around the World in A Lifetime (AWAL), sponsored by the Foreign Service Youth Foundation (**www.fsyf.org**), provide a forum for overseas students to discuss their experiences. AWAL also helps students with the process of transitioning back to America—a process that often presents its own set of challenges.

In addition to enlarging one's view of the world, several international school alumni comment that living outside the U. S. teaches students what it means to be an American. Many claim that only after leaving the U. S. were they better able to appreciate the advantages, opportunities, and values of the United States of America. Ralna remembers living in Southeast Asia where the monsoon rains would occur for several months each year. Directly across from her school, several nomadic families built their shanty homes from cow manure. One afternoon there was a powerful rainstorm and all of the homes were washed away. There was nothing left to even suggest that just a few hours earlier, homes had been standing there. This experience profoundly impacted how Ralna now views the world. She commented: "Sometimes we take the smallest things for granted, when there are many in the world that do not enjoy the simplest luxuries."

Embracing global education

Though it sometimes seems that Foreign Service families are giving up the security and roots of a hometown, in reality, they are exchanging one opportunity for another. In adopting an internationally mobile lifestyle, overseas students gain a broader perspective of the world and a better understanding of themselves. Most Foreign Service students enjoy a normal, productive, satisfying, educational experience in an extraordinary setting. Despite the challenges and difficulties of studying abroad, most overseas alumni agree with Ralna, Christian, Patrick and others when they say, "It was worth it!" That growing up overseas was a positive experience is reflected in the fact that many Foreign Service children choose to continue an international lifestyle and pursue international careers.

To be successful, Foreign Service families must accentuate the positive. Researching new assignments is also critical as it provides the information needed to set realistic expectations. Not every experience will be exactly the same for every family. With an open mind and a desire to learn, Foreign Service students embrace the best of each new country, each new culture, and each new school. In becoming perpetual foreign exchange students, foreign lands become their classrooms and students of all nationalities their classmates. In the end, Foreign Service kids are normal kids studying overseas, but their experiences will enable them to make a difference in the world—wherever their adventures take them.

Jaimee Macanas Neel, a soon-to-be Foreign Service officer, was born in Hawaii and married Jim Neel while at Brigham Young University. After graduating from law school and passing the bar, Jaimee decided that becoming an inner-city schoolteacher would be more challenging. She joined Teach for America and taught in Anacostia (DC) and the Bronx (NY). At their first overseas posting to Sao Paulo, Brazil, Jaimee worked at the US Consulate and also reached out to a local orphanage—for which she received the 2005 Secretary of State's Award for Outstanding Volunteerism Abroad. Jaimee is excited to join her husband as a tandem couple as they prepare for their next post to Embassy Cairo. Jaimee has been trapped in the Great Pyramid, escaped a riot in Jerusalem, hitchhiked across Africa, snorkeled off the Cook Islands, slept in an Estonian bus station, heckled vendors in Tibet, studied law in Shanghai and biked among Taiwanese rice fields as a missionary. Jaimee now finds adventure and joy in showing her two-year-old son, Jimmy, the world.

No Place Like Home:
A Teen's Perspective

by Rachel Midura

I am the daughter of a diplomat. This past year—my thir-teenth—seems to have encompassed more changes than the previous twelve together. Not only did I become a teenager, but I went through one of those intercontinental moves that are so familiar to Foreign Service kids. My entire life was upturned, and I left the world that I had known for nearly a third of my life. And yet, somehow, I survived.

In the Czech Republic, we lived in a neighborhood known as "Mala Sarka," meaning "Little Forest" in Czech. It was a bit far from down-town, but walking distance from my school. I attended the International School of Prague (ISP) from fourth through seventh grade. I loved everything about the school, from its strange building-block structure to my very international friends. I had pals from Serbia, Kyr-gyzstan, Ukraine, and the U.K., as well as classmates from just about any country you could mention. It was a wonderful "melting pot" for various cultures and languages that formed a very safe and scholasti-cally-oriented environment. For many, school feels like a prison, but for me, it honestly felt like a second home.

In contrast to the U.S. system, middle school began in sixth grade at ISP. I went in with my best friends, Lana, Tijana, and Emily, and dur-ing the year gained a new best friend (also with the Foreign Service), Alexandra. Of course, I did still go through the normal soap operas that middle school life inevitably brings, but I felt very settled nonethe-less.

In seventh grade, knowing that the end of our time in Prague was near, I asked for a digital camera for my birthday. It was delightful when I opened it on that rainy November day, and I was raring to go. I started taking pictures at my birthday party. I got out a box of costumes, and we snapped silly photos while wearing boas and costume jewelry. Everyone had fun, and I made a silent vow to take pictures at every gathering that final year.

Time flew by. Before long, it was Christmas. I remember the last time I went to the Prague Christmas market with my family and two of my friends. That night will be one of my fondest memories for a long time. The Christmas carolers singing "Good King Wenceslas" on a stage in Old Town Square, the gigantic Christmas tree, and the little booths filled with everything from beeswax candles to tiny crystal animals all contributed to a magical ambiance. It was almost time for dinner when it started to snow. That was the icing on the cake, so to speak. There is nothing more beautiful than a European Christmas market with snowflakes dancing in the night air.

Other events came and went. Traveling with the Knowledge Bowl team turned out to be a very international experience. My Serbian friend Lana was on the team when we went to Sofia, Bulgaria for a multi-school competition. It was fun to buy souvenirs, but even more fun thanks to the lack of parents. Our team did not win the treasured gold trophy, but no one was disappointed with the trip.

I also participated in the ISP softball team that spring. Because of my past Little League experience, I managed to make it to the top-level team. The tournament was held in Prague, with visiting teams from Budapest, Sofia, Vienna, and Bucharest. After days of tough games, my team came out on top, winning the championship for the school. That was an event to be proud of!

Before I knew it, the big move was just a few weeks away. School ended with a lot of teary eyes, and one by one students left the school either for vacations, or permanently. Lana would also be moving that summer, back to her home city of Belgrade. We put our heads together to plan a final bash for the both of us. As moving was a common event at the International School, it was customary to throw a goodbye party. And as we had the same friends and approximately the same moving date, Lana and I decided to throw a twenty-four hour party that would be the grand finale of our time in the "city of golden spires." I spent a week organizing the digital snapshots I had shot over the last year, and created a slideshow that included pictures of the entire group of us to give to friends as a memento of the past year.

The party was a memorable one. Our friends brought thoughtful presents to remember them by. We spent half the day at my house, and then my dad drove us in a rented van to the Hotel Praha swimming pool (I think that that will be the last time my dad ever volunteers to chauffeur a dozen hyperactive teenage girls, but he survived the trip). The day ended with a sleepover at Lana's house, where we chowed down on Kentucky Fried Chicken and watched a "Friends" Marathon. That party is my most treasured memory of our entire tour in Prague.

Moving day was fast approaching. It wasn't long until the movers came, packing up all of our eclectic "ethnoplunder" (as my mom likes to say) and other possessions alike. We still had the Embassy furniture, but the house felt strange indeed. We had bought a house in suburban Washington, DC, not too far from where my friend Alexandra used to live. My mom tacked a map of the area to the billboard in the breakfast room, so that we could all gaze upon the strange new land that we would soon call home. Our plane tickets were purchased, and we were ready to go.

At the time, we had two cats called Huckle and Hobbes. We had grown so attached to the felines, there was no way we could leave Prague without them. So they were packed up in little cat containers, and loaded into the taxi with the rest of the luggage. I remember very sadly looking upon the house that was no longer ours. The taxi drive to the airport seemed like the longest drive I'd ever taken, even though it was less than an hour. I remember looking upon the neighborhood of Nebusice, and desperately trying to record all the sights and sounds as we passed them. I wanted to take mental pictures of them all, so that I would never, ever forget. But they passed in a blur, and then we were boarding the plane.

Hobbes and Huckle yowled so piteously I felt as though my heart would break. They were terrified of the noises around them, and it was a lucky thing that being pushed beneath the seats in their cages seemed to calm them somewhat. We settled down, and I took a book out of my backpack. We were all so accustomed to traveling that it was a no-brainer to pack an activity bag for any trip. And a long trip it would be, at nearly fourteen hours in total.

We had just began to watch a movie when we hit some serious and scary turbulence, and doing much of anything other than gripping the seat became impossible. When the pilot finally landed, some of the people aboard the plane clapped. I was such a bundle of nerves after everything from the turbulence to the time jump, I felt like I was just barely keeping from complete hysterics.

We went through the usual security in the American airport. It was a long walk down the many hallways, but we got our luggage back without any major disturbances. The cats were exhausted, and we were too.

The drive to the apartment was strange, to say the least. We rode in my grandparents' car, which they had kindly left for us at the airport. It was the exact same make and model as our car in Prague, but a different color. And the car wasn't the only thing that was eerily familiar, and yet different.

License plates from the different states. Warm, humid weather. Signs in English. All of these were very strange to me, and yet slightly exhilarating. Even after the horrible flight, I couldn't help but feel a slight sense of adventure. Here was a place from my past that would become the place of my future. My parents were excited, and as I had so many years ago, when my dad brought news of the move to Prague, I couldn't help catching a bit of it.

The temporary apartment was nice enough. I got my own room, which was a definite plus. I love my little brother, but the last thing in the world I would want is to share a room with him for three months. Sitting down on my bed, I opened the notes that my friends had given me to read as soon as I arrived. That, unfortunately, was not a wise move. Reading the comically worded notes of encouragement and various memories was too much for my already rattled emotional state. A wave of homesickness hit, and I was hit hard.

Unable to stop missing my friends and my home, I couldn't even enjoy the all-American pizza dinner at a nearby eatery. I cried and cried, and when I curled up to go to sleep in my foreign bedroom, I had to work hard not to let the visions of Prague wash through my mind. Huckle, who by then was probably in as much as a state as I was, curled up next to me on my bed, and began to purr. Stroking his soft fur, I felt the full medicinal effect cats seem to have. That and a couple of deep breathing exercises was all I needed to fall into a deep sleep.

Adjusting back to American life was not as hard as I first imagined it would be. I was disappointed in some areas, but pleasantly surprised in others. The strangest things were fascinating to me. Whenever we went in the car, I would read aloud the names of streets, and laugh at clever vanity plates on the cars besides us. The county library was an amazing experience indeed, and I checked out more books than I could carry. It was so fun to be able to understand the people around me, I'm afraid I did more than a little eavesdropping in public places. We ate all sorts of inexpensive ethnic food that you just couldn't get in Prague.

One of the best things about that summer was probably the camps. I attended a drama camp, and in retrospect, that was one of the best practices in re-integration that I could have done. It was very nice to meet people who enjoyed doing what I enjoyed, and I don't quite know how I could have made it through the summer without a little socializing with my peers. Being cooped up in a new environment with your family for three months is not good for a person, or so I believe.

Going to the camps was a good moral pep rally, and helped me prepare for the school social life I would be dropped into.

We moved into our house in early August. That entire summer, I had been planning my dream room, and we had been buying furniture. It was fun to see my sanctuary finally come together, and I couldn't wait to e-mail pictures of the house to my friends. I had planned a lavender room, for all the relaxing effects. It did help with the homesickness to have a real, permanent home.

The middle school I would be attending was humongous! It looked like the American high schools I only knew from television and movies. Being in eighth grade, I felt as though I should see younger kids, but everyone looked so much older. I knew right off the bat I would have trouble finding my way to classes. The simple design of the school was no help; it was easily five times as large as the middle school section of ISP.

My mother had made contact earlier with another parent at the middle school, and I had been her daughter's pen pal for several months. Joan had recently moved from Holland, and so we had something in common. It was great to see at least one familiar face at the open house.

The first day of school was a big event. I spent ages organizing my supplies and picking out an outfit. I was determined to make the best impression possible. I woke up even earlier than necessary, probably out of sheer nervousness. It had been four years since I first started a new school, and that had been a completely different situation. At the time, I had been moving to a smaller and more close-knit school, a school where students were used to new faces and teachers expected a large number of arriving students in each grade. That was not the case at my new middle school.

The day started off badly. I nearly missed my bus in the morning, and the noise level was excruciating. I am not the quietest of people, but being surrounded by all that rowdiness made me want to withdraw into a shell. Then I walked into the wrong classroom. It was five minutes before I realized my mistake, and I don't believe my cheeks have ever been quite as red as they were then. I slipped out, and then into the correct room. Everyone had formed little social groups already, and I didn't know where to go. So I grabbed a seat near the back of the room, and waited nervously for the teacher.

She gave us little organizers, which had everything from our homework, to our hall passes, to our locker combinations. Being prone to losing things, I was terrified already. She told us how we were not allowed to have backpacks after the first week, and any traces of excitement I had went out the door. I had never used hall passes before, nor had miniscule three-minute breaks. And to do all of it without backpacks? I was overwhelmed, and I had been at school less than an hour.

The day went by with several other mishaps. Luckily, the teachers were fairly understanding when I explained I was late because I simply didn't know my way around. I didn't make many new acquaintances, and really felt out of the loop as friends all around me reunited after the long summer break. When I came home, I crashed, and watched hours of television while downing ginger snaps and Coke.

Eventually, I learned my way around. I was careful to carry a map at all times, just to make sure I didn't get lost. I was always careful to check the room numbers. There were some subjects referred to in class that I had not learned the past year. I asked for worksheets from the teachers, so that I could catch up with the classmates who were attending the middle school for their second year. The opposite happened too; I was placed in a Spanish class that was almost identical to the one I had taken the year before.

Something that made all of the new places and things a lot easier was keeping in contact with my old friends. Using e-mail and IM, I was able to keep in touch very well. We even used voice IM'ing, so we could talk just like we used to on the phone. In Belgrade, Lana was experiencing the same moving problems as I was, and talking to someone else about the ordeals of moving made the burden a little lighter. It was nice to be able to open up about my feelings regarding my new school and new home.

Though I still had friends in Prague, I felt it was necessary to make friends here. I was tired of reading a book during lunch and sitting alone during class. I started conversations and signed up for activities. As I adjusted to everyday life, it began to improve. When Christmas had come and gone, I finally felt as if I could live normally once more.

Nowadays, I have some good friends here. I am active in school life, and yet I still keep contact with my friends abroad. I am working as a prop master in the Spring Play, and finally feel as though I can be myself again. Moving is a terrifying experience that I will be happy to miss out on for the next few years, but I would not give up my time in Prague for anything in the world. I can't wait to go to high school next year, and I actually feel as though my experiences with moving will make that adjustment seem like a piece of cake. I believe moving has made me a better person is some ways, since I feel that if I survived that, I am ready to take on whatever the world can throw at me. Because, hey, I've been thrown all over the world!

Rachel is a teen who can't wait to see what Fate has in mind for her, though she hopes to continue writing and reading her way through any English-language library she can get to. She's been to many places she wishes she could remember, including Guatemala, Lusaka and El Salvador. She now lives with her family and three cats, and hopes to one day return to Prague as a particularly nostalgic tourist.

Intercultural Marriages

by Janet Heg

It's well known that men are from Mars and women are from Venus. So how much more complicated does the situation become when the man comes from Moroccan Mars or the woman from Venezuelan Venus?

Whenever I mentioned this article to anyone, they almost invariably—and only half-jokingly—suggested that there were far greater differences between men and women than between an American and a European. Nevertheless, intercultural marriage is an important feature of life in the Foreign Service, and the constant need to adapt to new cultures adds an extra dimension to an already complex family situation.

At the end of an embassy-organized bunco evening in Mexico City, I asked how many of the women present were married to men from a different culture. More than half raised their hands. When I asked a State Department psychiatrist if I could talk to him about intercultural marriage, he estimated that 40 per cent of Foreign Service spouses were foreign born. When I married into the Foreign Service, I expected to be joining an American community. I was both surprised and delighted to learn that my new friends came from every part of the globe.

"I'm living with three cultures," explains a Mexican-born friend, currently based in Central Europe, "mine, my husband's, and the country where we're living. And when we arrive at a new post, my husband goes to work at the embassy, in a familiar, American environment, but I have to get to know the community."

Like many foreign-born spouses, she feels the wrench of living so far from her own family; she hasn't visited her home country in five years. While American diplomats working abroad are required to take regular home leave, foreign-born spouses have to pay for their own travel home.

Many Foreign Service family members report that they enjoy the enriched cultural diversity contributed by foreign-born spouses to embassy communities abroad. Unfortunately, however, there are sometimes suspicions that not everyone feels this way.

A Salvadorian woman explains: "I also feel there's this 'stigma' that many American women put on foreign-born spouses. I don't know whether or not this may be an unconscious reaction on their part towards someone who's been born and raised outside the U.S. and hence thinks, speaks and acts different from them."

She admits that this could be gossip, but her feeling is that at least some of this is true. "We lived in Colombia and there was a palpable feeling that American women would not invite non-Americans to their morning coffees unless they needed something from us, i.e., they knew they would be needing Spanish."

Another Hispanic woman believes this incident is the result of cultural differences rather than xenophobia. According to her, Latina women expect to be personally invited to a social event, and don't consider a poster in the embassy or an announcement in the newsletter to be sufficient—this is typical of the hidden and subtle cultural differences that people aren't even aware of.

Another foreign-born spouse came up with a different explanation for this attitude. "I have seen this happen, but I see it as these Americans feeling out of place or miserable being in a foreign country, so they bond together with only people very much like them. I have seen this now in the three posts I've been. There's a group of mostly American-born spouses and they are happy to hang out and gossip by themselves. Then there's a group of more open-minded spouses who like hanging out with international types like us too, and it seems to work out fine."

There are subtle differences, too, even when the cultures at first don't seem too far apart. An American Foreign Service officer married to a British man found that some of the traits that had endeared him to her at first became irritating. "I'm more direct; he has a wonderfully polite British way of communicating. You think they're processing something the same way. They're not, but you don't realize it until two or three days later."

Her husband concurs, noting that life in the Foreign Service increases the strain on any marriage. "I'm a stereotypical Brit; I don't talk about feelings. I find it difficult to cope with stress because of my national character."

However, he feels they did find it easier to blend their family traditions and culture because they weren't too far apart, and they shared similar values. "Celebrating the differences can be a huge upside; I did enjoy learning about other cultures and customs, such as Thanksgiving, or that you're a redneck if you put tomato sauce on eggs. Plus we have fun teasing each other—remember the time we burnt the White House or that it took you so long to get in the war. Language is fun too—'I have been burglarized' still cracks me up."

A Filipina woman, married to an American she met at college, also felt that shared values strengthened their marriage. "I am an only child, but growing up middle class in the Philippines (as a minister's daughter) taught me to be frugal. John comes from a family of six which taught him to be frugal. We also had the same religion—we don't go to church anymore, but at least we have the common background."

Another American found the opposite to be the case when he married a Colombian woman during his first tour overseas. "There's generally no middle class in Latin America, so the women are used to living in large houses and having lots of servants. That's fine when you're serving in South America, but it can be hard for them to adapt to middle class life in the U.S. or Europe."

An American diplomat might seem like a "great catch" to many non-U.S. families at first, but when they realize that their child is going to move to another country, they begin to have doubts about the relationship. Family ties can be stronger in some non-American cultures, and grown children, especially daughters, may be expected to live at home until they are married.

The psychiatrist I interviewed knows only too well how difficult it is for any family to make the move to a new country. "It takes at least six months to settle in at a new post, but the foreign-born spouse can find the American community is less supportive. Plus the transition is tougher because the spouses don't come from the same ethnic background as their partner's peers. At each post you have to recreate yourself, and that's exhausting."

He also feels there's a difference in the social interaction between large and small posts. "In a large embassy there's anonymity, a high turnover and housing which is generally spread out. But in a small embassy or consulate, with just a handful of Foreign Service officers, you depend more on each your spouse and a small number of other officers." In addition, both partners can adapt to the new country in different ways and at different speeds, which can also create tension.

Locating employment can be more challenging for foreign-born spouses. Aside from the language barriers and possible differences in background and skills, if they have not become U.S. citizens, they do not receive hiring preference within the embassy and cannot take a job requiring a U.S. security clearance. According to the psychiatrist, however, a marriage can be more stable if the accompanying spouse is working, because it strengthens his or her own identity.

Another tough situation is the first posting in Washington, where an officer has married while overseas and then returned to DC. The high cost of living there makes it almost essential for both partners to work, yet the spouse may not have the necessary skill sets or language proficiency.

Nor is life in Washington easy if the spouse stays at home with young children. "You have to work long hours in DC," recalls one officer, "and she's home all day with the kids—in a strange country—and hardly sees her husband. It's a bewildering and very competitive world there."

One success factor in a cross-cultural marriage, according to the psychiatrist, is ensuring that the spouse makes regular visits home, but that is not always easy to arrange. "My wife insisted that she could not visit her family on her own—she had to travel with me and the children and that made it too expensive. It seemed like she would lose face if she came home without her husband."

Home leave rules can make such visits hard to arrange, even if the spouse's home country is close to the United States. Once the family has spent the required period of time in the U.S., there is usually neither the time nor the money to visit another country, with the officer under pressure to return to his or her existing post or to report for duty in a new country.

Once children arrive on the scene, there can be further cross-cultural issues, over the way they are brought up. "You have to choose your battles," explains one U.S. diplomat. "Americans more focused on making sure they don't use drugs and get into a good school, but whether or not they say please or thank you is slightly less important."

There's one more explosive ingredient to throw into this mix—the stepfamily, now commonly referred to as the blended family. "This results in lots of transitions and challenges," explains the psychiatrist. "You need to find the right wavelength, and that's even tougher when you come from a different culture."

An article in the *Washington Post* ("The I Do's and Don'ts of Intercultural Marriage," Rebecca R. Kahlenberg, November 22, 2001) identified three key areas of difficulty for cross-cultural relationships:

- Speaking styles: "People are so oriented to psychological interpretation that when a wife feels her husband isn't paying attention to her, she doesn't realize it's because he has a different way of listening or of being involved in the conversation" (Tannen, 2001).

- Childrearing: "Two people may be attracted to each other because they found their differences to be a source of pleasure, yet bringing up children differently from the way they grew up raises an awareness of otherness which can create tension, anxiety and even fear of difference" (Siegel, 2001).

- Attitudes towards the extended family, such as the assumption of a Hindu family that they would join the newlyweds on their honeymoon. "To the Hindu family, marriage was not about two individuals but rather about two families. Thus it was incomprehensible why the whole family could not come along and have all their meals with them" (Rosenbaum, 1994). Conversely, some parents may not be able to appreciate the ways in which their adult child is broadened by or attracted to the partner's culture.

Anyone reading the comments here might think that intercultural marriages are permanently stressful and unhappy. They're not. Marriage and the foreign service are both difficult and stressful, but not unrewarding. While combining the two factors might add an extra layer of stress, they also result in an incredible cultural richness. All the people I spoke to are still married to their foreign-born spouse, except one, and his new wife is foreign-born too.

"I was born in the U.K. but grew up in the U.S.," she explains, "and I never felt I quite 'belonged' in either country. But when I became part of the Foreign Service community, I felt right at home—I wasn't the odd one out any more."

America is often described as a melting pot, so on the whole it seems fitting that those who represent the country overseas should embrace wholeheartedly the concept of cultural integration.

Janet Heg's introduction to the expat life came at the age of five, when she moved from London to New York. Her father's three-month assignment turned into a long-term career, and Janet grew up in New Jersey. After obtaining a degree in journalism, she returned to the U.K. for what she thought would be a year and ended up staying for 25. She married a U.S. Foreign Service officer in 2003 and accompanied him on assignment to Mexico City the following year. Janet has continued to work as a freelance editor and media analyst for U.K. companies and has also worked in the housing office at Embassy Mexico City. Between them, Janet and her husband have five children, who at one point were attending five different schools in three countries. They are now looking forward to their next post, Jamaica.

References

Kahlenberg, Rebecca R., "The I Do's and Don'ts of Intercultural Marriage," *Washington Post*, November 22, 2001.

Books cited by Kahlenberg and in the present article:

Rosenbaum, Stanley Ned and Helene Rosenbaum, *Celebrating Our Differences: Living Two Faiths in One Marriage*, 1994, Ragged Edge Press.
Siegel, Judith P. *What Children Learn From Their Parents' Marriage: It May Be Your Marriage, but It's Your Child's Blueprint for Intimacy*, 2001, Quill Press.
Tannen, Deborah, *I Only Say This Because I Love You: How the Way We Talk Can Make or Break Family Relationships Throughout Our Lives*, 2001, Random House.

Single in the Foreign Service

by Marcia Anglarill

Desperate Housewives may be a popular show in America, but being single will always have its own share of challenges. Add to that a life spent predominantly overseas where you are moving every two to four years, and you can see how being single in the Foreign Service (FS) could merit its own television series.

It's hard enough to date in a place where you know the language, the culture and the people well. Granted, you could argue that dating in New York City is inherently easier than dating in Omaha, Nebraska, whether you grew up in one or the other. However, you could also argue the exact opposite. This is no less true among Foreign Service officers (FSOs), where one, for example, may find Port-au-Prince to be the equivalent of a dating desert island, while another may see it as a romantic paradise.

Though dating and relationships in general tends to be a popular topic, I've found that single life in the FS is often not talked about publicly. Privately, however, it is often the main topic when single FSOs get together. When I was soliciting feedback from single FSOs, the comments were few and slow to come at first. But soon came the deluge. It seems this was something a lot of single officers had something to say about—and even the married FSOs had opinions as well.

So, what *do* single Foreign Service officers have to say about being single in the Foreign Service?

The good, the bad and the ugly

According to one veteran single FSO: "There are wonderful aspects of being single in the Service—you control your time and your money. Singles tend to do the most traveling. Singles also can make assignment decisions without having to weigh [the] desires of others."

On the other hand, the same FSO notes that "FS life is far, far lonelier than most folks are willing to admit. The stress of living away from the U.S. must be harder for people who are not in good marriages." Loneliness does seem to be a recurring theme, particularly in some of the hardship posts. One single FSO in Kathmandu summed up her experience this way: "Single life in Kathmandu is, in a word, sad ... when I went on R&R recently, I realized in the Tokyo airport en route to the States that I was staring at all the men. Even the unattractive ones. Like I had been on a desert island for nine months." Another FSO in Peshawar, Pakistan, had a similar account of her experience. She reported that there really wasn't any dating life there, due to the traditionally conservative culture and the lack of an expat community.

Nevertheless, the diversity of places and situations for dating is very broad. A single FSO in Islamabad, Pakistan had very different observations from those of her colleague in Peshawar. In fact, she saw Islamabad as a "swinging-singles post." The difference, in her view, is that it is an unaccompanied post with a large Defense Department contingent. Thus, there are many single males, though she also notes some are "pretending" they are single. She observes that "opportunities for 'casual' dating abound," but also shares the view that the "prospects for long-term relationships are pretty slim." Similar accounts of Baghdad as a "good" singles post have also been circulating, with descriptions ranging from "Melrose Place" to "college-life revisited."

He said, she said

It is also no secret that the single life for male and female FSOs can be radically different, particularly if one is looking for a long-term relationship or marriage. Despite worldwide changes in women's status, it still appears to be much harder for a female FSO to find a partner willing to accompany her on future overseas tours. A single female FSO in Mexico offers her opinion: "Thinking longer term, for women, I don't think a Mexican man would follow you around the world. Men, I think that a Mexican girl would pick up and go with you." A married FSO in Paramaribo had this advice: "Do not come here as a single female if you are looking for love. All the Surinamese men marry young but have a 'Buitefrauw,' i.e. 'outside woman' or mistress—some Foreign Service Nationals in the embassy even introduce them as such in public." She goes on to report that she has heard many stories of single women getting involved with someone, only to find later that he is married (an experience, according to other single female FSOs, that is not limited to Paramaribo). Yet, she also notes that it is a good post for single men, given the number of male officers there who have married local women.

Another single female who has been in the FS for nineteen years had this to say: "I've noticed that when someone's wife leaves post for some reason, everyone falls over themselves to invite the husband over for dinners, barbeques, etc., acting as if he couldn't possibly feed himself while his wife is out of town. Single men are treated this way too. On the other hand, I never have received invitations because I'm single, unless I have to simply fill a seat at a representational event table."

A single female who entered the FS mid-career and mid-level found being single in the FS even more challenging than did those entering earlier in their careers. She states that while serving in Buenos Aires many years ago, she found that "single men at post went off on their own, don't know where (or with whom!), while the single women, who tended to live in downtown apartments, ended up forming their own cluster(s). Getting to know Argentine nationals was certainly much harder as a single woman, since the culture (at least at that time) was strongly family-based. In other words, single women had to fend for themselves." She further claims that when given the chance to return to that post as a much more senior officer, she declined, in part because she felt it would be "much harder to find satisfying social outlets with a much more visible job."

This experience—that single life is easier for men than for women in the FS—is one that many female FSOs shared over and over again, from a wide range of posts. Nevertheless, some single, male FSOs admit to having their share of challenges when it comes to dating abroad. As one male FSO in Hanoi candidly declared, "even though there are many beautiful women in Hanoi, dating here has many land mines." He describes the experience of meeting two attractive local women in a club and having to resort to writing in order to converse over the loud music. He claims, however, that the conversation abruptly ended when one of them wrote down 400,000 dong ($25) for the both of them. Another experience he shares is that of having some women believe they are in a committed relationship with him and showing signs of jealousy, although he has gone out with them only once or twice.

Another male FSO at a different Southeast Asian post reports similar experiences: "My internal radar has malfunctioned a few times and I've spent the whole night buying drinks and dancing with what turned out to be a hooker." He further admits, "I've dated anything from a lawyer to a woman who washes mangos for a living." However, he also points out that his dating experiences have been abundant and varied, specifically because before arriving at post he promised himself he would try harder and be more open to new dating experiences. Among the single male FSOs, this "pro-activeness" seemed to be a common attitude. As one male FSO noted: "single life wherever you are is what you make it … you can have a really lousy time in London, just as soon as in Bujambura."

Going native

As one may well imagine, another significant challenge when dating locals is learning to manage the cultural differences. An FSO in Mumbai writes: "The weirdest side to dating [here] is that people are really open. [There is] no game playing. If they like you, they will call you every day and want to see you every day. When I first started going out with my boyfriend, I thought he was a stalker because he called so much, but my good Indian friend assured me that his behavior was normal for India. He couldn't understand why I thought it was weird that he called every day when we first met."

A single FSO in Manila found he also had to make some adjustments when it came to dating. He wrote, "When I first got here I was getting shot down left and right, which was not too good for my ego. There is still a strong traditional Philippine way here, and the old customs of dating mainly meant group dating. Filipinos hang out in groups, and group members don't start 'dating' until they are getting serious. So my early attempts at dating freaked out a few women, since it was the American way of meeting once and asking them out, which they took as wanting to get serious. Eventually I smartened up and tried other things which have worked better."

Of course, FSOs dating overseas also face issues of security and privacy. The line between work and social life can become very thin, especially since Mission-sponsored functions and going out with your colleagues are often the easiest and most common social outlets. At many posts, FSOs are required to report any relationships with locals. At Critical Threat Posts, which include communist countries and those with a high terrorist or security threat level, the reporting policy is very stringent. For example, the Contact Reporting Policy for all American personnel serving in Vietnam states: "Any romantic, non-sexual relationship with a Vietnamese national must be reported," and "Any relationship with a Vietnamese national which involves sexual contact on more than one occasion must be disclosed. This is true even if there is no expectation of future contact." Such a policy is enough to make anyone think twice before even batting an eye at a local!

Single and then some

Another issue for some single FSOs is that of being a single parent, or having a non-traditional family, in the Foreign Service. One single parent who has been in the FS for over 20 years states: "The FS does a great job supporting traditional families; it does not support singles or single parents well, yet. Just think about all the administrative details of moving in or out of a post … admin days allotted are not near enough to pack, etc., if one is single and must tend to both home and office. The same is true on a daily basis—the FS demands long, long hours. If you are single, that leaves you holding the bag on everything—financial planning, tax forms, shopping, cooking, washing clothes." However, some might argue that being a single parent can be easier overseas than back home, at least in places where domestic help is inexpensive and reliable.

Another veteran FSO had this observation: "The emphasis on family-friendliness and tandem couples [within the FS] has disadvantaged single men and women in simpler ways too. While the housing space standards are based on Washington norms, and at post are based on position rank, the fact is that a single person is entitled to a maximum of about 30–40% less space than someone with two dependents. It's also rare for a single person or couple to get a house with a yard—whether you have a pet or not."

She further notes that "the emphasis on assigning tandem couples together where possible disadvantages singles and couples (where one partner is not working or is not a [FS] employee). The personnel system must work long and hard to justify assigning me to a great job in Paris or Vienna when someone bidding on the same job has a spouse who MIGHT also get a job at that post. The pressure is on the personnel system and posts to assign tandems together."

Another FSO with sixteen years of experience had this observation: "I have found that the higher concentration of families [at post] makes for a not so fun tour.… I find that there seems to be a dismissal of singles' needs by the CLO [Community Liaison Office] and post administration if there are a lot of families at post. In this 'family friendly' environment, little attention seems to be paid to the hardship that singles experience." She further noted, "I also believe that singles bear an undue burden at work.... [A]t one point when I was in Amman, the Front Office considered sending home all non-essential staff and told [everyone in the] office to come up with a plan if we had to evacuate all but a skeleton crew. I was told by my boss that since I did not have a family I would be the last to go. I guess my parents don't count as family."

This perception, that the FS tends to favor families, particularly traditional families, is sometimes shared by gay FSOs as well. There is no question that the cultural differences at many posts can be challenging for both male and female gay FSOs when it comes to dating. However, living as a couple in the FS can be even more challenging, given the current lack of recognition for gay partnerships. The partners of gay FSOs cannot qualify as "eligible family members," a status which bestows all kinds of benefits, such as relocation costs and medical care.

On the other hand, some married FSOs point out that having a family in the FS can also make life more difficult. Depending on the post, issues such as scarce jobs for FSO spouses, a lack of good schools or inadequate health care for special needs can also be stressful challenges that most single FSOs are spared.

How to deal

As a first-tour junior officer in Ho Chi Minh City, I am finding being single in the FS to be about what I expected—exciting, lonely, challenging, busy, fun and frustrating all at once. My friends back home have dubbed my present life here *Sex and the Ho Chi Minh City*. Indeed, at times it does seem to parallel the ups and downs of the main characters' lives in that (in)famous show. Yet now, eight months into my first tour and with the summer bidding cycle about to begin, I am realizing that bidding on a "good" post for single females for my next tour will be high on my priority list. "Good," however, is in the eye of the beholder.

As one FSO claims, "I don't think there are particularly "good" posts for singles or couples, because all posts are what you make of them—the hobbies and interests you have inherently, love of travel or not, social abilities, good manners/social skills, etc. Some posts are considered 'good' because of access to other single people, the night life, access to alcohol, etc."

Another single FSO reports: "I've noticed that I've had the best social times when I've had a small cadre of close single friends/acquaintances. We've socialized together, sat around in our TV rooms in our socks talking, knitting, drinking, eating, organizing movie nights/dinners, traveling together, etc.… When you're a family you travel around with a built-in social network and have built-in love/comfort/occasional strife. When you're single, you have to work harder to make new friends and acquaintances, keep yourself entertained, keep in touch with family and friends elsewhere, and keep yourself from being alone."

On the topic of social networks, another FSO notes: "It may be that technology—the availability of e-mail, cheap long-distance telephone calls, and easier travel—now provides sufficient connections to existing friends and family that singles at any level or age can in a sense take with them their own support system."

Life in the FS is a challenge whether you're single, married, gay, male, female, old, young, entry-level or senior-level. The challenges may be harder to bear in some posts or circumstances, easier in others. As some would argue, the dating opportunities, or lack thereof, may depend on one's perspective. But even for those who don't find romance, life in the Foreign Service seems to offer plenty of other things that keeps them going. The FSO who has found dating in Kathmandu to be "sad" sums it up best with this additional insight: "And yet, life here in Kathmandu is wonderful. Great friends, good front office, exciting policy and political tensions. I'll take that over a man any day. Of course, I'd also take both!"

Marcia Anglarill is a single Foreign Service officer currently on her first tour in Ho Chi Minh City, Vietnam. Previously, she has lived in San Jose, Costa Rica, as a Peace Corps Volunteer; Paris, France as an exchange student; and Santa Cruz, Bolivia, her parents' homeland. She enjoys sports, movies, reading, dancing, listening to music, travel and adventure.

Foreign Service Highlights from a Family with Young Kids

by Michele Hopper

When people hear about our vacation travels, they often shake their heads. Exotic places are well and good, but when there's cheap full-time nanny care available at post, why drag four kids along to out-of-the-way corners of the globe? Because traveling as a family is what we do. The real question is, why live halfway around the world from home if not to expose our kids to everything wonderful and different along the way?

At our first post, Manila, Philippines, the islands called to us. We took three-day weekends to Mindoro, Bohol and Palawan with their clear waters and blue skies. We chased pods of dolphins, collected starfish, dodged sea snakes and watched black tip sharks cut through schools of fish along the shore. The older kids took an introductory SCUBA course and all four learned to snorkel. What aquarium touch tank can compare?

During our visit to Cebu, the country's second-largest city, rather than hit the typical beach resort, we delved into world history. We saw Magellan's Cross, planted by the famous explorer while attempting to circumnavigate the world and convert indigenous peoples to Christianity along the way. We explored the Lapu-Lapu shrine on adjacent Mactan Island, dedicated to the chief who killed Magellan because (more or less) he wasn't all that keen on being converted.

Our first adventure beyond the shores of our little archipelago was a long weekend in Hong Kong and Kowloon. We poked around the bird and goldfish markets, rode a nauseatingly steep tram up to Victoria

Peak and spent a day at the Ocean Park amusement park and aquarium.

For our official rest and recreation (R&R) trip, we chose New Zealand as our destination. We crisscrossed the North Island in a rented RV, ferried to the South Island and rode the TranzCoastal train to Christchurch. Along the way we raced through 3-D mazes, rode horses, hiked through geothermal parks, panned for gold, saw kiwis (both fruits and birds), floated through caves, went zorbing (a New Zealand sport involving rolling down a hill inside a giant inflatable ball), soaked in hot sulfur springs, and explored a Maori village and Hobbit holes. During our journey back to Manila, we spotted "Nemo" in the Sydney Aquarium and rode through Singapore's Night Safari. Over our three-week journey we all enjoyed new taste sensations from roadside meat pies to kangaroo steak.

A few months later we departed again for a week, to Thailand. Exploring the power of photography, the youngsters took great shots of temples and statues from their unique perspectives. Whether puttering through the canals of Bangkok or riding elephants in Chiang Mai, we kept everything hands-on. Even something as simple as chilled pineapple from a street vendor in Bangkok turned a long city walk into a treat.

Our second post, Togo, is a country with limited travel opportunities for a family of six. So, we put a lot of effort into planning our summer R&R. This time, we're heading to Helsinki, Finland and bussing our way through the Baltics with a final destination of Krakow, Poland. Castles, amazing food and perhaps even some indoor bobsledding await us.

As State Department parents, some of the adventures we face—from the moderate annoyance of delayed household goods to the drastic issue of host country unrest—aren't the kinds we're eager to share with our children. But traveling the world with their energy and eyes to guide us is without compare. It gives us all the opportunity to see the world and each other through new eyes.

Michele Hopper was born in Belgium in 1974. As an Army brat, she grew up in (the former) Zaire, Algeria and Niger before returning stateside for high school. While attending college in Virginia, she spent a semester abroad and traveled through western Europe, filling her bag with Greek Ouzo, Italian leather and Swiss chocolate. She is now creating her own family of GlobeHoppers, with the help of her Foreign Service officer husband, Ian Hopper. They have been posted to the Philippines and Togo, and are hoping either to head to the Middle East next or return to Asia Pacific.

PART IV
Employment Options for Accompanying Partners

Family Member Employment: At Work in the Mission

by Shawn Dorman

The two-career family has become more of a norm than an exception, and the Foreign Service is lumbering along attempting to catch up with that reality and figure out how a two-career family can succeed under the unique circumstances of Foreign Service life. Until the 1970s, the spouse (back then, almost exclusively wives) was considered by the bureaucracy to be an arm of the employee rather than an individual or professional in her own right, and the wife's performance in such endeavors as representational entertaining was included in the employee's performance evaluation reports. Spouses were not paid for their role as supporting actors, but were expected to work at that job. A 1972 Department of State directive "liberated" spouses from employee evaluation reports, and in 1978, the Family Liaison Office was created to further assist Foreign Service family members.

Since then, more and more spouses have taken on paid employment inside and outside U.S. missions. "At any given time," says FLO's Katie Hokenson, "there are 2,000 family member employees working inside our missions overseas."

Family member employment is a key issue for foreign affairs agencies seeking to recruit and retain the best employees. The new generation of Foreign Service employees wants and expects adequate employment options for their spouses. Management does seem to recognize that to keep employees satisfied, it has to be engaged in trying to satisfy the employment needs of family members. Some of the most exciting developments on the family member employment front are tied to employment outside missions. However, over 75 percent of family members working overseas work inside U.S. missions, and most family members still express a preference for work inside the missions. This article examines the status of those employment options.

We spoke with Deputy Assistant Secretary for Human Resources John O'Keefe, Family Liaison Office Director Faye Barnes, Overseas Employment Personnel Management Specialist Vens McCoy and FLO Employment Program Coordinator Katie Hokenson. In addition, more than 70 family members responded to our request for input on their own experiences with mission employment.

Deputy Assistant Secretary O'Keefe explained that improved family member employment is one element of the director general's current strategy. He said that management is aiming to help family members find more "professional-level" employment. A recent survey of 2,400 Eligible Family Members (EFMs), O'Keefe explained, helped illustrate clearly that "we have a real talent pool" inside the Foreign Service community; one that can and should be utilized.

Preference for Mission jobs

Of the 70 family members who responded to our request for comments on family member employment, a surprisingly high majority expressed the view that they would rather work inside the embassy than outside. This preference comes despite numerous bitter complaints about mission jobs, focusing on low salaries, lack of professional options and frustrations about treatment by post management. The reason most often cited by survey respondents for their preference for mission employment was, ironically, "salary." Many pointed out that jobs on the local economy in most parts of the world, while potentially more interesting than embassy jobs, offer unacceptably low compensation. Other reasons for their preference for embassy jobs include: the ability to accumulate retirement pay and other benefits (for certain types of positions), a secure environment, ease of commuting with their spouses, contact with the embassy community and the ability to be more "plugged in" to what is going on in the community.

More family members work inside missions than outside. About 25 percent of all family members overseas work inside missions, and 10 percent work outside, according to data from the Family Liaison Office. FLO data for 2004 showed that 35 percent of Foreign Service family members overseas were working, and that 50 percent would like to be working. Data from 169 posts, reported by FLO in their December 2004 Family Member Employment Report, show that the total number of spouses overseas was 8,413. Of those, 6,680 (or 79 percent), were women and 1,733 were men. The total number of spouses working overseas was reported to be 2,907: 2,092 working inside the mission and 815 working outside. The goal of State management, through the office of the director general, the Human Resources Bureau, the FLO and post management, is to help increase the number of working family members to 50 percent, which would meet the current demand.

The family members who responded to our survey expressed a wide diversity of attitudes about mission jobs. Their experiences were strongly influenced by how they felt they were treated by post management. Some were extremely pleased with their mission jobs, while others either did not find a suitable job in the embassy or were frustrated by the ones they did find. There is no one uniform family member employment system at work in all missions, and no uniform group of family members seeking work at all posts. The success or failure of each family member employment program appears to depend on the actual needs and resources at the post, combined with the level of commitment to fostering opportunities from post management. This can explain the wide diversity of experience family members have with mission employment.

Hiring categories

There are numerous hiring mechanisms under which spouses are brought on board for embassy employment (see sidebar for a guide to some of the most commonly used acronyms). Eligible Family Members who are American citizens and considered "AEFM," or Appointment-Eligible Family Members, have the broadest options for mission employment. An AEFM is a U.S. citizen spouse or U.S. citizen child at least 18 years old, on the travel orders of a U.S. citizen Foreign or Civil Service employee or military service member assigned to a U.S. mission. Non-American-citizen spouses are EFMs but are not eligible for spousal preference as outlined in the statute on preference. "Members of Household" and other non-married partners of Foreign Service employees overseas are not considered to be EFMs. Most State Department mission jobs are limited to those with AEFM status, as they require a security clearance. Non-sensitive positions with other agencies are open to all EFMs.

In March 1994, the State Department established the **Professional Associates Program** to open up unfilled junior officer positions to EFMs. In the same year, State also implemented the Rockefeller Amendment, which allowed embassies and consulates to employ expatriate American citizens and family members in positions formerly available only to foreign nationals, and gave preference to American-citizen family members over other applicants for these jobs.

One of the most important developments in family-member mission employment was the creation of the State Department's **Family Member Appointment** hiring mechanism in 1998. Prior to the FMA, spouses were hired under mechanisms that were, literally, the pits. The **PIT** (part-time intermittent temporary) appointment, used for many State embassy jobs, usually meant a low salary, virtually no benefits, no advancement and no continuity of career. The PIT has been replaced by the **TEMP**, "temporary appointments" for up to one year. These appointments are reserved for U.S. citizens and come with some benefits.

Another hiring mechanism that has long been used by a number of agencies is the **Personal Service Contract**. Family members hired locally by USAID are often hired on a PSC. There is no standard set of benefits that come with a PSC, and much depends on local practice and host-country laws. Most agencies, aside from USAID, now prefer to use the State Department hiring mechanism called the Personal Services Agreement instead of the PSC. The PSA is not subject to Federal Acquisition Regulations, which prohibited performance of certain types of duties including cashiering. The PSA was originally created for local hiring of non-Americans. It has been expanded to include American hires, and for them, it is called the PSA Plus Program. PSA and PSA Plus are identical except that "plus" includes Americans. Non-AEFMs are eligible to apply for both PSA and PSA positions.

The creation of the Family Member Appointment hiring mechanism represents an effort to standardize what have to date been very localized and varied employment programs for family members. There is no doubt that the creation of the FMA—a result of about 20 years of advocacy by the FLO and AAFSW (now the Associates of the American Foreign Service Worldwide)—was a big step forward. The Family Member Appointment is defined as a Department of State hiring mechanism used to employ appointment-eligible family members accompanying career employees on assignment abroad. The FMA, according to State materials, is "a five-year limited, non-career appointment," that allows family members to earn benefits. The benefits include annual leave, sick leave, retirement (FERS), health benefits (FEHB), life insurance (FEGLI), Thrift Savings Plan participation and non-competitive eligibility status for U.S. government jobs.

In 1999, a year after the creation of the FMA, 34 percent of family members working inside missions (of 150 posts surveyed by the FLO) were in FMA positions. By early 2005, the percentage had risen to 73. Clearly, the FMA hiring mechanism is taking hold.

The standardization of hiring mechanisms could help with a long-standing problem of employees leaving post without receiving a written performance evaluation. An employee with no performance record to carry to the next post, or, more importantly, back to Washington, where further U.S. government opportunities may depend on adequate documentation of previous work, is at a disadvantage when seeking onward employment.

"Either CLO or clerical"

Foreign Service family members looking for upwardly-mobile career paths should probably not look to the embassy for employment. As one FS spouse put it, "It's either CLO [Community Liaison Office] or clerical." This is an exaggeration, but does describe the typical perception of mission jobs—that they are not "professional" jobs. While it may be possible to aim for similar types of jobs at different posts, usually a family member looking for mission work has to take what is available, which will at best be a continuation of a type of work done at another post, and almost certainly not be an advancement up a career ladder.

Typical embassy jobs with the State Department include consular associate, consular assistant, community liaison office coordinator, information management assistant, general services assistant, office manager, administrative assistant, housing coordinator, newsletter or website editor, security escort, etc. The U.S. Agency for International Development has non-Foreign Service positions, which tend to be highly-coveted development jobs.

Consular Associates—family members working in consular sections around the world who have gone through the full basic consular course—have helped embassies and consulates with the heavy consular load and visa adjudication. There are currently between 150 and 160 CAs at work around the world, and the incumbents have held wide-ranging responsibilities similar to those of consular officers.

However, with the implementation of new security measures, CAs have no longer been permitted to adjudicate visa applications since September 2005. It is still unclear what impact this will have, but it is clearly a denigration of the authority that was invested in the position. Management has sent word to the field that post management should try to ensure that EFM consular positions are not eliminated in connection with the changes, and to try to minimize the impact on the CA jobs.

Some of the best mission jobs are the **USAID jobs,** seen as more professional in nature than many State jobs open to family members. "USAID is far more amenable to hiring people as professionals, giving them work in their area of expertise, and paying them accordingly," says an EFM working for USAID. "State has jobs for spouses that are basically secretarial, never professional, and mired in the 1950s view that a spouse has no professional track in mind other than a secretarial one." Many family members believe that most of these USAID jobs are unofficially reserved for USAID spouses, something a number of State family members point to as a source of great frustration.

Under the **Professional Associates Program,** originally established to open vacant junior officer positions to EFMs, the focus has now shifted to unfilled mid-level Foreign Service positions in the "hard-to-fill" category. (HTF positions are those that lack sufficient qualified Foreign Service bidders.) Every year, State management sends out a bid list for HTF jobs open to EFMs and Civil Service employees. When hired under the PA program, the EFM is hired on an FMA and receives commensurate benefits and a salary based on his/her qualifications. This year's list of State Department Hard-to-Fill Program positions was released in February, earlier than usual, in an effort to facilitate EFM participation. The 2005 list was particularly long and included a number of fairly high-level (FS-1) jobs. Although the EFM applicant is limited by the spouse's post of assignment, the list does offer one more set of potential job opportunities.

During the period of severe shortage of junior officers, before the State Department began hiring under the Diplomatic Readiness Initiative in 2000, State reached a maximum of 30 spouses hired under the Professional Associates program. FLO Director Faye Barnes indicated that original estimates had 50 PA positions filled, but that goal was not reached. In the interim, she says, the program almost disappeared until FLO picked it up again under the hard-to-fill category. Because family members are limited by the post of assignment of their spouses, few have been able to take advantage of the program.

About money

Post budgets play a major role in determining EFM employment options inside the mission, because EFM positions other than those in the Professional Associates Program are paid for out of post funds. In the 1990s, the severe budget strains on the foreign affairs agencies that resulted in a hiring freeze at State for several years and a reduction-in-force at USAID led to a shortage of entry-level employees at embassies worldwide. This led to more job opportunities for family members, many of whom began filling vacant State Foreign Service positions in consular sections as consular associates and professional associates.

During his tenure, Secretary of State Colin Powell brought budgets back to functional levels, and increased State Foreign Service hiring dramatically. More entry-level consular slots began to be filled by officers again. However, because the workload has grown substantially in recent years, the new influx of FS employees does not seem to have had a significant negative impact so far on the number of EFM jobs available. But foreign affairs agencies are again facing tight budgets, and other types of EFM jobs at posts under severe budget strain may be affected. "FMA jobs are often the first cut when the budget is tight," says EFM Patrick Fogarty from Nogales, Mexico.

Now more than ever, EFMs represent a highly skilled, though extremely diverse, work force, seeking salaries matching their abilities. Overseas, these hopes are rarely met. Most family members surveyed noted that embassy jobs usually pay better than those in the local economy. Yet many expressed annoyance that mission salaries are lower than those of their Foreign Service colleagues in the embassy. As a general rule, an EFM who wants an FS-level salary for an embassy job would be best advised to try to join the Foreign Service.

Although family members tend to view embassy jobs as more lucrative than outside jobs, salaries for jobs with international organizations such as the United Nations, international and U.S.-based NGOs and U.S. or multinational companies tend not to be based on the local economic norms. Thus, many of these jobs pay much better than embassy positions.

When hired under the FMA, EFMs are eligible to receive salaries based on the "highest previous rate" calculation. Yet there are two major "ifs" at play: *if* the post budget allows, and *if* the position is not classified for a maximum salary below the HPR level. According to the survey respondents, the HPR is in fact often used for FMA hiring, but not always. Post budgets are a limiting factor, and may not allow for payment of a particular EFM's HPR. Even the HPR is often seen by EFMs as too low, because it only takes into account previous U.S. government employment, not all prior experience and salary history.

Many spouses expressed frustration at not receiving the salary level they felt they deserved. A typical comment from an EFM in a Middle Eastern post was that when she was hired for an embassy position the "human resources officer single-handedly decided that my previous work experience did not matter and that I would start at the lowest grade for which the position was announced."

EFM salaries can also be affected by the relatively new "CAJE" system, the Computer Aided Job Evaluation, which is being used to reclassify FSN positions around the world. EFM Joyce Otero, in Prague, explains that she was hired for an embassy job in the security office with a salary based on her highest previous rate. "But after one year, this all changed when the position was CAJEed at a lower grade." Her salary will be reduced because her pay level was higher than the highest rate available under the newly classified position.

Post budgets can be affected by the needs of other posts. An EFM at a Latin American post pointed out that the Iraq war has affected employment: "Cost-cutting measures are under way here, supposedly due to the cost of Iraq.... I've been told that upper managers try to save money to 'look good,' letting support staff be overworked even when there are back-up workers available to help them, at a much lower rate."

Local economies

Many family members complain that in competition for embassy jobs with locals, they usually lose. This is the case despite the statutory preference for AEFMs in hiring for embassy jobs. There seem to be plenty of ways around hiring an EFM, if the post prefers a Foreign Service National. Often it comes down to money, because in most of the world, it's cheaper to hire a local than an EFM.

In many cases, however, there are other reasons for a post to prefer to hire a local over an EFM: Foreign Service assignment cycles dictate that EFMs will not stay on the job nearly as long as most FSNs; FSNs are usually native speakers of the host-country language; FSNs tend to know the local environment best and have vital contacts and access to the local community and/or government officials that an EFM usually would not have.

The issue of which positions should remain Foreign Service National slots and those that should be filled by family members is a contentious one. The department is working to open more FSN positions to family members to increase EFM employment opportunities. According to current department policy, all non-sensitive positions should be open to qualified EFM applicants. A pilot program being tested by the Western Hemisphere Bureau aims to bring more EFMs into FSN positions.

Many family members point out that post management often uses language requirements to ensure that FSN positions are filled by local applicants rather than American EFMs.

In most regions of the world outside of Europe, FSNs earn substantially lower salaries than Americans, because FSN salaries are based on (the high end of) local-salary norms. When an EFM is hired into a position previously encumbered by an FSN, the cost to the post, in most parts of the world, is higher because the EFM is paid on the American compensation plan. So, while the salary may be low compared to FS colleagues in the embassy, it is high compared to most FSN salaries.

Because locally-hired staff get paid out of post funds, there is an obvious preference for hiring at the more affordable local rate. The opposite is true in Europe, where the local compensation plan, and the Euro and British-pound exchange rate, translate into higher costs than in most of the rest of the world. One EFM in London noted that "the hourly pay levels for most EFM positions in London were more than 20 percent less than for the FSNs in the same positions, and less than what is paid to a good cleaner."

The hiring process

The hiring process varies from post to post. Some posts hire EFMs sight unseen, some without an interview. Others do not. The attitudes held by management at individual posts seem to play a strong role in determining how the selection process for EFM jobs works. A Post Employment Committee can help manage the process. Not all posts have a PEC, even though they are all, according to Foreign Affairs Manual 3 regulations, supposed to have one. Each post is also supposed to have a written "post employment policy" as well, but many do not.

Many embassy jobs require a security clearance, and the acquisition of a clearance can take a long time and delay hiring by months. In late 2003, Diplomatic Security implemented an interim clearance process, which allows posts to give temporary clearance to a spouse based on the Foreign Service employee's clearance. Posts must request the interim clearance from DS, and if all goes well, DS can grant an interim clearance within a few weeks that allows the EFM to begin work while the full clearance process continues.

The FMA hiring mechanism has helped many posts speed up the hiring process for EFMs, though more than a few family members responding to our survey had complaints about delays. One of the key benefits of the FMA hiring mechanism is that it allows the EFM to carry a security clearance from post to post, thus avoiding the time-consuming and costly process of redoing a security check. A security clearance granted for an FMA position can be revalidated for up to two years after the employee leaves the job. Before the FMA mechanism, a new clearance was required by each new post. A number of EFMs told us that they have successfully reactivated a security clearance at a new post, and were able to save time in the hiring process for a new job. Marlene Nice, one of the editors of this book, reports that she went into intermittent-no-work-scheduled status (known as "INWS") when transferring from Montevideo to Zagreb, and "it took just a matter of days to renew my top-secret clearance." Others told of having trouble reinstating a clearance at a new post. The success seems to depend largely on whether the management section at post tries to make it work.

Training

Many family members receive training outside the mission for embassy jobs. Some, especially consular associates, receive training before going to post. FLO's Katie Hokenson explains that training for family members prior to arrival at post (usually in connection with consular associate positions) is on a space-available basis. It has been somewhat more difficult for EFMs to get into consular courses during the past several years due to the increased hiring of Foreign Service employees under the Diplomatic Readiness Initiative.

EFMs who work as community liaison office coordinators usually receive training away from post. Others who often receive training out of country are APO postal employees, consular associates, voucher examiners, and those in other management positions in human resources and finance. Several EFMs working in website management positions reported being extremely pleased with training opportunities.

There are good positions for EFM nurses at many posts. Several nurses responded to the survey, none of whom had received training for the job. Obviously, to be hired as an RN, you must already be a trained nurse. However, the Foreign Service nurse does have unique responsibilities based on country-specific health-care availability. EFM nurse Alison Rowles recalls landing in Niamey without much information about her job: "I was handed a radio upon landing and told I had a deathly ill patient to deal with at the local hospital. I didn't even know where my home was, let alone the hospital! It didn't stop from there." Of respondents who had worked for USAID, some received outside training, and others did not. Training for USAID positions varies widely from post to post and job to job.

Attitudes: "just because we're here"

Many family members in embassy jobs complain that they feel underutilized, unappreciated and underpaid. "All the talk in the State Department about the importance of spousal employment does not amount to a hill of beans for anyone that has more than a high school education," says a male EFM at an African post. "I have been told and have read a million times that if I'm flexible enough and try hard enough that I will be able to have a rewarding career as the spouse of a Foreign Service officer, and it is really just not true. I have tried every category possible, and most positions have either required I get paid a ridiculously low salary or that I work at a level well below my experience.... EFM positions are usually low-level, administrative positions. Most spouses these days show up with university and graduate degrees and salary histories that just do not make the available EFM employment opportunities appropriate or interesting." One frustrated EFM says: "I will never apply to work as an EFM on a Family Member Appointment again. I was not treated as a person who could advance professionally but rather as a spouse who had been given the gift of a job that I should be happy to have, like social welfare."

Many EFMs express frustration at the identity they have inside the embassy community. The term "dependent" still has a negative connotation, one that seems to strip away any prior professional experience. Bernard Huon-Dumentat, an EFM in Lisbon who writes about issues of family member employment, had this to say: "The department still views FMA jobs as opportunities that the U.S. government has created to keep spouses happy. Therefore the attitude is that EFMs should be satisfied with whatever pittance they receive in salary and whatever pitiful regard they receive for their real input to the organization. There is no long-term vision." Another family member who has been watching the issue for years, Terri Lawler Smith, notes: "I have to tell you that over the last 20 years a lot of lip service has been given to all the positive changes that the State Department has made in EFM employment, but in reality, very few concrete changes have taken place since the old PIT days."

A view from an East European post was more optimistic: "I think working conditions and appreciation for EFMs have improved. An EFM working in an FMA position is not seen as being 'just the dependent' anymore but as a 'real employee.'" And from a first-tour EFM at a hardship post: "I have been very impressed with the importance that post management has put on family member employment. I am at a hardship post, and since I have been here I believe that almost every spouse that wanted to work in the mission has a job here." A family member new to the Foreign Service, who runs her embassy's website, says: "I have been overseas for seven months now, and have seen many opportunities for family members. I post all the jobs on the website so I have seen all of them. I believe HR works with all family members to find positions suitable and enjoyable for them."

So much depends on the management team at post. The key players determining the employment situation at a post are the ambassador and deputy chief of mission, the management officer and the community liaison office coordinator. The players and the dynamics are different at every post as American personnel cycle through from year to year and as the needs of each post change. Therefore, opportunities for family members can vary widely from post to post, and from year to year at any given post.

"Outside the fold": when a family member is ineligible

The FMA hiring mechanism is only open to AEFMs who are not receiving a U.S. government annuity, so there are many family members who do not qualify. This is a point of stress for those family members outside the AEFM box, including Members of Household, other unmarried partners and non-U.S.-citizen spouses of Foreign Service employees.

"The program of employment for family members fails to address the needs of the significant portion of spouses who are not U.S. citizens," says USAID Health Officer John Dunlop. "These people find themselves plunked down in a foreign country without even real cultural ties to the American community, much less the local community. They cannot work in the embassy, which can lead to a very isolating situation of forced unemployment. This is very hard on the family as well as the spouse."

There are nepotism considerations that preclude other categories of family members from gaining access to embassy jobs, including family members who would serve under the chain of command of their spouse if they served in an embassy job. As the Foreign Service employee rises in rank, the options for the spouse become more limited due to the wider authority under the employee.

There are also conflict-of-interest concerns that can limit employment options. The Foreign Affairs Manual requires that spouses ask permission to accept a job in the local economy. A family member is not supposed to work in a position involving duties that could overlap or conflict with those of the Foreign Service employee spouse. This can limit work options both inside and outside the mission. The American Foreign Service Association (AFSA) heard from a family member in April who had to decline a lucrative private sector job offer because the work might have involved issues her spouse was working on inside the embassy. Management saw potential for a conflict of interest. The implementation of the rules on this vary from post to post.

What's new or improved?

In a March 2005 message to all chiefs of mission, entitled "Supporting Our People," Director General W. Robert Pearson laid out eight specific suggestions for helping validate the commitment to "improve the quality of employment life for our family members throughout the world." Half of the suggestions focused on mission employment, and requested that chiefs of mission: endorse the USAID/State pilot project to place qualified family members of USAID and State employees into professional positions; endorse the current department policy of family member preference in recruiting locally engaged staff; "keep an eye on" consular associate positions as CAs lose their visa-adjudication authority in September 2005; and ensure that every family member employee who works at post receives a performance evaluation.

The FMA hiring mechanism is providing spouses employment benefits never before available to them in mission jobs. Since its 1998 inception, with support from the director general, it has become the hiring mechanism of choice for many EFMs and managers.

A **pilot program under State's Bureau of Western Hemisphere Affairs** is aiming to increase opportunities for EFMs by implementing hiring preferences for "locally employed staff" positions. Announced in December 2004, the pilot project is a collaboration between the Family Member Employment Working Group and the executive office of WHA. (Note: The FMEWG is comprised of representatives from the FLO, the Office of Overseas Employment, Employee Relations Office and the Office of Policy Coordination, all under the director general's office.) Under the pilot, as of Jan. 1, 2005, WHA posts have been obliged to use a recruiting policy giving hiring preference to AEFMs and U.S. veterans for positions that have traditionally been seen as Foreign Service National positions. The WHA pilot could help increase job opportunities for EFMs in Western Hemisphere posts. Vens McCoy in the Overseas Employment Office tells us that feedback on the pilot has been positive, and they expanded the program to the East Asian and Pacific Affairs Bureau in January 2006. As soon as funding is available, the program will be expanded to more bureaus.

Another new initiative, based on a **cooperative agreement between State and USAID,** looks promising. USAID and State sent out a joint message (04 State 199609) stating that "USAID joins the Department of State in reaffirming its strong support for employment opportunities for the family member of U.S. government employees assigned to posts abroad. Employment opportunities should be available to qualified EFMs.... Family member employment has been an established feature of life at Foreign Service posts for decades, and providing such employment opportunities for them throughout the course of their time abroad has become increasingly important to all the foreign affairs agencies.

"In support of family member employment overseas, USAID is implementing a policy to make a significant number of additional positions available for EFMs, to be filled through USAID selection at post to include review by the Post Employment Committee.... USAID directors are expected to make locally established positions available to EFMs.... Directors of missions with up to five U.S. direct hire positions must, at a minimum, identify one local position for primary staffing by an EFM." The message gives special emphasis to identifying "professional-level positions."

USAID has often been the source of professional-type jobs for family members, who have in the past been hired primarily under the PSC authority. The new initiative calls for USAID to hire under State's FMA when the employee desires. Several EFMs who commented on

FMA hiring noted concern that if USAID positions are put under the FMA umbrella, the positions might be downgraded. One noted that the conversion to FMA for the higher-salaried USAID jobs might actually bring down the salaries to more typical FMA levels.

A brief mention of employment options outside missions must be made, for it is in this realm that a number of exciting programs are underway. The Global Employment Strategy has recently been launched by State. GES, according to the FLO, which runs the program, "seeks to increase spousal employment opportunities by establishing a global network of potential employers from multinational organizations and NGOs."

Another new program, called "E-Entrepreneurs," has come online to train family members to run their own portable businesses. The first pilot training was offered in May 2005. The Strategic Networking Assistance Program, known as SNAP, has moved out of the pilot phase, and is being covered by ICASS funding. SNAP aims to help connect family members with opportunities for local employment outside the mission, and to help with career development and planning, resume writing and honing interview skills.

"Walking the walk"

Family member employment has long been an issue fairly low on the list of management priorities, when it's been on the list at all. State management now seems to recognize that family member employment opportunities are a key element in efforts to recruit and retain the best employees. Embassy jobs will never be able to satisfy all the employment interests of family members. These jobs are but one piece of an expanding network of options.

Members of the Foreign Service community must understand that the foreign affairs agencies will probably never be able to ensure that all family members who want good jobs can get them at every post. "Heretical as it may sound and as much as I wish it were not so," long-time family-member advocate Mette Beecroft says, "there are couples whose joint career aspirations simply will not flourish in the Foreign Service. Especially in cases where an employee has had long-time aspirations to join the Foreign Service, it can be difficult to admit that the Foreign Service might just not be right for them."

To be blunt, the most exciting innovations and opportunities emerging for family members come from the world outside the embassy. The Internet—which vastly expands the options for continuity of contact with all types of employers and clients—will probably prove to be the single most valuable asset to a Foreign Service family member seeking some semblance of a career. Realistically, family members should not expect to have a traditional professional career path working in mission jobs. But they should be able to expect good-faith assistance from post management in their efforts to find the best employment possible.

The director general has gone on record asking chiefs of mission at all posts to make family member employment a priority, and he has laid out specific ways that they can do this. Obviously, this will only succeed if post management around the world takes it on as a priority. We have seen that management can talk the talk. Let's see if management will give it teeth and require posts to walk the walk.

Shawn Dorman, a former Foreign Service officer, is associate editor of the Foreign Service Journal *and editor of the book* Inside a U.S. Embassy. *This article originally appeared in the* Foreign Service Journal. *Reprinted with permission.*

An Acronym Guide to Family Member Employment

AEFM: Appointment Eligible Family Member, U.S.-citizen spouse or child over 18 on travel orders of U.S. citizen Foreign or Civil Service employee

	or military service member assigned to a U.S. mission
CAJE:	Computer Aided Job Evaluation, created to reclassify FSN positions
CLO:	Community Liaison Office, supports family members at posts
CS:	Civil Service employee
EFM:	Eligible Family Member, a dependent of a USG employee on travel orders
EOE:	Executive Order Eligibility, a 3-year window for a qualifying AEFM to apply for U.S. government positions in the U.S. under category of "status candidates" or "non-competitive eligibles"
FAMER:	Family Member Employment Report, produced by FLO
FLO:	Family Liaison Office, State Department office supporting family members
FMEWG:	Family Member Employment Working Group
FMA:	Family Member Appointment, a hiring mechanism
FSN:	Foreign Service National
GES:	Global Employment Strategy, a new employment program from FLO
HPR:	highest previous rate
ICASS:	International Cooperative Administrative Support Services, the program requiring cost-sharing among agencies at overseas missions
INWS:	Intermittent-no-work-scheduled status, for those leaving FMA positions
LES:	Locally Engaged Staff, another term for Foreign Service National

MOH:	Member of Household, an FS employee dependent without EFM status (yet).
PA:	Professional Associate, an AEFM who is selected to fill a Foreign Service position overseas
PEC:	Post Employment Committee
PIT:	Part-Time Intermittent Temporary appointment, a term no longer used by DOS, is now called a TEMP, or temporary appointment.
PSA:	Personal Services Agreement, a State Department hiring mechanism used by many agencies
PSC:	Personal Services Contract, a hiring mechanism used by USAID
RH:	Resident Hire
SNAP:	Strategic Networking Assistance Program
TEMP:	Temporary Appointment, formerly PIT

Flexible like a Contortionist: Pursuing a Career While Trailing a Diplomat Around the World

by Chris D. Stuebner

To a brand-new junior officer, the idea of pursuing dual overseas careers when both partners are professionals may seem quite feasible. However, the Foreign Service lifestyle presents a unique set of challenges and obstacles for those seeking employment outside of U.S. missions. Though finding gainful local employment in your field is possible in some countries, it comes at a price. Finding a job on the local economy of a host country takes a commitment to stay with the job search, flexibility, and often a willingness to accept a lower pay scale than in the U.S.

The majority of spouses who choose to work outside the U.S. Embassy are employed in the field of education, often as English teachers or staff members at international schools. However, in this article, I will focus mainly on local employment in professional fields other than teaching or training. The perspectives I will share range from that of a first-tour spouse who worked for a year as a statistician on three short-term assignments, to that of a securities lawyer who has worked in multiple countries over the past 22 years. The goal is to provide a reality check to dual-career couples (and hopeful singles) who are contemplating joining the Foreign Service, as well as to offer practical encouragement to spouses who are already committed to the mobile Foreign Service lifestyle.

Factors complicating a job search

What are some of the factors, specific to the Foreign Service lifestyle, that make a job search on the local economy so difficult? One experienced observer notes that "newcomers and people considering the Foreign Service should know that working locally is harder than they might think, due to work permit restrictions, low salaries, etc." Others' experience, my own included, suggests that additional factors come into play.

Duration of overseas assignments

Junior officers serve two-year tours, while assignments for mid-level officers and beyond average two to four years. This can impact the job search process for spouses. In the U.S., a job search takes an average of six months. Overseas, the process may take even longer.

Alexandra, who sought work in Mexico, wrote "I consider myself relatively adept at networking and exploring possibilities, and I proactively applied myself for over six months before something even potentially viable came up." My own experience has been similar, with job searches taking a minimum of four to five months.

Even after meaningful work has been found, the short time in-country may negatively impact employment. Kathryn, who has found local employment at three different posts, observed that she felt a "very constrained time frame as a Foreign Service spouse searching for a job. I was limited to how long I could work for a company or how long I could work on a project." However, she found a way to turn the time constraint into a 'positive reason' to hire. "It was a pretty easy sell, if targeted correctly. Consulting firms, advertising agencies, Internet companies, etc.—all like a short-term commitment."

Unanticipated changes in assignments

After spending five months looking for work and weathering those stressful first months in the new job, my spouse came home one evening and said, "Looks like we're going to [country] sooner than we expected!" I had been in my new position just three scant months. I literally did not know whether I was coming or going!

My spouse's employers had solid reasoning for their precipitous decision. The officer my husband was designated to replace in a year had been re-diagnosed with cancer and had to curtail. My husband already had the language from a previous tour and was eager to head back overseas.

Fortunately, senior management at my company offered some supportive advice. They pledged to handle the personnel resource planning issues. In the meantime, I should say nothing to my immediate supervisor or team members. Together, my new team dove into an intense four-month project driven by customer needs. Only toward completion of the project, when my impending relocation was just weeks away, did I make public the fact that I would be leaving. As it turned out, the customer strongly encouraged the company to keep me on board as a telecommuter, despite my relocation.

Narine's experience was more frustrating. After an eight-month job search, she joined a Ukrainian non-governmental organization as its executive director. Six months later, anticipating the end of her husband's contract with USAID, she resigned her position. Two months after that, she learned that he had been extended for another year! By then, the organization had found a new director, and so her employment search began all over again.

Throughout Foreign Service life, assignments can change at the last minute. Medical clearances get hung up. Immediate family members fall ill or elderly parents suddenly require assistance. If the officer originally slotted for a position cannot go, a replacement will need to be found—and that can start a domino-tumble of reassignments.

Wars and evacuations also wreak havoc with routine bidding cycles and regular summer rotations. However, the officer will still have a job, even if it turns out to be in a new location. In such cases, spouses have to be flexible—even if they or the companies they work for are left empty-handed by the unforeseen circumstances. Flexibility and a positive attitude helps, but it is not always easy to react this way.

Ellen was fortunate. She had been working as a teacher at the International School, well outside her preferred specialty of securities law, because "China had restrictive employment regulations and a surveillance system sophisticated enough to find those that contravened regulations." At the same time, she had been searching for ways to stay involved in her field. She lined up a part-time consulting job in Hong Kong, several hours by train from the Consulate in Guangzhou. She wrote: "Immediately prior to the official start of the job, I was evacuated from China, due to the problems in 1989. I decided to stay in Hong Kong and worked full time until the evacuation was lifted." The International School, on the other hand, was left without a teacher.

Legal status of diplomatic spouses

Diplomats' spouses differ, in their legal status, both from ordinary expatriates and from citizens of the host country. Work permit status depends upon the specific bilateral treaty or de facto work arrangement. In some countries, like China, the host government does not allow work permits for spouses of diplomats, even though ordinary expatriates can obtain employment status. Even when the work permit is not an issue, the fact that laws tend to be 'gray,' rather than black or white, can be a source of frustration to employees and employers alike.

Alexandra explained, "My husband and I were married after he was posted to Monterrey, and thus my paperwork as a diplomatic spouse was initiated several months after we arrived in Mexico. When I was offered the job, my status was not yet official with the Department of State, and according to Mexican law, the process for applying for work papers for diplomatic persons is different from that for regular non-Mexican applicants."

While both processes were expected to take minimal time, Alexandra had to choose one process or the other. She chose to wait for the correct paperwork from State, in order to receive her work permit as a diplomatic spouse. Unfortunately, on top of her six-month job search, that process took an additional five months.

Ellen found that "Indonesia did not permit people holding diplomatic visas to obtain work visas, but two male spouses were working there with work visas in their regular passports." Nonetheless, someone from the administrative section of the embassy requested that she "not give them any trouble" by working on the local economy. So, she explained, "I turned down a job with an American law firm, but accepted another offer working as a consultant on an AID-funded project—a job that did not require a work permit.

In my personal experience, while I was in Prague, I had no difficulties from the Czech side. The embassy submitted a diplomatic note informing the Ministry of Foreign Affairs (MFA) of my intent to work and the MFA's acknowledgement effectively constituted my work permit. However, well-intentioned 'corporate risk managers' in my U.S.-based employer never did resolve their concerns about potential foreign tax liability, even as I departed post, two years later.

Why seek employment outside of U.S. missions overseas?

Spouses who have successfully found employment on the local economy describe a host of advantages, including professional development, broadened social networks, exposure to local culture, fulfilling activity and, in some cases, even higher salaries.

Professional development

Finding local employment in one's area of expertise can be a unique experience that enhances professional development. Jessica successfully navigated the challenges of a job search and landed a position consistent with her background, conducting social work in an educational setting: "My previous job was working with inner-city youth in Indianapolis, Indiana. I was responsible for after-school activities (both educational and social), as well as summer and holiday time activities. I was so fortunate to find a job in Dublin that was completely related to my background. I worked in a disadvantaged/low-income area of Dublin ... with the children who were at risk of dropping out of school.... Activities ranged from basketball teams to family therapy/counseling to homework assistance."

Ellen, with her background in securities law, clearly relished the intellectual challenge of engagement in her field, and found legal work wherever she could. "In Hanoi, there were two American law firms and a few other Western law firms. There were work restrictions, but because there were no Vietnamese to take the job offered to me, the issue of a work permit was never raised. I was hired by a small International/American firm to be in charge of its Hanoi office. My boss worked in the firm's Ho Chi Minh City (Saigon) office. While working at the law firm, I also became involved as a director with two local organizations: the American Chamber of Commerce and the United Nations International School. I wrote several articles on corporate law during those two years, and spoke before local and expatriate audiences on trade law and other issues affecting businesses in Vietnam."

Jaco stated that his work overseas was an incredible professional development experience. He explained that while statistics seems pretty specific, there are, in fact, many different types of statisticians. He considered himself "very lucky" that he found three different projects in his area of specialty: survey sampling and questionnaire design. From Thailand, Jaco traveled on "a very exciting collection of assignments ranging from data collection in the hills of rural East Timor ... to consulting with the Nepalese Ministry of Education." He observed that "[I] would never have had that kind of responsibility/experience staying at my company stateside." Jaco also observed that "once I came back to the U.S. for an interview, the first question out of everyone's mouth was 'Wow, why did you up and move to Bangkok?' This gave me a great jumping-off point for my love of development work, international statistics, and related topics. It really stands out compared to all the other applicants who never leave the DC area."

Salary

Often, jobs on the local economy mean lower salaries than in the U.S. However, many spouses, even those working in developing countries, reported satisfaction with the compensation they received from their local economy jobs. For instance, Patricia was working within the embassy but was dissatisfied with her career development prospects. She explains: "I saw the Baker/McKinsey ad in the little English-language newspaper that came out weekly in Almaty … We used to advertise there for the embassy's local staff positions and all expats read it. I felt I'd gone as far as opportunity would take me as a spouse in the mission, so I decided to call about the job. I'm always open to something that would be more professionally challenging. They offered me the position (with substantially more money, I might add). I looked at our college fund and took it!"

Kathryn observed, "I was lucky to have negotiated contracts that paid me locally, but very decent salaries. I negotiated by pointing out that I did not need housing, health benefits, etc.… and that I would be satisfied with a decent salary (always in U.S. dollars) and flexible vacation time. Usually, the companies I worked for were flexible. It was a win-win situation since they got an expat employee with expertise without the high costs involved. This type of negotiation works best if the company is small. I also worked for large multinationals. They tend to be less flexible since there is a salary range for the position they are trying to fill. However, you can still negotiate to be paid in U.S. dollars and to receive longer vacations than locals."

Ellen reported that in Hanoi, "the salary was lower than what a firm would have paid in the U.S., but in return I negotiated a shorter work week." In Muscat, Oman, "the salary was on par with law firm salaries in the States, and the hours were much better." In Jakarta, "Because I was a contractor on a U.S.-funded project, Price Waterhouse determined my contract fee based on my experience and prior salary history. The fee I received was in the range of what I would have earned in a government attorney job in the U.S." Once she moved to Hong Kong, the "Security and Futures Commission offered a terrific expatriate package. I received a better salary than I would have in the U.S., plus a very generous housing stipend."

Broader social networks

For Ellen, however, another significant benefit was social. When discussing her two employment positions in Saudi Arabia, she explained: "The law firm paid me an hourly rate for work done, which on an annual basis if I had worked 40 hours a week, would be roughly equivalent to what I would have earned in a job with a large law firm. However, the work was erratic. The bank paid a substantially lower salary for a 40-hour week, but I wanted the opportunity to work in the bank as well as the opportunity to get out of my house and into a professional work environment."

Jenna observed, "… I prefer to work outside the embassy, even if it means a lower local wage, to be able to develop my own professional and social network. I think it makes life more interesting in a country."

Jessica explained, "As we were the only family at post without children (and the post was somewhat small to begin with), it was crucial for my sanity to find some friends with our same demographic!" Her sentiments echo those of Karin, for whom salary took a back seat to social contact. She worked as the deputy director of a local language school for a very minimal salary, but, as she wryly observed, "it was cheaper than therapy."

Kathryn observed that work in the embassy and on the local economy both have their rewards: "Working in the embassy provides stability, U.S. benefits such as social security, vacation, etc., and usually, very good hours. Working on the local economy can be challenging because of the long work hours (in China, Hong Kong and Santiago), and less vacation time, but it can broaden one's horizons. We were able to expand our network of friends to include locals and also expats outside of the embassy community. That made our tour so much more fruitful."

Exposure to local culture

Even beyond social contact, working locally provides a different vantage point. Jenna liked the fact that "I was able to get around the country on my own, which was particularly interesting in Bangladesh since it is not a tourist mecca and it isn't really set up for tourists. So visiting project areas as part of my job, I was able to get a more in-depth look at the people and country. I also liked being invited to U.S. and other nationality embassy receptions in my own right, as a consultant of the Asia Foundation rather than as a spouse."

Jo found her experiences in Japan "great fun and a real eye-opener." She elaborated: "I taught English over the phone at home from 8:00 p.m. until 11:00 p.m., with students all over the country calling me for 15-minute blocks of time. One student was the only English speaker living on her island in the south of Japan. Another student, proud of his country's ingenuity, once asked me whether we in the U.S. 'have anything like Tokyo Disneyland'! I taught at a prestigious public high school and went on (more or less mandatory) weekend trips with my fellow English teachers, some of whom would not ever speak English in the classroom … too self-conscious. I helped two translation companies 'get it right,' changing the translators' English into 'real' English. The subjects included everything from golf magazine ads to nuclear power plant cleaning manuals." Over the nearly five years she worked, she clearly relished the insight she gained into Japanese life and culture.

Jessica said she only came to appreciate this sort of access once she was already working. "I truly *lived* in Ireland and was able to see a side of the Irish that not many of the Americans at the embassy were able to experience or appreciate." In addition, she added, "Spouses that work locally are like ambassadors for the U.S. The Irish always had questions about the U.S.: what it was like being from the U.S., what it means to be an American, on and on. A couple of my colleagues even told me that they weren't real fond of Americans but now that they knew an American they realized that we're not that bad! I represented America without even realizing it."

Fulfilling activities

We all define "fulfilling" in different ways. For me, it is a combination of organizational mission, personal remuneration, intellectual challenge, and social interaction.

Initially in Prague, I worked from home as a telecommuter. For nearly six months, I continued in my U.S.-based job with MITRE, a federally funded research and development center. It was an odd arrangement. My colleagues, secretary and supervisor were all based in McLean, Virginia. Our customer, the U.S. Treasury Department, was based in Washington, DC. Not surprisingly, my responsibilities shifted when I crossed the Atlantic. No longer was I visiting customer sites and gathering system information; rather, my contribution took the form of critical comments or additions to others' drafts.

The arrangement seemed ideal: job continuity, flexible hours, plus a U.S. salary and benefits, in an economy with depressed wages, and no real market for systems engineers. However, I found the experiment tremendously unfulfilling. Engagement with my surroundings added absolutely no value to my work. In fact, even normal social interaction carried a cost. A trip into town to meet a new acquaintance for lunch meant two hours unbilled that day. The two halves of what I had enjoyed most about previous research and work experiences—intellectually satisfying challenges and meaningful social engagement—had become oddly disassociated.

My next position, working as the technical sales account executive for a U.S.-based telecommunications software firm, represented a substantial step forward. Still based in Prague, I was on the road two weeks of every month, visiting customer sites and attending trade shows across Europe. Extensive interaction with customers and colleagues during these trips tided me over during the off weeks, when I worked first from a home office and then from a small office in Old Town. Nonetheless, when I began my current job in Kiev, the aspect I most enjoyed was the social interaction with multiple colleagues, most with language or science and engineering backgrounds, all working in the same office!

Ellen accepted a pay cut in order to move from home into a real office. Jo abandoned self-employment as an editor, in order to try a job in the Consular Section. She wrote, "I thought I would most likely give it six months and then get back to my business of editing. Turns out I really enjoyed the work and people from the first day and I am still there after 11 months."

It seems fitting that a discussion of the benefits of employment on the local economy comes back full circle, to employment in the embassy. The spouses who sounded happiest about their patchwork careers were those who viewed meaningful, fulfilling employment as the goal, and embassy or non-embassy jobs as complementary means to attain that goal.

Finding work

The spouses who consistently found work on the local economy have plenty of advice to offer others.

Learn the language

Jenna sums it up: "Definitely try to get a bit of language before you go. I was fortunate to have had five months of Bengali from [the State Department training program] and that certainly helped me in my job. It wasn't the make or break issue that got me hired but it was a huge bonus for The Asia Foundation and it was extremely useful when I had to run meetings with leaders of multiple organizations and they would all break off and speak in Bengali. It was also necessary when I went out into the field and met with people in the communities, many of whom did not speak English."

She added, "Any amount of language is great." I agree, wholeheartedly. It is far easier to compete for jobs available to local applicants if one can say "I'm learning" or "I speak a little and am improving," rather than "I don't speak any."

Ellen's biography captures her sense of the importance of having language: she spent nine months in Indonesian language study before heading to Jakarta; she invested another nine months studying Vietnamese before their tour in Hanoi; and she left work at the Securities and Exchange Commission, in DC, to train in Chinese language, before her tour in Guangzhou/Hong Kong.

I have not been nearly so dedicated about learning in advance. I was fortunate to have started Russian in seventh grade, and I picked up Serbo-Croatian and Slovene once in country. However, before our tour in Prague, I squeezed in fifty-six hours of one-on-one instruction in Czech after work, and I listened to Czech music tapes on my commute all that summer. Once in Prague, while I was telecommuting, I hired a personal tutor both for social companionship and to continue my efforts. Four months after I arrived, I had enough to begin placing cold calls to companies in the IT/Telecom sector. One of those calls ultimately yielded the offer from the Czech systems integrator.

Leverage existing relationships

I have found it easier to walk confidently into a job interview while still gainfully employed. While telecommuting proved less fulfilling than I had hoped, taking my U.S. job with me overseas offered significant advantages as a transition strategy. First and foremost, I was still employed, and still bringing in a significant portion of my U.S. income. However, because I had shifted to an hourly schedule, I could also make time to handle the logistics of our move, learn the language, and search for a local job. When I did accept a new offer, six months after arriving in country, my supervisor and colleagues wished me well and asked that I consider rejoining them once I returned to the U.S.

Ellen has also used existing work to transition into her next location. Working for a U.S. law firm in Muscat, Oman, she had an advantage obtaining a follow-on job when she returned to the U.S. Upon arriving in DC, she worked for the Washington office of that firm for a year, before returning to work at the Securities and Exchange Commission (where she had worked for six years prior to heading overseas). Similarly, when she transitioned from Jakarta to DC, she continued working "for six months or so as a consultant to the Ministry of Finance of Indonesia from Washington."

In Washington, DC, before studying Bengali at the Foreign Service Institute, Jenna had worked for IFES, a democracy and governance organization. Once she got to Bangladesh, she said, "I was able to do a short-term assignment (one week of on-the-ground logistics for an assessment team of two American consultants that was coming to town). The timing was great and I ended up completing this assignment shortly after arriving in Bangladesh. Through the meetings that I set up for the two consultants I was able to meet a number of organizations that I had previously been in touch with from the U.S. during my exploratory networking. What was most helpful was that they were seeing me now in a professional/on-the-ground capacity rather than the faceless job seeker from afar. The day my one-week assignment ended, I was offered a job with The Asia Foundation as a consultant."

Jaco found his first consulting assignment through a colleague at the company where he worked before he left the U.S. "One of my bosses was well known enough in the field to be on a first name basis with the director of U.N. statistics. I met the guy during a conference and he set me up with a gig (temporary job), which was great. Then an old professor that I have always kept in touch with e-mailed me to ask if I'd be interested in doing some work in East Timor (temporary gig #2), working for CAVR, but indirectly for UNDP. I got that job basically without any formal interview because that old professor happens to be the head of the American Statistical Association now. When that project came to a close, I touched base with someone that I had worked with at ESCAP who was starting a small statistics group at UNESCO."

Network

I asked Kathryn whether, as she had looked for work in Hong Kong, Beijing, and Santiago, her search methods/approach had differed at all from a job search in the U.S. She replied more succinctly than most: "The search process was quite similar—relying on contacts and networking first."

Jo explained, "Six months before going to post, I requested that the embassy newsletter be sent to me weekly. Community members who wanted to pass along jobs were advertising regularly, so I got a feel for some of the opportunities. When the time drew near, I contacted the Community Liaison Office (CLO) coordinator, and she agreed to pass on letters that I wrote (no Internet in those days!), which hooked me up with some possibilities. In some cases, I learned more about the jobs and decided not to take them. In others, they worked out and were 'mine' for almost five years."

Jenna expanded, "I strongly believe in networking and information gathering before going to a new post. Find out as much as you can about what the industries are and be creative about what you might do in a post. Talk to as many people as you can about the country you are going to because you never know who knows someone who is there, was there, knows others there, etc."

My search, from Washington, DC, for opportunities in Prague was discouraging. Internet search engines yielded few clues as to which Czech sites might be useful. When I finally found some Czech job sites, most of the openings were quite technical: hard-core programming and database development, for which I had neither the qualifications nor interest. Slightly more useful were the insights gained from English-language business publications directed at expatriate management. The handful of contacts my husband knew from his previous tour also yielded no leads.

Seek locals' guidance and continue networking

Once I got to post, the most productive step I took was to ask a local employee in the embassy's Commercial Section if she could review my resumé and provide any suggestions. Her American boss, whom I had contacted months before, had offered no ideas. Hanna, however, went through her index of business cards and photocopied a page of her contacts in information technology and telecom. These served as the starting point in my cold-calling campaign, which yielded a firm job offer that matched my U.S. salary (and improved substantially on my part-time wages!).

The other offer came through precisely the sort of casual conversation Jenna mentioned. After a brief chat at a party hosted by one of my husband's colleagues, one of the few non-government types there invited me to lunch. An account executive for a telecom software company, she felt my eclectic background, which included some light-weight programming and systems engineering, as well as research interviewing, was well suited to technical sales. Her company hoped to expand its business in Eastern Europe, and so I received a call from the head of technical sales in London. The fact that I had a competing offer likely helped to improve the package offered. Ultimately, I was hired onto the company's New Jersey payroll, which enabled them to provide me a U.S.-level salary and withholding and enabled me to maintain my U.S. security clearance.

When I moved back to DC temporarily, from our next post in Kiev, the fact that my security clearance was still on record made a huge difference. One week after arriving in DC, I had two offers: one from the company I worked for prior to leaving four years before, and the other from the parent corporation of the telecom software firm I'd worked for in Prague. I was able to start work immediately, and so made very good use of the four months prior to my daughter's birth.

Jessica also used the pre-existing networks she found. "When we arrived in Ireland, I met with the principal at the school the kids from the embassy went to. He looked at my CV and gave me a few pointers. I also talked with the Human Resources office in the embassy. This wasn't necessarily for a job in the embassy—but since the office was made up of Irish, I turned to them for advice. For example, they gave the name of a few Irish job banks and websites as well as advice on my CV and interviewing. I found job listings on the Internet and sent my CV and cover letter to a handful of places. I did contact them by telephone, also, as a follow up. I was just so lucky that one of these leads called me in for an interview and they later offered me the job."

Alexandra also found more success when she focused on building her own local network of contacts: "My field is in international development. Prior to arriving in Mexico with my husband for his first tour, I had managed business development efforts at a large USAID contractor. My experience also included positions in organizational development.

"Monterrey has one of the largest universities in Latin America, and so I decided to conduct informational interviews with professors who might be able to tell me more about their fields and possible work in the area.... Through my contacts with professors, I eventually spoke to a department at the university regarding their interest in finding someone with experience in nonprofit management and was hired.... I had the general skills for adapting to this position and was able to draw on my skills working with NGOs and others to help the department design and implement a business plan. I was not, however, interested in the substance of the job and eventually wound up leaving post for a more rewarding position outside of Mexico."

Get out into the community

Jo found her first job in Sweden through less-strategic networking. "While walking my dog, I met someone in my neighborhood who soon began giving me editing to do, encouraged by my editing background from Japan and my human resources educational background. She showed me the ropes of starting my own business; I had the embassy apply for the proper tax number to allow me to get a work permit, and I began to learn how to handle the advantages of business-based tax deductions."

Jenna, who had resigned her first position in Bangladesh to stay home with her new baby, was volunteering one day a week, counseling students who wished to study in the U.S. Participating in a panel talk hosted by the Public Affairs section, she met another panelist, the director of career counseling at East West University in Dhaka. During a second meeting, they together hammered out a proposal for Jenna to develop and teach a course on job searching skills, and he arranged for her to meet with the administrators of the university. She observed, "I was paid a reasonable U.S. hourly rate based on my consultancy daily rate but probably could have asked for more if I had had more time to research what type of salary would be acceptable in this type of situation. I also underestimated how much preparation time I would need for the course. I ended up teaching four separate sessions of the six-module course I developed and it was very well received by the university."

Don't give up

Before I left Prague, I determined that my company had no interest in having me based in Kiev. My supervisor in London directed me to devote my remaining weeks to finding another position. I started with an intense search across our parent company's intranet, looking for any reference to any project in Ukraine. I jotted down clues as I went along—references to individuals, divisions or tasks. Progressively, I drew a 'map' of the corporate activity, which suggested eight disparate parts of the organization had, at some point, conducted work in Ukraine.

My next step was to e-mail, and then interview by phone, division managers from each of these groups. While none were currently engaged in the region, a few provided leads, primarily to former competitors. Not until I got back to the U.S. did I succeed in talking to the manager of the only group that was still active in Ukraine. Ultimately, his team agreed to pick me up. We completed the transfer paperwork from the telecom subsidiary to the parent corporation five weeks after I'd arrived in the U.S. (and just one week before our scheduled departure to Kiev).

However, once I got out to Kiev, that job, so hard sought, was put on hold. The customer, a U.S. government agency, had not succeeded in reaching a diplomatic accord with its counterpart Ukrainian ministry. For the next four months, I spearheaded corporate fundraising for the International Women's Club charity Christmas Bazaar. This volunteer work met my immediate needs for fulfilling engagement and teamwork, while providing a clear picture of the (relatively bleak) commercial scene. While I was back in the U.S., working on customer premises, I ran across a lead to my current position, at a multilateral mission. As the diplomatic agreement was no closer to signature, my new division granted me personal leave, and so I signed a two-year contract to the end of my spouse's planned tour in Kiev.

Use your differences to your advantage

I asked several spouses whether their Foreign Service affiliation made any difference to prospective employers. Jessica replied, "I don't think my affiliation with the State Department made any difference. I think that being an American helped me stand out in the applicant pool. I wouldn't say that I know what I was doing in this whole job search. I was just persistent in researching and following up. Most importantly, I was creative in figuring out how to take advantage of the limited resources I had available to me."

Jo noted, "At the time I was in Tokyo, there was a cachet to studying or practicing English with a native-speaking diplomat." She then clarified, "The advantage was being a native speaker PLUS being creative. One really needed an angle, e.g. energy, humor, being willing to walk across town to deliver translation 're-writing' if the fax did not work, taking an interest in each high school student as if they were the only one."

Jenna observed, "The university thought it was quite prestigious to have someone affiliated with the embassy, but I found they were more impressed with my educational background (Harvard undergrad, Fletcher graduate school). I say 'impressed' because in Bangladesh those types of credentials are highly regarded. I was always being introduced as the lecturer from Harvard, when in fact my affiliation with Harvard was simply that I did my undergraduate there so it was a bit misguided."

Ellen used her relatively unusual professional affiliation as a calling card: "In the smaller posts, the whole city of expats seemed to either know I was coming before I came or learned soon thereafter that I (with my particular skills) had arrived. Therefore, the jobs often came to me without a great deal of searching (I'm exaggerating a bit)."

Building a career

In 1995, I thought I had a problem parsed. I knew I wanted to live and work overseas. The typical Foreign Service tour, two to three years per country, seemed perfect: long enough to learn the language and get to know the culture, but not long enough to get bored. The challenge was finding a spouse who would agree to follow me around the world. The closest candidates—a physicist, a computer scientist, and an electrical engineer—were fine friends, extroverted and interested in meeting people from other cultures. But their jobs were not portable.

Experienced Washington hands warned me that joining the Foreign Service as a single woman was an unlikely path to marital bliss. To their (and my) complete surprise, I met my future husband, then a mid-level officer, just one week into my first tour. Too soon, we bumped into an expectation that in a tandem relationship, the junior officer's career should take precedence over the senior officer's, until tenure has been granted. With little appreciation for the magnitude of the new challenge I was embracing, I resigned my commission.

Never would I have imagined the string of job titles that followed: Senior Information Systems Engineer; Technical Services Account Executive; National Security Analyst; and Project Coordinator for Sustainability Promotion. For better or for worse, and despite my liberal arts credentials, I had become the 'engineer' married to a diplomat. Pursuing a fulfilling, independent career, while at the same time trailing my spouse around the globe, has required the flexibility of a contortionist.

As others' stories attest, my experience has not unique. The small number of spouses who have worked in multiple full-time positions outside the embassy describe a string of jobs loosely linked, at best.

Kathryn, who has worked successfully in China, Hong Kong and Chile, wrote, "My resumé tends to be all over the place because I had to take what I could get in some places. However, I gained extensive international experience in all of the jobs and I tried to build my resumé in marketing and business development."

Ellen wrote, "Although I have had great jobs, I have also compromised a lot when it has come to salaries or benefits. I have done so on the basis that it WAS a good job that would help me get my next, even better, job where we moved next." She explained that several factors have recently changed her attitude. Given the recent experience of not working for an entire tour, she now places more value on the opportunity to pursue more leisurely pursuits, such as involvement in the international women's community. In addition, her age and experience have led her to set a higher price on her availability to work. She concluded, "I have a narrow focus for my job search this time around. I want either to work at the OECD or teach at the university level."

Jenna, despite her initial success, has also re-focused: "I am doing the Fast Train teacher certification program at George Mason for elementary education. I will be finished with the basis coursework and will have a provisional license that allows me to teach overseas by the end of my husband's one-year language training. While I love development work, my priorities have changed since having children and I would like to work in a field that mirrors their schedule more, i.e. summers off, same holidays, etc. So I am looking to shift careers into one that is also very portable for Foreign Service spouses."

For those spouses who are committed to building professional careers in areas outside public diplomacy or the international schools, the following suggestions may be useful:

1. **Make current decisions with a view to long-term flexibility.**

   Given two job offers, choose the organization with wider geographic reach, better name recognition in subsequent job searches, or more promising career development. The ability to retain security clearances should not be underrated. However, working in a foreign, rather than a U.S. company, can be very culturally rewarding.

2. **Market your flexibility.**

   Some potential employers will appreciate varied experience. Some will shudder at the apparent lack of focus. Fortunately, as one gains experience, hiring decision-makers tend to be more senior and, often, to think more strategically. From their vantage point, proven ability to thrive under varied conditions is an asset!

3. **Network backwards.**

   Maintain contact with former colleagues and employers. You never know when you might be brought back to Washington, DC unexpectedly, or return to a foreign country for a second tour. Leveraging a global network of contacts increases the likelihood of success in each new job search.

4. **Plan forward.**

   Even "regular" careers tend to move two to three years at a time. Develop mentoring relationships and new skills with a view to the future.

5. **Take inspiration from earlier 'blocks' in the patchwork quilt.**

   If there is no market for the 'red'-toned blocks, see if there's a market for the 'blue' ones. Ellen's long career included blocks of teaching and blocks of law. I've alternated between systems engineering/technical work and more policy-oriented employment.

In conclusion

Ellen commented, "I think the State Department, through the Family Liaison Office, has come a long, long way in its effort to make it easier to work on the local market. There are a lot of exciting projects in the pipeline and now in effect. However, I think that the embassies have to be nudged regularly to evaluate their own roles in the process. At my various posts, I have seen complacency, indifference, and just plain refusal to recognize the need of spouses to work as an issue to be addressed. It has taken an increase in the number of male spouses at posts—and females in the Foreign Service—to spur some of these Ambassadors and Deputy Chiefs of Mission (DCMs) to push the bilateral work agreements or otherwise try to open doors to spousal employment."

I have to agree with the conclusion of Douglas Kerr, who wrote in the first *Realities of Foreign Service Life* book about the "Plight of the Pantoflarz": "Those [trailing] husbands who've had the most success to date are the ones who initially recognized the full scale of the difficulties they would face and that they alone would have to surmount those obstacles…. Knowing that they would have to beat the bushes for any and every opening, they have arrived at post predisposed to do so. They hit the ground running, with a fully formed assessment of the difficulties they would face."

Male or female, an accompanying spouse who wants fulfilling employment will be most successful when he or she takes full responsibility for making that job search work. The embassy can help lay the groundwork—negotiating work agreements and sharing its institutional knowledge about the local market. However, the spouse's own efforts, networking, perseverance, creativity, and flexibility play a far more important role. Setting out with eyes wide open to the challenges is the best preparation for a journey that, like most adventures, can be draining, exhilarating, brutally hard, and sweetly rewarding. Best of luck!

Chris D. Stuebner grew up wholly in the U.S., as the daughter of an IBM engineer and a homemaker/nurse. She traveled overseas for the first time as a second-grader, tagging along on a rare business trip to Germany. Her next trip was not until her junior year of high school, when she toured Moscow, Kiev, Odessa and Leningrad with the Russian class. A scholarship from the U.S. Information Agency enabled her to spend her senior year in Rijeka, Yugoslavia. She attended college and grad school in the U.S., but spent several semesters and summers abroad: in London; Tartu (Estonia); Odessa and Kherson (Ukraine); Ljubljana (Slovenia); and Skopje (Macedonia). Since joining the Foreign Service community, she has lived in Almaty, Prague and Kiev.

Conversations with
Tandem Couples

by Patricia Linderman

In the Foreign Service, a "tandem couple"—evoking the romantic image of a pair pedaling a bicycle built for two—is simply any married pair of career foreign affairs agency employees. Some 11% percent of Foreign Service officers, along with a full 30% of Office Management Specialists abroad, are tandems. But how does this work in practice? They benefit from two professional salaries and retirement plans, of course—but are they also entitled to two shipments? Two houses? How hard is it to be assigned to the same country? Can they work together on the job? If they have children, how do they balance their work and family lives, with frequent moves and possible separations?

I spoke to a diverse group of tandem couples in order to find out. Among them were:

- June Tang Williamson, who is a Foreign Service Specialist in Information Management, as is her husband;

- Cheryl Payne, an Office Management Specialist, whose husband is a Security Technical Specialist;

- Greg Delawie, Deputy Chief of Mission in Zagreb, whose wife, Vonda, is also a high-level Foreign Service officer;

- Ambassador W. Robert Pearson (former Director General of the Foreign Service) and Margaret ("Maggie") C. Pearson, an officer in the Senior Foreign Service.

I combined their answers with information provided by other sources (sometimes omitting names to protect privacy) to address some of the most frequently asked questions about tandems.

Q: How does one become a tandem couple?

Numerous variations are possible, of course: some couples join at the same time, while some are already in the Foreign Service when they meet and marry. Often, a partner starts out as an accompanying spouse and later joins the Service.

The Foreign Service exam is routinely given at embassies overseas, so that accompanying spouses need not return to the U.S. to take it. Although spouses are not given preference in hiring as Foreign Service officers or Specialists, their experiences abroad can definitely be helpful as they take the exams.

After June Tang Williamson's children grew up and started their own families, she and her husband decided to work together for the first time in their 30-year marriage. Since they both had master's degrees in the computer field, they decided to apply as information systems specialists and were both accepted.

Cheryl Payne notes: "We joined separately and did not know each other. We met at our first post; I was doing a temporary duty (TDY) assignment at the embassy. Later, he came to my post and we established a relationship by phone, e-mail and visits, ultimately marrying."

Greg and Vonda Delawie met in the same A-100 (junior officer training) class and got married four and a half years later.

Ambassador Pearson was the first of the couple to join the Foreign Service, but Margaret Pearson had always had a strong interest in overseas service—in fact, she applied to join the Peace Corps when she was only 13. (They advised her to come back later!) At their first post, Auckland, Mrs. Pearson took the Foreign Service exam. She was hired as a USIA [U.S. Information Agency, now Public Diplomacy] officer and sent for language study and training.

Q: How does the assignment process work? Are tandems routinely assigned together?

On this issue, the State Department combines two rather contradictory principles: "worldwide availability" and a family-friendly assignment process. As stated on the Department's website: "In cases where both husband and wife are foreign affairs agency employees (a tandem couple), both are expected to be willing to accept assignments to a post other than that of the tandem spouse in order to meet the needs of the Service. The Department recognizes the importance of family unity and will make every effort to assign a tandem couple to the same post at the same time."

In other words, tandems are not routinely assigned together, and in order to advance their careers, they must be willing, in theory, to accept separate assignments if they are needed elsewhere. In practice, tandems can usually find positions in the same country, especially if they are willing to compromise. For instance, one partner might accept a less-challenging position or one that is out of his or her usual specialty. The jobs also may not begin and end at the same time, so that the partners may spend a year or two apart. It is also possible for one partner to go on leave without pay (LWOP) status for a limited period in order to accompany the other partner.

Cheryl Payne and her husband have faced all of these difficulties in their search for posts together. She describes their experiences during the most recent bidding cycle: "I had a handshake [on a job] but they would not give the post to him. So I vacated the assignment, we talked and decided I should bid on my own and he would follow on LWOP status. Fortunately, and this was not a plan on our part, the post I was offered had a position opening for him during winter cycle [both were previously on the summer cycle, meaning that they transferred in summer]. We are still waiting for him to be paneled [confirmed for the assignment]."

Greg Delawie notes: "We would not consider separate tours, and we have been fortunate enough to date to have avoided leave without pay. The main challenge has been to find two jobs of the appropriate grade and cone [specialty] in the same city. We have found that it is easiest to arrange this when in Washington; we have spent about 50% of our married careers in Washington, with one tour out and the next tour in Washington."

The Pearsons made a decision early on that they would not accept separate assignments. This has led to plenty of anxiety at assignment time. Often one job started 2–3 months before the other, but their periods of separation have always been 6 months or less. Along with their personal policy of not accepting separate assignments, they had to decide whose career would take precedence in case they were unable to find two good jobs in one place. (His, hers, or alternating?) In practice, they have given priority to Ambassador Pearson's jobs, saying that Margaret "chose flexibility." However, Mrs. Pearson has also done extremely well, rising to the Senior Foreign Service. One of her most challenging assignments was press spokesperson for the U.S. Mission to NATO, where Mr. Pearson was also assigned.

Sometimes career considerations and the desire for professional challenges motivate tandems to choose separate tours. Tatiana and Michael Gfoeller, in their article "A Career Built for Two" (*Foreign Service Journal*, May 2002), describe their dilemma as they both rose higher in the Service and wanted positions at the level of deputy chief of mission (DCM). They were still too junior to be assigned to this position at a large post with several missions (such as Brussels), and the smaller posts to which they could aspire did not have two jobs at this level. They write: "Making the best of the situation, we each bid on DCM positions in two relatively small embassies, Ashgabat, Turkmenistan (for Tatiana) and Chisinau, Moldova (for Michael). Having enjoyed those management challenges, we followed up those assignments with a DCMship in Yerevan, Armenia, for Michael and a posting as deputy principal officer (as well as acting consul general for half a year) in St. Petersburg for Tatiana."

Q: Can tandems work together? What about the problem of having one supervise the other?

The Gfoellers took advantage of a unique opportunity to work together: team-teaching for one year under the Virginia and Dean Rusk Fellowship at Georgetown University, a program for which tandems are especially encouraged to apply.

June Tang Williamson and her husband work together in the Information Management section. She notes: "People in our own shop had a hard time dealing with us at first. We made sure that we don't do the same job at work. Vacation time is another hard deal."

As junior officers, tandems may work together in the same area, such as the consular section. However, nepotism rules prohibit one member of a tandem couple from supervising the other. This often becomes more of an issue as the tandem officers rise in their careers.

Fortunately, there are usually ways around the problem. Greg Delawie notes: "After 16 years of marriage, we finally encountered a situation where one of us could not supervise the other because one of us was assigned as a Deputy Chief of Mission (DCM). Fortunately the Ambassador and the Bureau were willing to agree to an alternate supervisory arrangement, whereby the non-DCM member of the couple is supervised directly by the Ambassador."

When Mr. Pearson was DCM in Paris, Maggie Pearson served as press attaché and information director, reporting directly to the Ambassador, so that her husband did not supervise her. When he was assigned as Ambassador to Turkey, however, Mrs. Pearson could not bid on the post directly. Nevertheless, an arrangement was worked out allowing her to live and work in Ankara: she was officially assigned to Washington and supervised there on a telecommuting basis. Her assignment was to serve as Special Adviser for Central and Eastern

European Property Affairs, overseeing the return of property confis-
cated during the Nazi and Communist eras. In addition, she took nine
months of leave without pay while in Turkey, pursuing opportunities
such as travel and volunteering, which she reports finding "also very
satisfying."

Q: What benefits do tandems receive?

According to the State Department website, "Each employee is
independent of the other, i.e., each member of a tandem couple maintains their own separate orders and entitlements (except housing)."
This means that tandem couples are entitled to two household shipments (or a double weight allowance), but only one house or apartment, of the size appropriate to the number of people in their family
and their responsibilities for official entertaining.

For posts where unfurnished housing is provided, each tandem partner is entitled to a shipment of 18,000 pounds. For furnished posts,
the figure is 7,200 pounds each. However, State Department transportation official Mette Beecroft cautions: "You should not plan on each
taking 7,200 pounds. You would have far too much to fit into ONE
dwelling. As for UAB [unaccompanied air baggage, also known as air
freight], now each of you is entitled to 250 pounds, the amount to
which the first traveler is entitled. If you have children, they would be
put on the orders of one of you, not on both parents. You are also each
entitled to an automobile. Though a word of caution here: In some
countries, if two cars belong to the same family, the local government
will say, in effect: 'OK! Your family has imported your first car—and
that's the limit.' They will levy taxes on the second car. The concept of
the tandem couple is not understood everywhere. In any case—something to watch out for."

*Q: Are two foreign affairs employees who are living together but unmarried
considered to be tandems?*

No. As the GLIFAA (Gays and Lesbians in Foreign Affairs Agencies) organization notes: "The Department does not consider unmarried couples to be 'tandem couples' for bidding and assignment purposes. Thus, you and your FSO partner would have to bid on positions at the same post, and would be considered as two separate bidders. It is certainly possible for you and your partner to be assigned to the same post, particularly if you make your wishes clear during the assignments process, but there are no guarantees that two officers will be assigned together, even if they are a traditional tandem couple. The needs of the service and the system's efforts to best accommodate the interests of all bidders play an important role in the process" (**www.glifaa.org**).

Q: How do tandems with children manage moves, separations and childcare issues?

Greg and Vonda Delawie, with two children, report: "We have always had a live-in babysitter, and we have not had assignments which required a great deal of regular overtime."

When Maggie Pearson was hired as a USIA officer, she was pregnant with their only child, Matthew, at that time. The transition to Beijing, Mr. Pearson's next post, was their most difficult move in the Foreign Service. Mrs. Pearson wanted to be assigned to Beijing as well, but it was very difficult for her to get an assignment. After much negotiation, she was given a junior officer position in the consular section (she later switched to a USIA job). Some colleagues in the Department, she reports, actually advised her to leave her baby with relatives in the United States, because she would be "too busy" as a junior officer to be a mother.

At home after work, the Pearsons alternated studying Chinese with caring for their young son. The family had a nanny from the Philippines and hoped to take her with them to Beijing, but the Chinese government denied her a visa. They ended up with a Chinese nanny chosen for them by the government. Later, the Filipina nanny joined them again for the Pearsons' assignment in Brussels.

When Matthew was older, they were able to find good after-school programs for him, and the work-family balance became easier. Of course, transitions can always be hard on Foreign Service kids: when the family transferred to a new post in the summer when he was 13, he accused his parents of "ruining his life," but by Thanksgiving, he had adjusted quite well.

When the Gfoellers took separate assignments for four years in a row, they originally planned that their son, Emmanuel, would alternate years with each parent. However, he settled in so effectively in Ashgabat with Tatiana—enjoying school, friends, amateur archeological expeditions and camping in the desert—that they decided not to move him mid-tour, so he spent two years with his mother in Turkmenistan and the next two years with his father in Yerevan, Armenia.

Q: What are some of the main advantages of being a tandem couple?

According to June Tang Williamson, who joined the Foreign Service along with her husband later in their careers, the most enjoyable aspect is "being together and sharing the experience. We did not have much time to do things together when the kids were young." Cheryl Payne notes: "Double the weight allowance, a spouse who understands what you do and why you work the way you do. Also, why there are some things you can't discuss." In Greg Delawie's view, "The main advantage is that we both are able to work in our chosen profession."

The Pearsons cite two main benefits: both spouses have the chance to work and advance in a professional career, and at the same time they have many shared interests, since they are active in the same field. The Gfoellers find their "partnership" approach exhilarating and satisfying, writing that "having a tandem career is great, despite all the challenges, and maybe because of them."

Q: What are some of the disadvantages?

Cheryl Payne points to "limitations on where we can go—posts I would love to go to and cannot bid on until he retires." According to Greg Delawie, "The main disadvantage is that tandem assignments are more difficult to arrange. The pool of jobs is much more limited. Although it is difficult to quantify, we have probably been promoted more slowly because we made some compromises in the assignments we accepted."

The Pearsons identify one potential pitfall they believe they have avoided: letting their life as a couple and a family be swallowed up by work issues. They've counteracted this by actively maintaining "a life outside of work," including cultural interests, hobbies and family activities.

Several respondents mentioned a lack of understanding from some non-tandem officers and family members. "There are people who are envious because we are a dual-income couple and people who resent the double weight allowance," says one officer. Another adds: "The current attitude appears to be anti-tandem: we should not be kept together and just accept that. This is from non-tandems, but probably people who have spouses who do not work and there is no question of their being separated unless the FS employee is assigned to a position where family cannot accompany them. I think the FS is non-family friendly."

Greg Delawie notes: "A tandem couple is a good deal for the Department, with one house instead of two, and two happily employed professionals. But as a member of a tandem couple, I do not endorse special deals for tandems (by which I mean jobs for which an officer is not truly qualified) because it is not fair to the post or to non-tandem officers. I know that we have never had a tandem assignment for which either of us was not qualified. Nevertheless, there is a perception among non-tandems that tandems do get special treatment."

Q: Do you have any advice for new officers who are starting out as tandems?

June Tang Williamson advises: "Try to work in different fields. You must be very flexible and open-minded." Cheryl Payne notes: "You have to make the decision on separation. Will it happen during your careers? And, whose career will take priority—and how to handle that."

In their article, the Gfoellers counsel tandems to "volunteer for tough assignments." For one thing, if a post is not highly sought-after, tandems are more likely to get the assignment of their choice. They also recommend that tandems "bid on posts where there are several U.S. missions." In addition to increasing the range of jobs available, having several missions reduces nepotism concerns.

According to Greg Delawie, "The couple needs to decide whether staying together is their top priority, and if so, to accept the disadvantages (minor as they can be) that go along with that. Probably the couple would also be wise to invest in a house or apartment in the Washington area, because it is likely they will be serving there on a regular basis."

Patricia Linderman, one of the editors of the present book as well as the first volume, is co-author of The Expert Expatriate: Your Guide to Successful Relocation Abroad *(Nicholas Brealey Intercultural, see www.expatguide.info) and Editor in Chief of* Tales from a Small Planet, www.talesmag.com *. A Foreign Service spouse since 1990, she has lived in Port of Spain, Trinidad; Santiago, Chile; Havana, Cuba; Leipzig, Germany and Falls Church, Virginia with her husband and their two sons.*

Foreign Service Highlights

by Kevin Ogley

A career in the Foreign Service offers many different opportunities, not just for the diplomat but also for the spouse and children. We've found that interesting and wonderful things now happen far more often than in our previous lives.

Here are some of my highlights:

- My wife and I have met a variety of politicians, officials, and foreign diplomats. The opportunity to speak to the people whose decisions shape the world has been fascinating.

- Being in the Foreign Service makes it far easier to meet local and international celebrities. During our first year in South Africa, we met Brad Pitt, NBA basketball players and famous local television presenters, and we were guests at a reception for England's National Cricket Team (I'm English and this was a particular highlight for me; wonderful embassy staff arranged our invitation).

- We have an amazing, big house with a swimming pool, provided by the Embassy, and we can afford full-time domestic help.

- The adventure of exploring the culture and sights of the host country has included everything from stroking the tummies of white lion cubs to romantically wandering the countryside and historic cities.

- We've had fantastic help in sorting out the little (and big) things in life. We have experienced a strong community and benefited from the wonderful people whose job it is to help you. People deal with your potentially stressful situations and make your life easier. If you need anything from advice on a restaurant, repairs to the house or help finding your spouse a job, there are people at the embassy who can help.

- We've been able to offer our friends and family fantastic opportunities for holidays and experiences they never would otherwise have had.

In short, we have seen and done a great number of things we would never have experienced if we were not part of the Foreign Service, and the most exciting aspect is that there is always more adventure and excitement ahead.

Kevin Ogley is a freelance journalist and a Foreign Service spouse currently living in South Africa with his wife Dina. They are expecting their second son and have a 20-month-old boy called Kevin. As well as writing, Kevin is heavily involved in promoting and improving sports within the government school system in South Africa and is a partner in a sports management and coaching business.

PART V
Challenging Moments

Truth or Policy: Speaking Your Mind in the Foreign Service

by Justin P. Friedman

It was the make-or-break question in the interview. "There are going to be times when you personally disagree with U.S. government policies. What are you going to do about it?" We hired the woman who answered, "It's all a question of professionalism. I will follow U.S. policy. If I felt I could no longer do so in good conscience, I would have to resign."

Working for a foreign government, our Locally Engaged Staff like Vlatka face this question every day. I doubt that most Foreign Service officers (FSOs) ever come close to resigning over a policy dispute. However, at least three FSOs made very public and, for the Bush Administration, very embarrassing resignations in the months prior to the Iraq War. This was one of the largest policy-induced exoduses from the Foreign Service since the Vietnam War. It raises the question: what would it take for you, or me, to decide to abandon a fascinating and rewarding career?

For most of us, the answer is, "a heck of a lot." I have never thought seriously about resigning in my eleven years in the Foreign Service. I love the work and I love the intellectual challenge of having my own ideas put to the test by sharp, well-informed people. However, every once in a while some issue crosses my desk and I wonder if I've gone crazy or if my colleagues are suffering from a mass case of collective stupidity. The question is, how do you cope with that grey area of issues where there are no absolute rights and wrongs? And, for most of us, how do we decide how far to push our personal views versus swallowing our pride/ego and shilling for some policy with which we may personally disagree?

FSO—one job or two?

Every year, some political pundit (either from the right or the left) says that the Foreign Service is "disloyal to the President and his policies." What these pundits fail to understand is that being an FSO is actually two jobs at once.

When we're inside the secure walls of the embassy overseas or at Main State back in Washington, we have a duty to "tell it like it is." If you don't have the guts to go against the flow and challenge received wisdom from inside the policy-making system, how critical are you going to be of what you are told by foreign officials? After all, that's what the U.S. taxpayer is paying us to do. We have to go beyond the obvious, pat analyses of the blow-dried, 24 hour cable news correspondent and explain the real sources of foreign behaviors and how we can influence other societies and governments to advance America's interests. This is true whether you are explaining why the current government cannot sign an important agreement with us or why it really does take three workers to change a light bulb in the ambassador's residence.

As a group, FSOs tend to score as strong critical (skeptical) thinkers on psychological or personality profiles. In my experience, that's a good thing. My bosses have always challenged me to do my best to punch holes in their best ideas. Call it survival of the fittest policy, but if you aren't willing to tell me I'm wrong, even if I outrank you, than I really don't want to work with you. But the reverse is also true. If you don't have the intellectual honesty to admit someone has a better idea and then support it wholeheartedly, there is no place for you in the Foreign Service.

When we're talking outside the embassy, however, we have to explain and defend U.S. policies in a way that our audience will understand and, we hope, sympathize with. In public, there is no "gosh, I really don't agree with our policy on kumquat subsidies; if I were back in Washington, I would try to change the President's mind on this one." We support U.S. policy. Period. No winks or twitches. Just as a lawyer must use every tool at his or her command to serve the client, a diplomat must use every fact and argument at his or her disposal to advance the official U.S. view. That is professionalism, plain and simple, and most of us thrive on the challenge.

Where the job gets frustrating—dealing with foreign audiences or inside the building—is when the person you're talking to fails to understand which job you are doing. Let me share a couple real-life experiences I've had in my eleven years in the Foreign Service to give you a flavor of how this works in practice.

Inside the Controlled Access Area—"just say no"

At an embassy overseas, the Ambassador is the personal representative of the President of the United States. This means that he or she outranks everyone at the mission and, from a protocol standpoint, just about any official American who comes for a visit. I've worked for Ambassadors (and senior officials in Washington) who can handle this responsibility and will always challenge you not to agree with them too quickly. I've also worked with people whose sense of personal power seems to have weakened their willingness to accept limits on their authority.

On two of my tours overseas, I worked as a consular officer, issuing visitor visas to qualified foreign citizens and denying visas to just about everyone else. I once had a young applicant who needed to travel to the U.S. to get some very expensive cancer treatments unavailable just about anywhere else in the world. When I realized that the company that was promising to finance the treatment was on a list of businesses suspected of being controlled by organized criminals, I denied the visa. The next day in front of the embassy's senior leadership or "country team," the Ambassador asked me why the son of a very highly placed government official had been denied a visa. I explained the suspicious source of financing, but the Ambassador instructed me to issue the visa anyway on his personal authority because of the importance of the government official. I screwed up my nerve and said, "Sir, you don't have the legal authority to issue visas. And even if you did, it would be a mistake because this person can be permanently excluded from entering the U.S., along with his father (your contact) for being connected with organized criminals." The Ambassador started to object, but I was rescued by the Deputy Chief of Mission (#2 in an embassy) who recommended that we get an advisory opinion from Washington.

The moral of my story: it's okay to say no to power, but be sure you're on solid ground. Oh yes, and it doesn't hurt to have a powerful ally.

The kicker: we asked Washington for that advisory opinion. However, we could only show that the money for the treatment passed through a criminal organization in a third country. The claimed source of the money was suspicious, but as yet not proven to be a criminal organization. We were instructed that we could not deny the visa on the grounds I had cited. I put my tail between my legs and issued the visa.

When you just can't agree with the policy

So, what happens when you've done your personal reality and morality checks and still can't agree with the official U.S. policy. Do you throw away a career you love and quit the Foreign Service? Fortunately, there's another option: the dissent channel.

The dissent channel was created in order to allow officers to make principled challenges to official policy without having to have their message approved by their chain of command. These messages go directly to the top of the State Department—and they are read.

So what happens if you write a dissent message—are you shipped off to nowhere and never get promoted? No. Some of the most distinguished professionals in the State Department have written dissent messages and gone on to become Ambassadors. I've had the honor to work with several officers who wrote a dissent message objecting to

U.S. policy in the Balkans in the early 1990's of standing by while Slobodan Milosevic and his cronies carved up Yugoslavia. These people are still in the Service, getting desirable assignments, and moving up the career ladder.

The kicker here: it took a while, but eventually their recommendation to lift the arms embargo against Bosnia and use U.S. airpower to strike at Serbian targets became U.S. policy.

Out and about among friends—it's still a free country

Just because you've joined the Foreign Service does not mean that you've given up the right to make your own political choices. In my experience, FSOs politically run the full range of the ideological spectrum. At my first post overseas, one of the other first-tour officers had previously served as an intern for Senator Edward Kennedy (known to be about as liberal a politician as they come in U.S. politics) and the other had left a job at the Heritage Foundation (a very conservative Washington think tank) to join the Service. No one can be expected to abandon his or her personal beliefs when doing the job. However, there are right times to keep your personal values to yourself and right times to let them shine.

When talking to family and friends I follow two basic rules: tell them the truth and tell them the truth. When asked, I always try to explain the rationale behind U.S. policy, pointing out a clear U.S. national interest and a well-thought-out strategy. In these cases I am fully comfortable taking the "official line." For example, before the start of the Iraq War, I told my friends—who asked quite often—that I fully supported our policy of giving teeth to UN Security Council resolutions requiring Saddam Hussein to prove he had fully disarmed himself of chemical, biological, and radiological/nuclear weapons.

On controversial issues such as this, I have found that the debate is rarely about what the U.S. interest is, but rather how we go about pursuing that interest. Sometimes elements of our national strategies and tactics are driven by the specific values of the current President, Secretary of State, and/or influential members of Congress. Even on issues where I disagree with elements of the official policy, I do my best to explain that policy. Then I explain how my personal values do or do not line up with the policy and how that leads me to the same or a different view on the issue.

Public speaking—to a U.S. audience

Whatever your personal views might be, when you are invited to speak in public in the U.S., your audience will expect you to support official policies. That's the easy part. One of my jobs gave me the opportunity to participate in a number of public events in Washington, DC, and I welcomed the opportunity to lay out U.S. policy on international oil and gas pipelines for an interested audience. My favorite challenge is participating in open question and answer sessions and I try to allow for this whenever the program format permits. So far, I've been lucky enough to emerge from the rough and tumble of explaining and defending official policy without making any major mistakes.

The hard part of speaking in the U.S. is when your audience wants you to criticize official policy. Not too long ago, I participated in the State Department's Hometown Diplomat program. Speaking to a room full of eighty or ninety students from my old high school, I got the very question with which I started this article. I'm happy to report that my answer was pretty close to what Vlatka gave us in her job interview. I think the student who posed the question was really asking why I hadn't resigned over the Iraq war. I hope she walked away with an understanding that reasonable people could support U.S. policy in this instance, even if she may not ever agree with that policy.

Talking to non-Americans

The best part of the job of diplomat, in my view, is explaining U.S. policies and actions to non-Americans. I've found, as I'm sure many others have before me, that the best way to reach a foreign audience is to find a link: a shared value that you can build on to explain a specific policy. I believe that our core national beliefs—in freedom, democracy, the rule of law and respect for the dignity of the individual—have been and always will be attractive to audiences from all nations and cultures.

So how do you connect to an audience and not undermine their trust in us and our core beliefs when discussing events like the abuse of detainees by U.S. military personnel at the Abu Ghraib prison in Iraq?

My answer is that the U.S. is a country ruled by law. We have a history of investigating and prosecuting crimes committed by our citizens, our military, and our leaders regardless of their power, prestige, or station in life. There is an established process to hold individuals accountable for their actions or failures to prevent actions such as those which occurred at Abu Ghraib. Our system has demonstrated its ability to police its own. Justice is probably better served if we do not abandon our responsibilities to an external legal body.

I may have left out a point or two, but my answer is essentially a restatement of the official line on Abu Ghraib. In this case, it's not just policy, it's what I believe. That doesn't mean that you have to agree with me to join the Foreign Service. However, I believe my best arguments are those I make not out of simple repetition of the official policy but out of sincere personal belief. Regardless of whether you repeat the official language or restate it in your own words, you have to be ready to answer hard questions with conviction. If you can't, you're not ready to serve your country as a diplomat.

Foreign Service officer Justin Friedman has served in consular and political assignments in Kiev, Ukraine; Ottawa, Canada; Zagreb, Croatia; as well as in Washington, DC, where he worked on the Russia Desk and as Special Assistant for Caspian Basin Energy Diplomacy. With his wife, Claudette

Friedman (also the author of an article in this volume) and their three children, he is currently on his way to Brunei Darussalam, where he will serve as Deputy Chief of Mission.

Duty Officer

by Paul Poletes

Being duty officer is a simple fact of Foreign Service life. Like packouts and Fourth of July receptions, it's something we all have to live with. But for the most part, pulling duty is a relatively painless experience. After lugging the duty bag around for a week, you thankfully dump it on someone else. In my last four years, working in Dhaka and Bishkek, I can count on one hand the number of duty calls I received that required anything more than a single, brief phone call.

But God help you if you're in a country visited by literally hundreds of thousands of Americans each year—all of them, it seems, just waiting to get into some kind of trouble like losing a passport or going to jail. These things happened all the time to American citizens while I was duty officer in a Western European country.

Being duty officer there was like re-living the American Citizen Services portion of the Foreign Service Consular Course, where officers are trained to deal with every possible calamity that can befall an American overseas.

On two occasions when I was not the duty officer, American citizens fell overboard from cruise ships that were in or approaching local waters. Unfortunately, both of the people died.

Being duty officer would have been much worse, however, were it not for the so-called "Security Receptionists." These receptionists were local employees who answered the phones after hours, and were the duty officers' best friends. The Security Receptionists spoke the local language, seemed to have every phone number in the country on hand, and were experts at deflecting frivolous calls.

Ironically, the toughest duty case I ever dealt with involved no American citizens at all. An Albanian man, living illegally in the U.S., had been arrested and was being held in an INS detention facility in New Jersey. Somehow, the poor man had fallen three stories from a raised walkway and fractured his skull. He lay unconscious and near death in a hospital, while INS officials scrambled to locate his family, who were living in my host country.

It was just past 6 p.m. on a Friday when the duty phone rang. (NOTE: All crises involving the duty officer seem to happen on Friday, just after the close of business [COB], when it's too late to arrange for someone to come in to the embassy in the morning.) The embassy after-hours operator put through a call from the Albanian man's daughter. The daughter explained what had happened to her father, and tearfully begged me to issue visas to her and her brother so that they could see their father before he died.

That night I was up until nearly 3 a.m., calling the daughter back multiple times. I called the INS district office in New Jersey, which fully supported the issuance of visas to the man's son and daughter. I called the hospital and confirmed that the man was in critical condition and could die at any moment. I talked to the Visa Chief in the Consular Section, who had no objection to my issuing emergency travel letters, which were used in place of visas.

On Saturday I met with the son and daughter and collected their passports and photos for the travel letters. Two hours later they had their letters and promptly left for the U.S. About a month later I received a letter from INS, thanking me for my efforts to help unite the Albanian family.

Another memorable case happened the following spring, as American tourists began flooding into the city. An elderly tourist slipped and fell at a historical site and broke her hip. She was taken to the hospital, where she and her husband (neither of whom could speak the local language) tried in vain to communicate with the doctors and nurses (none of whom could speak English).

The after-hours operator patched through a call to me from the woman's husband, who was nearly deaf. I had to shout as loudly as I could into the cell phone so that he could hear me. Finally, I just gave up trying to talk to him over the phone and drove to the hospital to meet with him in person.

I arrived at the hospital and quickly found the woman, who was being well taken care of, despite her inability to communicate with the nurses and doctors. She and her husband, in their eighties, were totally in the dark about what to do next and how long she would be in the hospital. I met with the doctor and discovered, despite my limited language skills, that the woman needed surgery to implant a pin in her hip. I broke the news to the couple, who took it surprisingly well.

I went out and bought some English-language magazines for the woman, whose only entertainment in the hospital for the next two weeks would be local TV. I gave her the magazines and promised to visit her again the next day (Sunday).

When I came back on Sunday the husband pulled me aside and said that he had to leave the next day to go back to the U.S. "to take care of urgent business."

"I'll be back," he said, "in two weeks when my wife is discharged from the hospital so that we can fly back together."

I was stunned. How could he leave his wife alone in the hospital in a country where they had no relatives or friends and she couldn't speak the language? But his wife seemed okay with (or had resigned herself to) the idea. Two weeks later, she was released from the hospital and went back to New York.

Since leaving that post, my life as an occasional duty officer has been an easy one. But someday, somewhere, my luck is bound to change. And when it does, I'll be thankful for the experience gained from all of those lost weekends doing duty work in Europe.

Paul Poletes currently works as the Montenegro Desk Officer at the State Department in Washington, DC. Paul is married and has two young children.

Going It Alone:
Unaccompanied Assignments in
the Foreign Service

by John Maxwell Carroll

When an officer agrees to join the Foreign Service, in reality the spouse, children and other Eligible Family Members (EFMs), if any, also sign up for the ride.

However, there are currently hundreds of overseas positions within the State Department—in the world's more dangerous or politically unstable areas—where EFMs are not permitted to go. Iraq and Afghanistan generate the most headlines, but Africa also features plenty of places where it's considered unsafe for the spouse and/or kids to live.

No EFMs are allowed in Pakistan, Saudi Arabia, Afghanistan or Iraq except for spouses with a job already lined up at post, and only adult EFMs are allowed in some places. And meanwhile, since the Department officially assigns its officers based on the "needs of the Service," the size or newness of the family is no barrier to an unaccompanied assignment. As State's website notes, "All officers are considered world-wide available and must be prepared to go where needed. While personal and professional factors are taken into account when making assignments, the needs of the Service remain paramount."

Just married, have some familiarity with Arabic? You may be closer to an assignment in Baghdad than a 20-year veteran who is fluent in Spanish and Russian. Have five children, of which three are in grade school, plus an at-home partner and three cats? That doesn't prevent your spending a year in Karachi.

Many of these unaccompanied tours are what the State Department calls "hard-to-fill": jobs that attract few volunteers and sometimes even remain vacant. With a new Department emphasis on staffing "hard-to-fill" jobs first, before any other assignments are given out, it is more likely than ever that a Foreign Service officer (FSO) will at some point need to leave his or her family behind and serve a year (or more) alone.

What can justify this time apart? Both the officer and the family members must find reasons to support the separation: perhaps patriotism; a genuine desire to make a difference; hopes for career advancement; extra hardship and danger pay (which can range up to 70% of the officer's base salary); the promise of plum follow-on assignments; or simply the pressure on the officer to accept an unaccompanied tour in order to continue his or her Foreign Service career.

> *"I went primarily out of a sense of responsibility to make right what we had done. Before it was attributed to Colin Powell, I was using his 'China Shop' principle of international obligation: you break it, you buy it … Since we don't have kids, it was easier for me to go than for most of my colleagues. Finally, as a development professional, I was curious and a little excited about the biggest development program since the Marshall Plan."*
>
> —*Thomas Rhodes, USAID Iraq*

Whatever the incentives that motivate you, one thing that will serve your family well is to ensure that everyone in the family understands the reasons, and no one feels "left behind."

> *"On the one hand, I felt it was my duty to support American foreign policy by supporting my husband's tour, and on the other hand, I wanted to give him the career support and experience he would obtain with this assignment. I just resolved that I would deal with whatever came as a result … and, of course, upon my husband's departure, our house fell apart. Our car was totaled in a freak storm, the computer died (…). That was certainly a good test of my new resolve!"*
>
> —*Alaina Teplitz, FSO and tandem spouse*

"It is always useful to think of the professional aspect for your Foreign Service partner. Going overseas in the foreign services is great for your spouse's position and increases chances for climbing the ladder in this field and excelling, especially if it is a hardship post. Even though the financial gain isn't more important than an intact family, focusing on the monetary advantages for you and your family can ease the separation."

—*Jennifer Riker-Alm, wife of a Diplomatic Security Agent*

Especially since unaccompanied assignments tend to be one-year postings, every bidding cycle for new positions features a large number of them. Foreign Service families must get ready for the pressure. For some, even though they understand the "needs of the Service," an unaccompanied assignment still seems like an unthinkable option.

"I can see that just because someone doesn't have children it shouldn't de facto mean that they get all of the nasty posts, the danger posts, or otherwise "unaccompanied"—and I assure you we have done our share of hardship posts even with the kids in tow, and always by our own choice (...). We do our time in the ways that we can, but unaccompanied is something else entirely. Simply put, it's bad for the family. And since I feel strongly that family is more important than work, I couldn't conscionably say that it makes any sense to deny my children their father for a year for the sake of the State Department."

—*Bonnie Carlson, spouse*

"I would suggest, with a young family, taking a post where the whole family is included and including support groups from the get go. Do not separate from your spouse, because being a father or mother is number one. Do it together. Make a difference together."

—*Jennifer Riker-Alm, wife of a Diplomatic Security Agent*

If the officer in your family does accept an unaccompanied tour, once he or she leaves for post the world will indeed be different. The other side of the bed is empty every night. You're aware that your FSO is in a stressful situation, and you can't just call him or her for help when a problem breaks out. You may suddenly find yourself living as a single parent. How will you manage and care for your children without your partner? Do they understand the situation? Are you responsible for everything you normally do in your family, plus everything your partner did?

Of course there is no one answer for how the "left behind" family lives. Every family has its own relationships, its own sense of "what makes a home," its own family issues and its own financial situation. Some choose to live in the Washington DC area and be closer to other Foreign Service families and resources; some choose to live nearer to other family members; and some choose to live in a completely different country.

> *"I wanted to remain as far from U.S. news and the opinions of some close friends and family as possible. Fortunately, we have lived on several occasions in France and have very good friends there whose country house I was able to use for the year. I tried to see the year as a sort of "sabbatical" for myself (I have been a French teacher for most of nearly 25 years) [and] a chance to live in the countryside (a lifestyle that is impossible in USAID) (…). I followed the French media, split and stacked firewood, read endlessly, gardened, and saw a lot of foreign films over the year. I also visited French friends and entertained French and American friends."*
>
> —Kimberly Rhodes, USAID spouse

> *"I was a mother of three children, three years and under. It was essential in my situation to move closer to family. Even though this lightened the burden I have to be honest and say it wasn't or isn't easy. Families want to help, but ultimately they have their own lives and their own opinions about raising children, which creates tension with those supporters. After all, the children are the responsibilities of both parents, not the extended family."*
>
> —Jennifer Riker-Alm, wife of a Diplomatic Security Agent

It's sometimes possible for a family to stay at a previous overseas post while the FSO serves a one-year unaccompanied tour, but it's your own decision about how helpful this situation might be. While you are separated, the family can receive an additional Involuntary Separate Maintenance Allowance (ISMA) in the officer's paycheck (you must apply for this), which is intended to help you manage the costs of being apart. (In May 2005, FLO's successfully advocated for a new Involuntary SMA with an 18% increase over the voluntary SMA, for families living apart due to "the convenience of the U.S. government".) The officer also receives periodic paid travel to an agreed-upon "rest and recuperation" location. The Family Liaison Office's Program Specialist for Unaccompanied Tours offers guidance and referral services for house and home issues, family counseling, and road maps of steps to take, starting well before the unaccompanied tour begins. But ISMA, travel vouchers and systematic plans for living apart only go so far; the stress of separation still takes its toll.

> *"I had a moment of real despair about midway through the first period before my husband came back for a visit. Something went wrong at work—an embarrassing mistake on my part—and it came home to roost as I was trying to get dinner together. I burned the main part of the meal because I was on the phone trying to solve this problem. While I was really chagrined over my mistake, I felt even worse over having mangled my kids' dinner. I didn't want this to be a sign of how our life might be without a united family. Fortunately, it was just the low point and not a typical day. I really could have used his help and support that night. Getting it via e-mail just made me feel even worse."*
>
> —*Alaina Teplitz, FSO and tandem spouse*

> *"The most difficult times during his year in Iraq were just after seeing each other, when I knew that I would not see Tom again for another 2–3 months. This I kept in perspective, however, by thinking of all of the families of soldiers stationed in Iraq, Afghanistan, etc. who don't see their spouse/parent for 12–18 months at a time!"*
>
> —*Kimberly Rhodes, USAID spouse*

> *"Weekends were the hardest for me, because most of my neighbors and friends would be doing things with their families and I had to get used to taking the kids out for fun outings, to restaurants, etc., by myself. The weekdays were usually so busy that we didn't notice his absence as*

much. It was a very stressful period for me and I was angry frequently, particularly when the medical issues of our baby would heat up or when I had to take the baby into surgery by myself. I felt very alone most of the time."

—*Theresa M., spouse*

One universal piece of advice seems to be: *stay in touch*. With the spread of Voice Over Internet Protocol phone systems, this is easier than ever; but no matter how it's done, frequent contact is a big help.

"We e-mailed at least once per day, and he phoned me every 3 or 4 days. This way, if I happened to see anything bad in the news regarding Iraq, I knew pretty closely where Tom was. There was only one time that I had to worry for any length of time: A helicopter was shot down in Baghdad when Tom was in the city, and I didn't know exactly where Tom was, or when he would be traveling by helicopter to/from the airport. Fortunately, he called that night, so it was only a six-hour period of worry.

While Tom described his daily life and also sent me pictures, it was very difficult to imagine what his routine and surroundings were like."

—*Kimberly Rhodes, USAID spouse*

"Keep up the link through e-mail, telephone, and snail mail. From my side, I consider the letters and boxes I send to be part of an umbilical cord supporting my husband so he knows his family is always thinking about him and I can feel like I'm contributing. From his side, I know it makes his day when he receives a postcard from our children. Watching their handwriting change over time or thinking about what they choose to say gives him a little window into our day-to-day life that he would otherwise miss.

There are days when I dread to read the news or times when I begin to get anxious if I don't see an e-mail, because I know exactly what the security requirements are and how they might be lacking. I just do my best to carry on."

—*Alaina Teplitz, FSO and tandem spouse*

Whether your officer wants to serve an unaccompanied tour or not, it's important to realize that it may happen—and do your best to be ready. Have plans in place for communication between officer and family, and for the family "going it alone" while the officer is at post. The family members interviewed for this article recommend that others in their situation be assertive and proactive in their planning and in their requests for information and help from the State Department (or anyone else). You will most likely be busier and under more stress while the officer is away, so explore in advance what your agency—and even your family and friends—can do for you.

> *"The more details of housing, job, family, pets that can be taken care of together, before the spouse goes to post, the better. State/USAID/etc. should increase the separation allowance, as it is very difficult to find work for just a year. I was lucky to have a house on loan for the year and therefore few expenses!"*
>
> —*Kimberly Rhodes, USAID spouse*

With both spouses feeling the strain of separation and looking forward to the end of the unaccompanied assignment, one might think that a kind of "second honeymoon" might follow the reunion. However, it seems more typical for the partners to experience some bumps as they readjust to life together as a couple and family. For that reason, the Overseas Briefing Center and Medical Office offer a two-hour "Out-Brief for High Stress Assignments" at the Foreign Service Institute on a monthly basis.

> *"My children haven't really verbalized what their father's separation meant to them. When he did come back for good, we all had to readjust our lives. He was used to doing his own thing, looking out for himself only and had to slowly adjust to being a part of a family again. (…) The experience has changed me in the sense that I know that I am capable of standing on my own, raising my kids alone, and I did appreciate my husband more when he wasn't here. But that said, our rela-*

tionship struggled as a result of the long separation. He was critical of my childrearing, how I kept house, etc, … and didn't have much appreciation for what I had gone through in his absence. And quite honestly, I was still angry that he chose an unaccompanied assignment at such a critical time for our family. Over the past two years we have melded our lives back together, but knowing that those unaccompanied assignments will very likely occur again is not a good feeling for me."

—*Theresa M., spouse*

"The huge downside of the unaccompanied experience from the perspective of someone married for 28 years was the "re-entry" process! Re-entry was much more difficult than any of us had ever imagined. It's been a year and half, and we are still having re-entry issues. I think that State Department needs to look at this carefully and spend as much time with the officer's re-entering the family as they do with their support and information about schools."

—*Michelle Ganser, spouse*

Although separated tours are clearly a hardship for both sides, affecting both the family and the marriage, there can also be some positive elements. As Theresa's comments show, spouses sometimes feel a sense of accomplishment and greater independence in getting through a difficult time alone. The feeling that the officer is doing something worthwhile can also make the separation easier for both partners.

"I was promoted from a [Foreign Service grade level] 3 to a 2 during the year, but I would have had a good shot at it anyway. I got my first choice of onward postings, despite the need for language training, but that's not unique either. There was a huge dump of responsibility that I was not fully prepared for, but to which I believe I responded reasonably well. However, the year was too fast and too weird to develop specific skill sets, etc. A nice, helpful, and constructive thing I got from the year is a sense of perspective. When you've been responsible for people's safety, for hundreds of millions spread across dozens of projects, for hosting Senators, Deputy Secretaries, the AID Administrator, and nationally-known press, it's clearer how much you have to worry about the

deadline for reviewing someone's talking points. I'm glad I went. I regret the disruption that it caused, but we got through it OK."

—*Thomas Rhodes, USAID Iraq*

"I think families need to go into these situations with open eyes, including a frank understanding of the danger to the assigned spouse and the anxiety and burden left with the remaining partner, particularly if there are children. If there is mutual support, everyone will come out (hopefully) that much stronger."

—*Alaina Teplitz, FSO and tandem spouse*

Resources for employees and family members facing unaccompanied tours

U.S. State Department Family Liaison Office
http://www.state.gov/m/dghr/flo
"Unaccompanied Tours: Support and Information,"
http://www.state.gov/m/dghr/flo/c14521.htm
Tel: (202) 647–1076 or (800) 440–0397
E-mail address for Unaccompanied Tour questions: FLOAskUT@state.gov
Associates of the American Foreign Service Worldwide (AAFSW)
www.aafsw.org
Special resources for those affected by unaccompanied assignments:
http://www.aafsw.org/una/una_main.htm

John Maxwell Carroll is a former television producer now committed to following his wife, a Foreign Service Officer in the Public Diplomacy cone, around the world. Their first posting was Matamoros, Mexico.

Anticipating Evacuation: Prudent Measures for Contemporary Diplomats

by Aubree Galvin Caunter

My husband and I moved to Istanbul in August 2003 and knew right away it could feel like home for a three-year tour. By November, we were already feeling comfortable: making friends, investigating neighborhood markets, and navigating our SUV through the narrow cobblestone streets.

It was fall in Western Turkey and I was flush with the possibilities of a new country. But like most autumns, I was also nursing a season-long head cold. So one morning—November 20—instead of heading to a street bazaar for vegetables, I succumbed to my sinuses and put myself back to bed at 10 a.m.

Suddenly, I was startled from sleep by windows and doors rattling in their frames. The dog, previously snoozing at my feet, began barking ferociously. I leapt up and turned on the television. The local stations began to show the carnage: nearly simultaneous bombs had ripped through the HSBC bank building and the British Consulate, injuring more than 400 and killing 27, including British Consul General Roger Short.

The live feed showed what remained of the HSBC headquarters: a hollowed shell and black crater. The building was only five blocks from our house; I was able to see the TV helicopters from my porch as they filmed the scene.

I called my husband, whose commute to the U.S. Consulate passes the HSBC building, and he said that all employees had been accounted for. Next, I tried in vain to reach a friend whose husband works at the British Consulate. I learned later that he'd sustained massive head trauma and been medically evacuated to London.

It was horrible: the bodies, the blood, the panic. Al-Qaeda was being blamed. American, British and Australian citizens were warned to be extra guarded. There was talk of evacuation. Family members and non-essential employees of the consulate might be asked to leave the country. I felt confused: I was scared by the bombings, but how could I leave this city I had come to think of as home?

While rumors flew throughout the community as to the status of the as-yet-unauthorized evacuation, my friends with children began preparations. They packed each child a bag, gathered school reports and updated immunization records. I sat and watched the news, willing the world to go back to normal.

A week passed, and then another. More bombs were detonated in the city, including one at a freemasons' lodge. But we were not evacuated. Some consulate community members resented the decision, feeling the danger to families had been great enough to warrant evacuation. Others, like me, were relieved not to be separated from their homes, pets and spouses.

Facing the reality of evacuation

At its core—no matter the outcome of each individual case—evacuation is divisive: it carves up emotions; it separates families. No one wants to be evacuated from post. But, these days, it is folly to assume that a career in the State Department would pass without having to experience an evacuation.

In fact, between 1988 and 2007, more than 265 posts have been drawn-down or evacuated. On average, some 14 posts are drawn-down or evacuated annually, with one occurring approximately every three and a half weeks during the past 19 years. Perhaps most revealing is that two-thirds of those posts were rated as low- or medium-threat just prior to evacuation.

"It is not easy being out in one of our embassies now," said former Secretary of State Colin L. Powell in his remarks to the U.S. Global Leadership Campaign in 2004. "More and more of our embassies are on authorized departure or ordered departure, where families are not there. It makes it harder for our Foreign Service families, but they put up with that hardship."

Indeed, as a U.S. government employee or family member, you must face the reality of evacuation. Reasons can range from terrorist threats and impending civil war, to health epidemics and natural disasters. No matter what the impetus, the State Department assures that "the primary purpose of evacuation of a U.S. Mission is for the safety and security of Mission personnel and their families."

Will I be forced to leave?

Though the justifications for evacuation may be infinite, the resolution is carried out in only one of two ways: by either authorized or ordered departure. Department of State spokesperson Richard Boucher, at a press briefing in 2002, explained the difference like this: "We do differentiate between voluntary departures and ordered departures. I think it just (has) to do with … the level of tensions, the kind of transportation available, the likelihood of future transportation, the environment for those who stay." In the simplest terms, an authorized departure is voluntary; an ordered evacuation is mandatory.

During an authorized departure, people are urged to leave, but ultimately the decision is left up to the individual. However, those who choose to leave post during an authorized departure cannot choose when to return. The decision essentially gives non-emergency embassy workers and family members the option of leaving with paid travel home. For example, when U.S. facilities in Saudi Arabia were under attack in 1996, the Department felt it was a "reasonable precaution" to allow the 118 spouses and children of employees to return to the States.

"There are a lot of people here who we believe should be given at least the option of coming back to the United States should they wish and having the U.S. Government assume the financial cost of that," said Department spokesperson Nicholas Burns at the time. "We just want to give them the option, should they so desire, given the fact that there have been two bombings, to come back to the United States and bring their children back to the United States."

In sharp contrast, an ordered departure is just the way it sounds: family members and non-emergency staff must leave. Of the decision not to order departure in Saudi Arabia, Burn said, "If we thought that there was an imminent threat to Americans—private Americans or official Americans or their dependents—that could not be controlled, and that could not be met, then, obviously, we would take a stronger measure than an authorized departure."

Deciding between authorized or ordered departure status "has a lot to do with the threat, but it also has a lot to do with the circumstances regarding our ability to protect people, the kind of housing that they live in, the availability of commercial flights. So it's not necessarily just a reflection of the threat," said Department spokesperson Boucher. The decision, he said, is also "based on our best assessments of the general security situation and the possibility of developments that would result—or the possibility of deterioration in that situation."

As Foreign Service members Michael and Mary Ann Darmiento discovered, ongoing political and civil strife in a host country can quickly escalate into an emergency situation that requires immediate evacuation. The Darmientos were posted to Belgrade, Yugoslavia, in 1994 when NATO launched air strikes against Bosnian Serb targets to force compliance with United Nations Security Council resolutions. Immediately prior to the attacks, family members and non-essential employees were put on ordered departure. Mary Ann and her newly adopted daughter needed to leave Michael, a Regional Security Officer, for the relative safety of Budapest, Hungary. Mother and daughter were evacuated twice that year: in February for ten days and again in May for five days.

Complicating matters during the family's first evacuation was unfinished adoption paperwork. "We had just had final adoption of our 1-year-old daughter from an orphanage in Belgrade on a Friday and the evacuation was effective that Sunday. She obviously did not have a passport, so she could not leave the country. The assistant secretary ordered me to leave by noon on Monday, with or without her," said Mary Ann Darmiento. Luckily, the baby's Serbian passport was issued that Monday morning at 11 a.m.

In some extreme cases, operations at post are temporarily suspended and the remaining staff is evacuated. Occasionally, evacuees are never returned to post. Knowing these possibilities, Darmiento was understandably tense. "We were always in a state of limbo not knowing if we were going to be allowed to return. And since my husband was still in Belgrade, I worried constantly for his safety. Obviously it was a very difficult time for us," she said.

Though the situation that year in Belgrade never warranted it, circumstances do arise when normal diplomatic operations cannot be resumed. If this occurs, the operating status of a post can be permanently changed. High-threat posts can be re-designated as open to only certain types of dependents: adult family members only; adult family members and minors under age 5; or no family members, also known as unaccompanied status.

With noted exceptions like the Darmiento case, evacuations are normally issued for at least 30 days with the average evacuation lasting three to four months. Post status is reevaluated every 30 days for up to six months at which point, if the mission is still considered unsuitable for families, it becomes unaccompanied.

Emotional baggage

Though there are as many reactions to evacuation as there are people who have been evacuated, the most common emotion is anxiety. Evacuation disrupts every part of your life—career, family and home—and individuals can feel powerless against a rising tide of uncertainty. At issue is control, or more accurately, loss of control. Often, the only defense against this feeling of helplessness is preparation.

When Sharon Marshall, an administrative officer with more than 10 years of experience in the Department, was evacuated from Riyadh, Saudi Arabia, she relied heavily on a plan she'd formulated with her family. The evacuation, which lasted from May to August 2003, was forced by Operation Iraqi Freedom in neighboring Iraq. "Because of the war, all of us had given some thought about what we would do for an evacuation," said Marshall. "The embassy in Riyadh gave many thorough briefings about evacuations leading up to the war, so that information was fairly fresh for the ordered departure."

The missions in Saudi Arabia were already on authorized departure. But following the bombing of Western residential compounds, which wounded some 200 people and killed 34, including seven Americans, the status was changed to an ordered departure. Marshall and her husband, also a Department employee, had three children aged 12, 10 and 3. "The girls were upset by the bombings—they knew friends in school that lived in those compounds," said Marshall. The degree of stress felt by evacuees is often in direct proportion to three factors: suddenness of crisis onset, relative exposure to danger, and duration of the situation.

Marshall's first thought was to make travel arrangements for her and the children. "Once flight reservations were secured, we were able to focus on the other things we needed to do. My husband did a power-of-attorney at the embassy and made sure I had that with me just in case I could not return to Riyadh and needed to buy a car or a house without him," she said. She also visited the health unit for medical and shot records.

Although well-prepared, the family still experienced anxiety about the evacuation, especially their youngest child. "Riyadh was the only home our son knew, so it was very hard on him," said Marshall. "He was too young to understand why we could not be there but his cats and his Daddy could."

Indeed, both the evacuated family members and those who are left behind face an emotional battle without each other's support. Those in the U.S. may be struggling with new expenses, temporary schools and lodging arrangements. Meanwhile, the ones remaining at post are dealing with increased danger and insecurity. "The waiting is hard on everyone—the ones evacuated and the employee left behind," said Marshall.

Evacuation in detail: spouses, children and pets

It's worthwhile to note that while most evacuations are carried out by commercial air services, there are cases in which airlifts are necessary. When the missions in Haiti, Jamaica and Cuba were threatened by Hurricane Ivan in September 2004, charter flights were lined up to evacuate stranded Americans who lacked shelter, food and water.

In such a situation, pets are of unusual concern. While it is the official policy of the Department not to evacuate pets, the reality is that pets are evacuated when possible. The planning and expense, however, is solely that of the employee. Because pet evacuation is most probable when transportation is arranged on a commercial airline, families with pets are encouraged to take advantage of authorized departures, when the opportunity to book cargo still exists.

As for families, evacuation most often means withdrawal to an employee's safehaven city. A safehaven, pre-determined at the time of arrival at post, can be anywhere in the world, but is most often within the continental U.S. Perhaps the most frequent choice is the Washington, DC metro area, given that personnel under ordered departure must report to work at their agency's headquarters.

To help defray the additional expense sometimes incurred with living back in the U.S., official evacuees are offered certain financial considerations. Allocations are made for subsistence allowances, lodging, meals and incidental expenses, and the benefits remain the same for both authorized and ordered departures.

Single parents and tandem couples—where both spouses are employed by the Foreign Service—must make special arrangements in the event of evacuation. During an ordered departure, employees who hold critical positions must remain at post while the children will be forced to leave. Prior planning for the care of children at the safehaven is of utmost importance, both for the safety of the family and the emotional state of mind for both parents and children.

Life after evacuation: moving on

The Department makes a concerted effort to help its employees and families deal with the inevitable hardships of evacuation. With premission training and at-post security briefings supplemented with updates on specific threats, the Department keeps employees well-aware of the potential for possible evacuation. This, coupled with support for evacuees from the Department's Family Liaison Office, forms a network that can be called upon during all matter of emergencies. Still, it remains the primary responsibility of the individual to prepare—both mentally and physically—for the event.

Living through an evacuation can make families a little wary at first. In the long term most come to terms with the incident as just a part of the many varied experiences afforded to a member of the Foreign Service community. In fact, evacuation veterans are often better prepared than their non-evacuee counterparts in the event of an emergency.

Veteran evacuee Marshall offers sage advice for her counterparts in the future: "Recognize it is a hard time and that everyone will deal with it differently. Be prepared for the unexpected. And, most of all, be flexible."

Aubree Galvin Caunter is a freelance writer and editor whose work has earned numerous honors, including an "Award for Excellence" from the Society of Professional Journalists and a "Best in Show" from the Maryland-Delaware-DC Press Association. Her most recent project is a collection of comedic essays lampooning life as a new mother. She has twice lived in London, England and is currently in Istanbul, Turkey with her husband Dave, a Special Agent with the Drug Enforcement Administration, and her 10-month-old daughter Riley Jane. You can read her blog at aubreecaunter.blogspot.com.

Your Health Abroad: What You Need to Know about Medical Evacuations

by Jessica P. Hayden

In 42 BC, Publius Syrus proclaimed: "Good health and good sense are two of life's greatest blessings." Of course, the diplomatic corps at that time wasn't much to speak of, but I'm sure he'd agree that in today's Foreign Service, you need both.

I generally consider myself a pretty healthy person, so when I started to experience pain in my abdomen about a year ago, I didn't think much of it. We had only been posted in Kazakhstan for a few months and I figured my system was still getting used to the changes in my diet. I had, after all, spent the last few weeks experimenting with the local fare, eating Central Asian delicacies like *kazy* and *kumus*, otherwise known as horse sausage and camel milk.

But after a few days of increasing pain, I decided to make a late night call to our Regional Medical Officer (RMO), Dr. Kim Ottwell. It would be the beginning of my introduction to the world of medical evacuations, or what most refer to as "medevacs."

Over the next week, I'd endure various forms of prodding (some of which I'm convinced would fall under the Geneva Convention on Torture) during my medical evacuation to Manas Air Force Base in Kyrgyzstan. I would also brave surgery in a makeshift military tent by Korean doctors who didn't speak English, spend a week of recovery on a cot, and ultimately return home to Almaty with my appendix in a jar.

While most medevacs are aimed at more civilized environments, like hospitals with four walls, there are certainly challenges unique to each experience. When you're posted in a country with a substandard healthcare system, the medical officers like to get you to adequate care quickly. From broken limbs to heart palpitations, if you find yourself injured or sick you may also find yourself on a plane.

Here's what you need to know.

Medical Evacuations 101

It didn't take long for David Bridges, a political officer in Kazakhstan, to realize something wasn't quite right. After eating mushrooms his wife purchased at a local market, he soon came down with-flu like symptoms and starting peeing bright orange. Add that to the fact that his dog vomited immediately after eating the leftovers, and it wasn't hard to deduce that he may have been poisoned.

After the RMO in Kazakhstan ran a few tests on David, she decided he should be sent to London for additional tests, fearing his liver might have failed as a result of the mushrooms. That night both the RMO and David left for London. He would stay in a British hospital for eight days, and then spend an additional five weeks in Washington undergoing a battery of blood tests and recuperating.

The general policy of the State Department is to provide the best possible care for employees at post. But local facilities are often not up to western standards, and in those cases, the RMO has the authority to medevac patients. In this case, the clinics in Kazakhstan simply didn't have the equipment necessary to diagnose and treat a possible liver failure.

While medical evacuations can sometimes be granted for non-emergency situations, generally the condition has to be such that treatment cannot wait. According to the regulations, medical travel can be authorized only when treatment, "cannot be postponed until the individual's next scheduled travel (e.g., transfer, home leave, rest and recuperation, or post funded travel)."

What kinds of illnesses or injuries warrant a medical evacuation? According to Dr. Kim Ottwell, it varies from post to post. She notes that, "the majority of illnesses/injuries that require medical evacuation are due to the fact that evaluation or treatment requires tests or procedures that we cannot perform in our ambulatory health unit. Additionally, if a problem is likely to require hospitalization of greater than 1–2 days, we cannot support [treatment] with our minimal resources." While serving in Kazakhstan, Dr. Ottwell found that injuries were the most common reason for medevacs, for instance orthopedic problems that required surgery. At her previous post, Bangladesh, infectious diseases were the number one cause of evacuation.

In addition to medical evacuations, "dentevacs" are also available in certain circumstances. While simple cavities probably won't get you a free ticket home, if you need, "care for a dental condition that causes severe pain or for which postponement of treatment would cause permanent damage to the teeth or supporting structure," you will most likely be dentevaced. Unfortunately, the State Department hasn't yet determined that getting your teeth whitened falls into this category!

To be eligible for medical (or dental) evacuations, you must be covered by the Department of State Medical program, which includes all Foreign Service employees and other U.S. government employees who are U.S. citizens along with their eligible family members (spouses, unmarried children under the age of 21 and disabled relatives) who are stationed abroad. Civil Service employees who are assigned on temporary duty abroad are also covered.

We all know how outrageous medical costs are these days. You may walk into a doctor's office with a medical problem and walk out with a financial one. But one of the great benefits of serving your country overseas is medical care. There is very little that you'll end up paying for out of pocket. David Bridges notes, "The only expenses I had to cover were the incidentals—in my case, about $300 worth of books purchased to keep myself occupied between blood tests."

When you are medically evacuated, the State Department will pay for all travel expenses as well as the expenses for medevac attendants. In addition, all hospitalization and related outpatient expenses are covered (above and beyond what your insurance pays). You are also eligible for per diem.

What about my medical clearance?

There are a variety of medical clearances for employees of the Foreign Service, but if you leave the United States in good health, you'll most likely be issued a Class 1 clearance, or "unlimited clearance for world-wide assignment." When an employee or family member is medically evacuated to the U.S., that clearance is automatically annulled and a new clearance must be obtained from the State Department's Medical office.

For those who are medevaced to other locations abroad, medical clearances are not necessarily canceled. Generally, patients must have their medical clearance reviewed by the Foreign Service Medical Provider (the doctor at the hospital or military base where they are being treated) before they can return to post. If a change in the patient's clearance is needed, the medical provider will notify the medical office at the State Department.

One important factor to bear in mind: whether you are medically evacuated to the United States or a medical facility abroad, it is your responsibility to initiate the clearance review with the State Department. If you do travel back to post without first renewing your clearance (or obtaining a waiver) you will not be eligible for medical benefits and related allowances, such as per diem and reimbursement for travel and hospitalization. In addition, your access to the Embassy health unit will be denied. So make sure you get your clearance squared away before you return to post!

Medevacs with children

When Sharon and David Harden adopted their five-year-old daughter, Kadi, from Sierra Leone, they soon discovered that Kadi had been exposed to tuberculosis. David, the USAID legal advisor in Kazakhstan, and Sharon were immediately faced with an onslaught of questions: Will our daughter be okay? How long will we need to be in the United States? Will we need to curtail our tour?

When a child falls ill anywhere in the world, it is tough on a family. But the implications of Kadi's diagnosis reached into every facet of the Hardens' lives, from David's ability to continue working in Kazakhstan to schooling for their other three children.

After the initial diagnosis, they focused on what they could control and quickly tried to figure out how to get Kadi back to the States and into the hospital, while still taking care of their three other children. They decided that their youngest daughter, Waverly, would accompany Kadi and Sharon, while David stayed in Almaty and looked after their two boys.

The decision to split up the family was not easy. Over lunch on a spring day in Almaty, Sharon explained, "When I decided to take Waverly home with me for Kadi's medevac, the doctor at post strongly recommended against it. I went ahead with it anyway and it turned out to be a good decision. You know your family best, and for us having a sibling there made Kadi feel less scared. It is a very individual choice."

"It was a stressful time," Sharon recalled. "We did our best not to make the entire event too disruptive for our kids." Some of the strategies they employed included keeping the children still at post on a regular schedule, advising teachers and guidance counselors about the situation, and buying special gifts from the United States.

Sharon and her two girls ended up staying in the U.S. for only three weeks before Kadi was cleared to return to post. Today, she's a healthy and happy child, keeping her parents and teachers on their toes.

Making lemonade out of lemons

When I first arrived in Kazakhstan, I had a friend who constantly joked about her valiant, but unsuccessful, attempts to get herself medevaced. "Do you think this hangnail looks serious enough?" she would ask with a mischievous grin.

At hardship posts, it is no wonder that the idea of a free ticket to London is enticing. But medical evacuations are not usually met with such enthusiasm. The stress of health problems is only multiplied by the disruptiveness to your life.

How can you mitigate the downsides? Follow these tips from the experts (or at least those who have survived the experience):

- When you first arrive at post, make arrangements with others to watch kids or pets if you or your spouse has to be medically evacuated. This can reduce the stress when you suddenly find out that a medevac is necessary.

- Keep your health insurance information together with your passport in a safe but accessible place. Make sure at least one other person has access to these documents in case you are unable to obtain them yourself in an emergency.

- If you are medically evacuated, keep a detailed expense log. This record will help you when you return to post and need to file the paperwork for compensation.

- If you are not going to be hospitalized, choose a hotel that is close to the medical facility to reduce commuting time. A hotel with meals included can also make life easier when you are spending most of your day at medical appointments.

- Stay in close contact with the State medical office in Washington. Providing them with regular updates on your case can help expedite your clearance to return to post.

- If you are in the States, have family and friends come visit you. While you may not be in the States under the best circumstances, use this time to catch up with those you miss.

- Bring along extra books and magazines that are not related to work. Use the time to relax and catch up on your personal life. Take care of both your physical and mental health.

Of course, a medical evacuation is not a vacation, and if you are ill, you need to be careful not to overextend yourself. David Bridges spent one afternoon at the British Museum with his father, who had flown to London to meet him. David remembers, "While my father looked at Celtic artifacts, I fainted gracefully near the Elgin Marbles, coming to severely embarrassed—and thankfully, unnoticed—at the foot of some lovely nude torso."

Know before you go

If you are particularly concerned about a certain post and its health implications, you can visit the State Medical office in Washington, DC and read about the post's medical capabilities. Dr. Ottwell recommends that officers consider their medical needs before bidding on a post, especially if they have children. Specifically, Dr. Ottwell notes for officers with children, it is important to think about the distance and time it takes to transport patients to medical evacuation centers. She adds that everyone should ask themselves, "Am I comfortable with the level of care that will be available at post, and is it appropriate for most of my family's needs?"

Your health, your control

While you may not have the choice of whether to stay at post or get medical attention elsewhere, ultimately you are in control of your health care decisions. For example, if you decide that you'd rather be treated by a specialist in New York rather than go to your post's designated medical evacuation point, you can ask the RMO to send you to your preferred destination. You'll be required to pay any excess travel costs, but if it is important to you, don't let bureaucracy get in the way.

Be proactive about your treatment and make your voice heard. Just because your family physician won't be the one treating you, there is no reason you can't take the same approach to your health as you do in the States. If you are unhappy about a doctor or a medical facility, ask for a second opinion. You only have one body, so make sure you are involved in the decisions about how it's being treated.

Jessica P. Hayden is a freelance writer. She spent two years in Almaty, Kazakhstan with her FSO husband, Liam. She is now completing her law degree at Georgetown University Law Center in Washington, DC.

Highlights from Foreign
Service Life

by Douglas Kerr

Perhaps ironically (and topically, since I'm writing this on the fifth anniversary of 9/11), one of my earliest Foreign Service "highlights" was the poignant and emotional outpouring of support and love for the 9/11 victims from the people of Warsaw in the immediate aftermath of the terrorist attacks in the U.S. And three months later, Embassy Warsaw's "Candles in the Snow" memorial service was a truly touching experience.

Poland was an easy first tour for our family. The kids had a great international school, where one day they met Lech Walesa. He told the students: "If I'd had the advantages you have, I would have won two Nobel prizes. But make sure you're good in this life, because if, when you die, you get sent to Hell, you'll find it's managed by Marx and Engels."

I welcomed a "challenging" writing assignment with the Warsaw Stock Exchange to produce a glitzy, almost sensationalist promotional brochure about ... the seventh largest derivatives market in Europe. And my "Please, Sir, how much is your cherry?" story (all true, see the first Realities book) is still one of my favorite moments. I played squash against a real-life James Bond (and won). The embassy softball team, often featuring Ambassador Chris "The Thrill" Hill in right field, became the champions of East-Central Europe at a tournament in Prague, and we sang "Bohemian Rhapsody" on the plane home.

We made the obligatory pilgrimage to Legoland, in Billund, and enjoyed beach vacations in the Canaries and Croatia, together with a couple of vacations in Hel (on Poland's Baltic coast) where World War II started. On the way there (yes, the road to Hel and back), we stopped off to see Walensa's old shipyard, where communism first started to crumble. We visited Auschwitz, Birkenau and Treblinka—unmissable, and again, incredibly moving.

Then followed three years in Bangladesh. A common joke says the best thing about Bangladesh is … Thailand. But Bangladeshis are a lovely people—warm, welcoming, friendly. We spent five days on a boat sailing through the Sundarbans looking for Royal Bengal tigers, only eligible for the "man-eating" moniker after feasting on 15 people (a mere 14 confirmed kills doesn't make the grade).

I had a great job writing for a health care project, and I thoroughly enjoyed diving into development work. We had dinner with the Prime Minister (and 2,000 others—"Hey Khaleda, pass the rice"), and met the England cricket team (to a U.S. audience, imagine meeting the baseball all-star teams). I had lots of fun and games, playing tournament bridge twice a week and squash almost daily, and the tour ended with another softball championship. Life was very full and great fun in Bangladesh. There were, of course a slew of third world "issues" to deal with, but this brief piece is supposed to focus on the positive. And when those issues became too wearing, there *was* always Thailand to escape to. Every other month.

And now Trinidad. Coming from a greater hardship post such as Dhaka to a legendary Caribbean paradise, we've all been trying very hard to keep expectations low ("'Tis a far, far better place I go than I have ever been …"—and look what happened to that guy). As I write, we've been here less than a month and have our air baggage (UAB), but are still without household effects and our car, which is tougher than usual but we're trying not to be too whiny. Trini-style rocks, or rather, calypsos. We've seen a couple of fabulous beaches, and we've enjoyed some unusual events/receptions, including one on a boat in the harbor. The national anthem played on the steel drums is a marvel.

But the "Path to 9/11" events, including the attacks on the World Trade Center in 1993, the two African embassies and the U.S.S. Cole, serve as a reminder that the true Foreign Service highlights for us are not all about peaches and beaches, but rather the chance to contribute to the foundational diplomacy issues of cementing cross-cultural friendships. In our own small way, I hope we have done (and will continue to do) a good job of representing the U.S. overseas the way the vast majority of Americans would want us to.

Douglas Kerr was born and grew up in London and has accompanied his wife Michelle Jones for the past six years on her assignments to Washington, Warsaw, Dhaka and Port of Spain. He has spent his time overseas as a custom cabinetmaker (see www.starpointwoodworking.com) and as a writer and editor, accepting a variety of commissions in both widely disparate occupations, thus illustrating the inescapable necessity that spouses must be highly flexible and ready to re-invent themselves, chameleon-like, with every new posting. He plays bridge, squash, badminton and softball, and on the most recent championship team was voted "least likely to swing."

For Further Information

Since resources are continually changing and those in print may become quickly out of date, we have not included a list here. For the most current information and a continually updated list of books, Internet references and other resources of interest to the U.S. Foreign Service community, please consult AAFSW's comprehensive website, **www.aafsw.org**.

About the Editors

Melissa Brayer Hess is a writer, trainer, and creator of Foreign Service Lifelines, **www.aafsw.org.** As a Foreign Service spouse for 22 years, she accompanied her husband on tours to Nigeria, Russia, Algeria, Egypt, and Ukraine. Melissa is currently the Deputy Director in the Crisis Management Training Division of the Leadership and Management School, National Foreign Affairs Training Center, Arlington, Virginia.

Patricia Linderman, a Foreign Service spouse since 1990, has pursued a highly portable career as a writer, editor, translator and language teacher. With her husband and two sons, she has lived in Trinidad, Chile, Cuba and Germany. She is currently Editor in Chief of Tales from a Small Planet, **www.talesmag.com** .

Melissa and Patricia have also co-authored the guidebook *The Expert Expatriate: Your Guide to Successful Relocation Abroad* (Nicholas Brealey Intercultural, 2002, second edition forthcoming in 2007, see **www.expatguide.info**), and co-edited the first volume of this series, *Realities of Foreign Service Life* (AAFSW, 2002).

Marlene Monfiletto Nice is a former newspaper reporter and editor. She followed her husband, Dennis Nice, into the Foreign Service when he became Facilities Manager in 1999. Since then she worked as an Eligible Family Member (EFM) in Ankara, Turkey; Montevideo, Uruguay; and Zagreb, Croatia, before becoming a Foreign Service officer in 2005.

978-0-595-45314-6
0-595-45314-7